Power and Principle

Power and Principle

The Politics of International Criminal Courts

Christopher Rudolph

Cornell University Press
Ithaca and London

First published 2017 by Cornell University Press

Printed in the United States of America

Library of Congress Cataloging-in-Publication Data

Names: Rudolph, Christopher, 1966– author.
Title: Power and principle : the politics of international criminal courts / Christopher Rudolph.
Description: Ithaca : Cornell University Press, [2017] | Includes bibliographical references and index.
Identifiers: LCCN 2016037079 (print) | LCCN 2016037906 (ebook) | ISBN 9781501705526 (cloth : alk. paper) | ISBN 9781501708411 (epub/mobi) | ISBN 9781501708428 (pdf)
Subjects: LCSH: International criminal courts—Political aspects. | International Criminal Court.
Classification: LCC KZ7230 .R83 2017 (print) | LCC KZ7230 (ebook) | DDC 345/.01—dc23
LC record available at https://lccn.loc.gov/2016037079

Cornell University Press strives to use environmentally responsible suppliers and materials to the fullest extent possible in the publishing of its books. Such materials include vegetable-based, low-VOC inks and acid-free papers that are recycled, totally chlorine-free, or partly composed of nonwood fibers. For further information, visit our website at www.cornellpress.cornell.edu.

For Jack
Reach for the stars!

Contents

Tables and Figures

Tables

Figures

Acknowledgments

This project began when I was a fellow at the Niehaus Center for Globalization and Governance at Princeton University in 2006–7. Many thanks to Helen Milner and the Executive Committee for giving me the opportunity to spend a wonderful year at the center.

I am indebted to many people for their contributions to this project. Thanks to Ken Abbott, Karen Alter, Boaz Atzili, Debbi Avant, Gary Bass, Cherif Bassiouni, David Bosco, Jeff Colgan, Meg DeGuzman, Kelly Greenhill, Joe Grieco, Emilie Hafner-Burton, Austin Hart, Courtney Hillebrecht, Miles Kahler, Robert Keohane, Yonatan Lupu, Jim Meernik, Luis Moreno Ocampo, Nick Onuf, Eric Posner, Rachel Sullivan Robinson, Wayne Sandholtz, Ben Schiff, Mike Schroeder, Anne-Marie Slaughter, Duncan Snidal, Jelena Subotic, Felicity Vabulas, David Victor, Erik Voeten, Celeste Wallander, and Alex Wendt.

Thanks also to Daniella Restrepo, Tetyana Sydorenko, Kate Tennis, and Brandon Brockmyer for research assistance and to Assen Assenov, Jess Chen, and George Panterov for technical assistance.

I am very grateful for the support Roger Haydon has given me and for his sage guidance during the publication process. I also wish to thank the anonymous reviewers for their insightful and very constructive comments on the manuscript.

As always, my greatest thanks go to my wife, Lori, for her love, support, and encouragement. I am indeed a very lucky man to share this life with such a special person.

Power and Principle

Prologue

Civilians have composed half of all war-related deaths over the past three centuries.[1] In the twentieth century, more than 170 million people—men, women, and children—"have been shot, beaten, tortured, knifed, burned, starved, frozen, crushed, or worked to death; buried alive, hung, bombed, or killed in any of the myriad ways governments have inflicted death on unarmed helpless citizens and foreigners."[2] When civilian war casualties are combined with those targeted by their own governments, the number rises to nearly 360 million people.[3] For those who experience or witness atrocities, shock and grief are often followed by an urgent cry for justice, a primal anguish born of human tragedy. During what some have called "the century of genocide," the global hue and cry for justice continued to grow . . .

Introduction

The Light of Justice

The dawn of peace must begin with the light of justice.

—Kofi Annan

Idealists argue that international society is witnessing a profound transformation. They suggest that the rise of international criminal courts over the past half century is not only evidence of the growing power of norms concerning human rights and principles of justice, but that such institutions may usher in an entirely new era of world politics. At a ceremony marking the birth of the International Criminal Court (ICC), Hans Corell, the United Nations (UN) Undersecretary for Legal Affairs declared, "A page in the history of humankind is being turned."[1] Although some of the hyperbole used by the court's most ardent and idealistic supporters may be salesmanship, it nonetheless suggests that there was widespread belief that the new institution represented a significant change in international politics: political and military leaders will no longer be able to victimize the innocent with impunity. They will now personally be held to account for their crimes in a court of law. Scholars have suggested that this shift toward individual accountability represents a significant transfer of authority from sovereign states to international institutions.[2] More broadly, proponents have lauded the rise of international criminal courts as a turning point in international politics, a stunning victory of principles over the realpolitik that characterize the Westphalian era. As one scholar put it, "The creation of the ICC denotes a pivotal historical moment in the development of international society."[3]

Scholars have used different terms to describe this transformation. For example, Gary Bass refers to a growing trend toward ideal-based legalism.[4] Similarly, Kathryn Sikkink suggests that the growing legitimacy of the norm of individual criminal accountability and an increase in prosecutions based on that norm are indicative of the emergence of a "justice cascade."[5] Along the same lines, Ben Schiff uses the metaphor of a "river of justice" to capture this sense of the inevitable shift toward a more Kantian rule-based order in international politics. He writes, "The river of justice widened from the inflow of norms as people broadened their conceptions of what it is to be human and to be civilized. They shaped their identities around consensus over an expanding set of normative conceptions. The currents included people's rights against sovereigns, the ethic of accountability, and the social responsibilities of both retributive and restorative justice."[6] For many, the ICC is a high point in a long process of global transformation toward a more principled order in international society.

Advocates of this view point to several seminal moments in this process. The first was the creation of the International Military Tribunal held in Nuremberg at the end of World War II. Though the victors of war have often tried the vanquished, the Nuremberg trials were notable for at least two reasons: first, they held the perpetrators of wartime atrocities to account for their crimes; and second, they afforded defendants the rights of due process that reflected contemporary standards of jurisprudence. A second key moment came in 1993 when the United Nations Security Council (UNSC) established the International Criminal Tribunal for the Former Yugoslavia (ICTY).[7] In contrast with prevailing legal norms regarding war crimes, this court affirmed the principle that international accountability was not limited only to those whose crimes are committed in the context of interstate war but applies equally in situations of intrastate conflicts.[8] Moreover, it also applies to situations where the government commits atrocities against its own people. In the case of Dusko Tadic, the court defended its jurisdiction over atrocities committed during internal conflicts by ruling that "the distinction between interstate wars and civil wars is losing its value as far as human beings are concerned."[9] The ICTY ensured that those guilty of these crimes could no longer hide behind the shield of Westphalian sovereignty. Moreover, the arrest and trial of Serbian leader Slobodan Milosevic suggested that justice finally would be brought to the highest echelons of political power. As reflected in the headlines at the time of his arrest, world leaders hailed the arrest and trial of Milosevic as the end of a turbulent era.[10] Scholars added that the arrest "was an amazing triumph for the human rights movement."[11]

Some critics argued that although the ICTY (and the International Criminal Tribunal for Rwanda [ICTR] that soon followed) was a significant step in the advancement of the application of international law, it still suffered from a degree of "victor's justice" because it was established by the powerful states of the UN Security Council. Thus, the creation of the International Criminal Court represents the third seminal moment in the growth of the international criminal justice regime. Under the terms of the Rome Statute, the ICC could independently investigate crimes, produce arrest warrants, and try defendants accused of the most heinous international crimes, including war crimes, crimes against humanity, genocide, and aggression.[12] Moreover, in contrast to the ad hoc tribunals that preceded it, the ICC is a permanent addition to the panoply of global governance institutions. Though there was much celebration among human rights activists when the ICC became operational in July 2002, significant questions remained regarding whether the court would succeed. Though the Rome Statute was able to gain the sixty ratifications necessary to establish the court, the majority of the world's nations had not yet joined the ICC and some of the most powerful actively opposed it.[13]

The fourth key stage in the process of institutionalization involved two separate events, each one signaling that the ICC has emerged as a functioning court. The first came on January 26, 2009, when the ICC opened its first case against Thomas Lubanga Dyilo, a Congolese warlord who served as leader of the Union of Congolese Patriots (UCP). In addition to committing crimes against humanity, Lubanga was accused of enlisting some thirty thousand children to serve as soldiers in the conflict.[14] The second came just over a month later, on March 4, when the Office of the Prosecutor (OTP) issued an arrest warrant for Omar al-Bashir, president of Sudan.[15] Bashir was accused of war crimes, crimes against humanity, and genocide in the ongoing conflict in Darfur.[16] Not only was the court up and running but it clearly showed its intent to hold the most powerful perpetrators accountable for their crimes.[17] As of 2015, the ICC has 123 states parties to the statute, is in the process of investigating crimes committed in nineteen situations around the world, and is adjudicating thirty-six active cases.[18]

If these events are indeed harbingers of a fundamental change in international order from one rooted in the rule of force to one rooted in the rule of law, their implications are profound and far-reaching.[19] Yet this wave of optimism still faces some grim realities. On February 3, 2015, a video began circulating on the Internet. The video depicted Lt. Moaz al-Kasabeh, a Jordanian pilot captured in December 2014 by the Islamic States of Iraq and Syria (ISIS), escorted at gunpoint to a steel cage. Dressed in an orange jumpsuit, the lone man is locked in the cage then doused with liquid. Moments later his captors set Kasabeh ablaze.[20] Less than two weeks later, another video emerged. The video depicts over a dozen Egyptian Coptic Christians dressed in orange jumpsuits kneeling on a Libyan beach, their hands cuffed behind them. Behind each prisoner stands an ISIS jihadist dressed in black. On cue, the prisoners are forced to the ground and beheaded en masse.[21]

Proponents may attribute the continued prevalence of brutality to the fact that international justice remains a work in progress. However, these events raise significant questions regarding the notion of an unstoppable river of justice moving international society toward a fundamental transformation. It strongly suggests that while much has been written about international criminal courts, important questions remain unanswered about their origins, form, and function. This book seeks to address three questions: (1) What factors drove the creation of international criminal courts? (2) Why did they take the specific form that they did, and who either supported or opposed such institutional designs? (3) How can we account for the behavior of the International Criminal Court? The answers to these questions may not only help us better understand the factors that shaped the emergence of international criminal courts but may also suggest the broader implications of their presence in international society.

Given what is at stake for international humanitarian law, it should thus come as no surprise that international criminal tribunals have garnered so much scholarly attention in such a relatively short period of time. Most of the available literature on international criminal courts focuses on the constitutional structure of tribunals, their practice, and their jurisprudence.[22] However, the questions posed here beg for the use of theoretical frameworks capable of identifying the most influential factors shaping outcomes. Theory prompts us to carefully define assumptions and key concepts, and to clearly articulate how these elements relate to each other. Sound theorizing requires that relevant causal mechanisms are well-specified and falsifiable, and that hypotheses generated yield unambiguous predictions.[23] This book develops and employs two types of international relations (IR) theory: mid-level theory and general theory. Mid-level theory focuses on narrowly defined phenomena.[24] In this case, its use is largely limited to explaining outcomes specific to international criminal courts. General theory encompasses broad classes of phenomena rather than variables specific to a narrowly defined domain.[25] The advantage is that developing such theory may not only be useful to explain outcomes related to the ICC or even a group of international criminal tribunals but to other international institutions more generally.

As mentioned previously, initial theorizing about the origins and design of international criminal courts has produced an emergent conventional wisdom in the literature.[26] Put simply, it explains these outcomes as primarily the product of growing human rights norms cultivated by norm entrepreneurs and unprecedented levels of grassroots civil society activism across the globe. Constructivist explanations that focus primarily on principles and norms are often presented in contrast to those that might emphasize the role of power. The predominant critique is pretty straightforward: because commitment to the Rome Statute cannot be seen as contributing to a state's material power or its strategic interests, many scholars argue that the creation of the ICC is evidence of the limits of any power-based theory.[27]

With regard to the question of the factors that shape the operation of the ICC, there is no well-developed theoretical literature to date. Of course, given the court's brief history of existence, it is only now that the court has established a sufficient track record on which one could begin to theorize about patterns of behavior. Given that the ICC was specifically designed to divorce power from principle by making the notion of equality under the law a cornerstone of the court, one might expect (or perhaps hope) that politics and political power would have little influence on the process of adjudication. Yet, a growing number of critics have charged that the ICC is little more than a pawn of powerful Western nations used to forward a political agenda against African nations.[28] These critics point to the fact that, to date, formal investigations and trials have only been established for cases drawn from African nations. From this perspective, power politics largely determines outcomes related to the operation of the court.

The empirical evidence presented in this book will show that both perspectives are extreme. The role of idealpolitik in the formation and design of international criminal courts is frequently overstated, as is the argument that the function of the ICC is dominated by realpolitik. Rather, *the politics of international criminal courts plays out at the intersection of power and principle.* Power politics play a significantly more important role in the creation and design of international criminal courts than is generally acknowledged in the literature, yet does not dominate the behavior of the ICC as some have asserted.

This book makes two principal arguments. First, it argues that the creation and design of international criminal courts are frequently as much a product of actors' interests regarding political power and influence as they are the product of norms of justice and the power of principled ideals.[29] International criminal courts have significant implications for state power, and preferences regarding institutional design may be strongly influenced by them.[30] These, in turn, influence whether an actor will support or oppose the creation of a court based on a given design. Second, the book argues that power politics can influence the behavior of international criminal tribunals, even those designed to be the most insulated from them, as is the case with the ICC. For the ICC, this has less to do with direct coercion by member states than it does on the weakness of the new court and its dependence on state cooperation. This dependence prompts the Office of the Prosecutor to internalize the preferences of states—including nonmembers of the court—whose cooperation is important for the court to fulfill its mission. The result is a prosecutorial strategy that takes a more pragmatic approach even as it maintains commitment to the principle of responding to the gravest violations of international humanitarian law. This book is intended to complement the existing literature by showing the interplay between power and principle in the politics of international criminal courts.

In explicating the political dynamics in which international criminal courts exist, the book does not propose a monocausal explanation of outcomes or argue for the superiority of a particular theoretical paradigm. Rather, it employs a more eclectic analytical approach.[31] This analytic eclecticism is reflected in the book's structure, style, and method. First, the book examines three distinct facets in the process of institutionalization: formation, design, and operation. Each of these facets is unique, although there is some overlap between them. For example, support or opposition to the creation of a new court is a function of design because this enables actors to determine the relative gains and costs associated with it.[32] Moreover, operation is influenced by design as well because institutional procedures are spelled out in the instruments of design. Given the high degrees of precision associated with international courts relative to other international institutions, the degree of this overlap between operation and design is likely to be more much more significant in legal institutions.[33] Formation, design, and operation are each addressed independently in the book's chapters, though these overlaps are acknowledged throughout. Thus, rather than having a single theoretical argument that is tested across a set of empirical chapters to follow, the book offers unique theoretical frameworks specific to each facet. Moreover, because each facet of institutionalization has generated its own specific literature, these are reviewed separately in each chapter rather than collectively in a single literature review chapter as is common in social science research. The second type of eclecticism reflected in the book involves epistemological style. The theoretical frameworks offered to explain outcomes all share a common emphasis on the role of power politics, but do so by combining specific elements drawn from the realist tradition in IR with other new or existing theoretical approaches.[34] These include regime complex theory and two-level game frameworks, as well as a new theory of internalization applied to the calculation of egoistic institutional interests. Lastly, the book's analytical approach is also eclectic with regard to method. Rather than employing one method of analysis, the book employs both quantitative and qualitative approaches at multiple levels of analysis. These include historical process tracing, textual analysis, nonlinear regression analysis, and event history regression analysis. Data used in these analyses are drawn from the creation of several original data sets, archival records, elite interviews, as well as an array of secondary sources.

The book is structured as follows. Chapter 1 presents a historiography of the period from 1945 to 1994 to explore the factors that affected the timing and shape of ad hoc international criminal tribunals. Much of the existing scholarship on the creation of these courts points to legal principles and norms as the primary reasons such courts came into being. In contrast to this prevailing view, this chapter shows how different elements of realpolitik motivated their creation. Once the decision to create a court was made, however, norm entrepreneurs had an opportunity to shape these institutions in ways that forwarded key principles of evolving international humanitarian law. The chapter begins by examining the creation of the International Military Tribunal (IMT) held in Nuremberg, Germany and the International Military Tribunal for the Far East (IMTFE) held in Tokyo, Japan at the close of World War II. The historical evidence makes clear that when considering options for dealing with their enemies at the end of the war, the Allied powers emphasized the role the tribunals could play in determining whether the Axis powers waged a war of aggression. Though the popular contemporary narrative regarding the IMT is that it was primarily a response to the horrors of the Holocaust and the crimes against humanity committed by the Nazis, the evidence suggests that this was not the initial rationale for creating the court. In short, the court's initial purpose from the point of view of the Allied leadership was to prosecute the *jus ad bellum* (the right to war).[35] Unpacking this crucial distinction between the *jus ad bellum* and the *jus in bello* (war crimes) enables one to see that the IMT was the product the intersection between realpolitik and idealpolitik because it involves legitimizing the use of force in war. Once the decision to establish the court was made, norm entrepreneurs then shaped its jurisprudence, and ultimately, its legacy.

Chapter 1 goes on to show not only how Cold War realpolitik served to impair further development of an international atrocities regime for decades but also how interests in the form of power intersected with human rights principles to shape their reemergence on the international landscape in the early 1990s. Some scholars have suggested that domestic outcry over atrocities committed in the Balkans and Rwanda prompted the UN Security Council to create the ICTY and ICTR. Yet the empirical evidence only partially validates this view. Chapter 1 suggests that for liberal democratic members of the UN Security Council that created the tribunal, creating the ad hoc courts was a way to respond to these crises in a way that involved lower cost and less political risk than more assertive policy options—particularly military intervention. For illiberal members of the Security Council, the decision to support (or simply not veto) these courts was a tactical decision rooted in a broader grand strategy predicated on forging closer relations with the United States and members of the European Community. As was the case with the IMT, once created, these ad hoc tribunals served as a vehicle for norm entrepreneurs to further develop the tribunal regime in ways consistent with evolving notions of international human rights law. By systematically analyzing the ad hoc courts from Nuremberg to The Hague, chapter 1 shows how power and principle intertwined to forge the growing ad hoc tribunal regime.

Chapter 2 examines the creation of the International Criminal Court, emphasizing the politics of institutional design. Much of the current literature on the creation of the ICC argues that support or opposition to the court can be largely explained in terms of growing support for principles of international humanitarian law. This offers a parsimonious but overly simplified account of the politics surrounding the formation and design of the ICC. In contrast, chapter 2 shows that for many states, interests regarding human rights were not necessarily their only concern during the Rome Conference. For a number of states participating in the negotiations, interests were at least partially defined in terms of power, and these strongly shaped their preferences regarding the institutional design of the ICC. These power considerations were far from marginal. In fact, they brought to bear questions regarding the architecture of international order and its institutionalized hierarchies. During the Rome Conference negotiations, a battle was waged between states seeking to maintain their relative position in the global hierarchy and those attempting to restructure that hierarchy in part by creating a specific type of international criminal court. This struggle was waged by several of the world's most powerful states and a coalition of "dissatisfied powers" engaged in a broader struggle to close the gap between the privileged and the marginalized in international society.

Chapter 2 explicates these dynamics by integrating two different strands of theoretical research. It combines insights from research that illustrate how power is vested in the creation and design of international institutions, with insights from the literature on regime complexes.[36] Synthesizing these frameworks shows how state power can be affected by relationships between institutions. This new theoretical framework is then used to explain state interests regarding a subset of Rome Conference participants and why the issue of Security Council control was so central to the negotiations regarding the design of the ICC. This political struggle centered on the question of whether the ICC would be nested within the UN/UNSC or would be designed independent of it. Using a combination of quantitative and qualitative methods of analysis, the chapter explicates the process of institutional design. This includes the PrepCom meetings (1996–98), the Rome Conference (1998), and the Kampala Review Conference (2010).

Although the empirical evidence presented in chapter 2 supports the hypotheses regarding the role of interests defined in terms of power in shaping the design of the court and who ultimately supported or opposed it, it also reveals several key outliers whose behavior seems at odds with what the structurally based theory predicted. Why was Guatemala the lone defector among the dissatisfied powers? Moreover, why did Britain and France both defect from the P5 consensus that sought a court largely controlled by the Security Council? Chapter 3 draws on Robert Putnam's two-level game framework to generate expectations regarding state preferences for each of the outliers.[37]

Scholars have suggested that domestic politics played an important role in explaining the shift in the British position vis-à-vis the Rome Statute and argue that this was a product of changing British values.[38] From this perspective, the rise of New Labour's "ethical foreign policy" in 1997 signaled a responsiveness to changing public attitudes in Britain that increasingly value humanitarian principles in the determination of foreign policy interests. The evidence presented in chapter 3 shows that this was not necessarily the case. It explains the British shift as a function of New Labour's electoral tactics created as part of a broad strategy to unseat the Conservative government and assume control over the government. Moreover, the evidence presented in chapter 3 shows that this use of principled rhetoric did not signal a fundamental shift in British attitudes, but rather, was a relatively short-term political tactic that was later discarded by those who employed it during the 1997 election. Chapter 3 goes on to explain how the change in the British position altered France's win set with regards to the Rome Statute. France was among the most ardent supporters of a weaker ICC with extremely limited powers to act independently. Like the British, French design preferences regarding the ICC were influenced by interests defined in terms of power, but at multiple levels. For the French, this was not a product of domestic politics, but rather, intra–European Union (EU) political interests. As soon as Britain changed positions, France faced the prospect of emerging from the conference as the lone holdout against the Rome Statute design among EU nations. Yet, even late in the game France was reluctant to budge. Ultimately, eleventh-hour design concessions offered by the Like-Minded

Group (LMG) served to bridge the gap with French preferences regarding the statute.

Unlike the cases of Britain and France, Guatemala's behavior regarding the design of the ICC has not garnered scholarly attention. Instead, the literature largely focuses on the Like-Minded Group, reflecting perhaps an assumption among scholars that this group represented largely homogeneous interests regarding institutional design. Like the other two outliers examined here, domestic politics are equally important to explain Guatemala's behavior regarding the ICC. In this case, reluctance to join the LMG in favor of a strong and independent court was a product of individual and party survival. The chapter explores the history of crimes committed during the reign of Efraín Ríos Montt and explains how his vulnerability to international prosecution pushed his Frente Republicano Guatemalteco party and their political allies to oppose the ICC. Once domestic political conditions changed in Guatemala, the government changed its position and has now joined the court.[39]

Chapter 4 goes on to show how the intersection of power and principle affects the operation of the International Criminal Court. Why does the ICC pursue some cases but not others? Moreover, why does it move the process of adjudication more rapidly for some situations and more slowly for others? The Office of the Prosecutor maintains that prosecutorial choices are made solely in accordance with accepted norms of jurisprudence.[40] Chief Prosecutor Fatou Bensouda stated emphatically that "we are a new tool, a judicial tool, not a tool in the hands of politicians who think they can decide when to plug or unplug us."[41] A growing number of critics have argued that the court is little more than a tool of powerful Western states utilized primarily to forward an anti-Africa agenda.[42] Is prosecutorial strategy driven primarily by issues of jurisprudence or politics? Though legal factors alone cannot account for the many inconsistencies evident on the court's docket, the empirical evidence does not support the notion that the ICC is the victim of "institutional capture" by powerful states.[43] Chapter 4 forwards a theory of prosecutorial strategy that explains why egoistic institutional interests may internalize the preferences of external actors. In particular, this theoretical framework provides a rationale for why the strategic interests of three of the most powerful nonmember states may be internalized by the OTP. Using a mixed-methods approach that draws on an original data set of legal and political variables, Chapter 4 shows how prosecutorial strategy emerges from the intersection of principle, power, and pragmatism. While international legal principles press the OTP to place greater emphasis on situations deemed to be the most grave, institutional pragmatism prompts the court to move much more cautiously in cases involving the strategic interests of three important nonmember states—the United States, Russia, and China.

At the time he took office, the chief prosecutor considered support from the permanent members of the UN Security Council to be "crucial" to its long-term mission.[44] The Security Council solely possesses the authority to sanction coercive military intervention to intervene in situations where grave violations of international humanitarian law are taking place. The Security Council is also the only body with the power to grant the ICC jurisdiction over situations involving the actions of nonmember states. As such, it alone holds the key to extending the jurisdictional reach of the court where doing so is necessary if perpetrators of mass atrocities are to be held accountable for their crimes. Moreover, the ability of the ICC to respond to humanitarian crises would be severely hampered should the permanent members of the Security Council seek to actively obstruct the court. Two permanent members of the Security Council, Britain and France, are members of the ICC and have offered consistent support to the court. With their support already in hand, it is rational for the OTP to pursue an institutional course aimed partially at forging better relations with the three remaining permanent members of the Security Council that are not members of the court: the United States, Russia, and China. Thus, it is in the egoistic institutional interests of the ICC to carefully consider the interests and potential reaction of these three countries as it considers is prosecutorial strategy. In other words, it is rational to expect that these interests may be internalized in the process of defining the institutional interests of the ICC. This internalization does not dictate that the prosecutorial strategy of the OTP is primarily driven by deference to American, Russian, or Chinese interests. Rather, this chapter suggests that these internalized interests may serve as a significant intervening variable in the process of adjudication. The findings presented in chapter 4 have significant normative implications. Although idealists are reluctant to sacrifice principle in the face of power, the realization of the court's important long-term goals relies on integrating power and principle through pragmatism.

The concluding chapter provides a brief overview of the key findings presented in the book, highlighting the argument that beneath the discourse regarding rights and justice that surround international criminal courts is a complex system of global power politics. As shown in the chapters that precede it, realpolitik and idealpolitik intertwine to shape the creation, design, and operation of international criminal courts. In addition to providing a brief summary of the book's major findings and their significance to scholarship on international criminal courts and international politics more generally, the concluding chapter returns to a basic question raised throughout the book: Does the creation of the ICC signal a transformation of international society? Proponents of the ICC have suggested that the adoption of the Rome Statute signaled a revolutionary shift in world order away from the realpolitik of the Westphalian system toward a more Kantian model, one based on core principles and the rule of law. A better understanding the role that power politics has played in the development of the atrocities regime prompts a more measured assessment of the impact international criminal courts have had on world order.

Do international criminal courts deter the commission of atrocities? Though it is certainly difficult to assess deterrence in any context, the anecdotal evidence is not compelling. The deterrent effect of potential tribunal action has done little to stem the commission of atrocities in places such as North Korea, Syria, Mali, and the Central African Republic. Moreover, the recurring violence in Mali and the Central African Republic even after the ICC has begun adjudicating those situations suggests that deterrence is elusive. In spite of that, the book does not suggest that international criminal courts are simply tools of powerful states as some critics of the ICC have argued. Nor does it suggest that international criminal courts will not contribute to global peace and the protection of human rights. Rather, international justice alone is not sufficient to realize these lofty goals—it requires the support of powerful states. Thus, principles of justice may need to heed the realities of international power politics by adopting a more pragmatic approach. International criminal courts have facilitated the articulation and diffusion of norms of human rights and individual accountability for conduct during conflict, both domestic and international. But the contemporary international order is based on another core principle: great power prerogative and special responsibilities.[45] Rather than attempt to supplant this principle of international order with one based on equality under the law, the ICC may find it necessary to accept some degree of great power exceptionalism in exchange for great power support so essential to a functioning legal institution. It seems that the OTP already has adopted this stance de facto, but is certainly not inclined to acknowledge it publicly. Although this has generated some criticism among human rights advocates, this course may be the most appropriate if international justice is to contribute to global peace and stability in the long run. Already, the United States has softened its stance against the ICC, and it is not inconceivable that it might someday join the court. China and Russia may be more reluctant partners, but they too have shown a more positive view so long as the court action conforms to current norms regarding Security Council control over issues of international peace. In short, the struggle between power and principle need not be decided wholly in favor of one over the other.

Chapter 1

Power and Principle from Nuremberg to The Hague

That four great nations, flushed with victory and stung with injury stay the hand of vengeance and voluntarily submit their captive enemies to the judgment of the law is one of the most significant tributes that Power has ever paid to Reason.

—Robert H. Jackson

On August 8, 1945, the governments of the United States, France, Britain, and the Soviet Union signed the London Charter, which established the International Military Tribunal (IMT) to prosecute major war criminals of the Axis powers in Europe.[1] Many scholars point to the Nuremberg tribunal as the cornerstone of the contemporary atrocities regime.[2] In Gary Bass's words, "Nuremberg remains legalism's greatest moment of glory."[3] Finally, perpetrators of atrocities would answer for their crimes while being afforded the due process rights and protections consistent with contemporary Western jurisprudence.[4] Justice Robert Jackson described the scene in the courtroom: "In the prisoners' dock sit twenty-odd broken men. Reproached by the humiliation of those they have led almost as bitterly as by the desolation of those they have attacked, their personal capacity for evil is forever past. It is hard now to perceive in these men as captives the power by which as Nazi leaders they once dominated much of the world and terrified most of it."[5]

This event would prove not to be an isolated one in the history of mankind, but rather a seminal moment in a more expansive process of justice and accountability. In 1993, another international criminal tribunal was established to prosecute perpetrators of atrocities in the former Yugoslavia, followed shortly thereafter by another tribunal for Rwanda in 1994. In 1998, the jurisdiction of the International Criminal Tribunal for the Former Yugoslavia (ICTY) was expanded to include investigation and prosecution of acts stemming from the conflict in Kosovo. The rise of international criminal tribunals was hailed by human rights activists, and scholars have pointed to their existence as evidence of the growing power of human rights principles and norms.[6] Before 1945, the dominant practice in the application of international law on matters relating to human rights was deference to the notion of domestic jurisdiction.[7] It now appeared that despots could no longer hide behind the shelter of state sovereignty.

A conventional wisdom has emerged in the existing literature on international criminal tribunals that explains their development in terms of principled politics and political activism. For example, Bass argues that "it is only liberal states, with legalist beliefs, that support bona fide war crimes tribunals."[8] Much of the extant scholarship concurs with this assessment. The basic causal logic revolves around the role of evolving human rights ideas and norms, facilitated by norm entrepreneurs such as Henry Stimson, Robert Jackson, Telford Taylor, and Benjamin Ferencz, just to name a few.[9] Norm entrepreneurs were the architects that oversaw the codification and expansion of international humanitarian law through such instruments as the Nuremberg Principles, the UN Genocide Convention, and the Universal Declaration of Human Rights following World War II. Among these, the Nuremberg trials established precedent for holding individuals—rather than states—accountable for gross human-rights violations.

As outlined in the introduction, several scholars have characterized the process of legal and institutional development using the metaphor of a river (or stream) of justice. For example, Benjamin Schiff writes, "The international justice river arose in the mists of time from divine and international law sources. As it grew and its current accelerated, legal engineers shaped its flow, and advocates broadened its appeal."[10] Similarly, Kathryn Sikkink conceptualizes the confluence of several streams of justice, including those related to the Nuremberg trials and to the rising prevalence of domestic trials for prosecuting gross human-rights violations: "Underneath these two streams of prosecutions, states and non-state actors worked to build a strong streambed of international human rights law and international humanitarian law that fortified the legal underpinnings of the cascade."[11] This, then, forms the basis of what she terms the "justice cascade," which she defines as "a shift in the legitimacy of the norm of individual criminal accountability for human rights violations and an increase in the criminal prosecutions on behalf of that norm. The term captures how the idea started as a small stream, but later caught on suddenly, sweeping along many actors in its wake."[12]

Using this metaphor of a growing "river of justice" brings into sharp relief the linkages that exist between the Nuremberg trials and subsequent legal institutions. This framework not only forwards a causal logic—one that explains subsequent developments in terms of a linked process of legal development—but also an evolutionary logic.[13] In this sense, subsequent forms of international criminal tribunals represent some form of advancement (i.e., improvement) from prior forms in the process of realizing a stronger "justice." Thus, the ad hoc international criminal tribunals established for the former Yugoslavia and Rwanda, although based on precedent set at Nuremberg, sought to move beyond the "victor's justice" that some thought characterized the trials following World War II. In terms of evolution, many proponents of international criminal tribunals saw the International Criminal Court (ICC) as the realization of a more perfect legal institution, in that it moved beyond deference to Westphalian sovereignty and inherent differentials in power in the Westphalian system of world order. For them, "The International Criminal Court is a milestone in the ongoing transition towards an international legal order that is less based on state sovereignty and more oriented towards the protection of all citizens of the world from abuse of power."[14]

Although the development of the contemporary human-rights regime and its impact on international criminal tribunals is well documented in the existing literature, explanations that emphasize the role of principled norms leave important questions unanswered. Many scholars have pointed out that the growth and development of the atrocities regime was stunted during the Cold War, yet few have rigorously addressed this period of institutional stagnation. All too often, scholars whose narrative emphasizes the growing "river of justice" pass over the Cold War in an extremely abrupt fashion. Frequently, this is done in as little as one or two sentences.[15] Since the Cold War superpowers were the ones who initially established the IMT, what aspects of the Cold War prompted them to oppose further development of the regime? Presumably, scholars emphasizing the role of liberal principles might point to the intransigence of illiberal states reluctant to institutionalize norms that they do not practice. From this point of view, the Soviet Union, which holds veto power as a permanent member of the UN Security Council (UNSC), is the likely obstacle to the creation of an international criminal court that is an official organ of the United Nations (UN). However, if principles and norms were determinative, why did the liberal democracies fail to move ahead with the creation of a treaty-based court as was the case with the ICC? If proponents of liberal norms indeed seek to lock in such commitments, why not create a court with jurisdiction over states in the Western sphere? Additional questions emerge regarding the creation of the ad hoc tribunals in the 1990s. The creation of these ad hoc UN tribunals is often attributed to the end of the Cold War and the pressure applied to liberal democratic states by civil society actors to respond to human rights crises in places such as Somalia, the Balkans, and Rwanda.[16] Yet, the tribunals were a product of Security Council action, and not all permanent members can be classified as liberal democracies. Why did Russia and China support the creation of the tribunals? Theories based on liberal principles alone have difficulty accounting for these outcomes because important elements are missing from such accounts.

This chapter focuses on the role of power to fill these gaps emanating from constructivist-oriented approaches that emphasize the role of norms and norm entrepreneurs.[17] Realist scholars of international relations (IR) have argued that states maintain a stable hierarchy of interests in which the accumulation of power is afforded the highest priority. This strong distinction between "high politics" and "low politics" arises because the ability of states to survive in an anarchic international system is directly related to their relative power.[18] This is not to suggest that states may not seek to attain ideological or ethical objectives, such as the protection of human rights. Rather, it suggests that when pursuit of ideals runs contrary to the pursuit of power, states will choose the latter. Moreover, states may aspire to achieve moral aims, but all require power to realize them.

This chapter explores how interests defined in terms of power intersect with norm development in determining the timing and shape of the emerging tribunal regime. Although the effect of power appears frequently in the expansive literature on international criminal courts, it is often underspecified and/or applied to very specific outcomes or issues. Moreover, the grand narrative in much of the extant literature typically characterizes realpolitik as the source of intermittent obstacles to the development and application of law rather than a fundamental factor shaping state interests and behavior. This chapter argues that elements of realpolitik provided opportunities for norm entrepreneurs to forward a principled agenda in designing international criminal tribunals. Interests defined in terms of power were an important factor at several key stages of regime development. This chapter reminds us what the original motivations behind tribunal justice actually were and how this narrative changed over time. The historical record shows that the initial motivations to create an international tribunal were based primarily on a desire to adjudicate the legitimacy of the war (*jus ad bellum*) rather than the specific war crimes committed during the conflict (*jus in bello*). Once the decision to establish a tribunal was made, however, the design of the court and its jurisprudence were put in the hands of those who could promote a basis for the court more firmly grounded in international humanitarian law.

This chapter also explicates how Cold War realpolitik served to stymie institutional development for decades, even as atrocities were well documented and the global movement for human rights remained very active. The point made is that powerful states, whether liberal democratic or not, would not support the creation of a tribunal that impaired their ability to conduct the Cold War on their terms. Moreover, this chapter explains how strategic interests shaped the timing of the emergence of the ad hoc tribunals in the 1990s. Human tragedy and public outcry in liberal societies may partially explain the pressure for powerful countries to respond, but it does not account for the specific choice of response (i.e., international tribunals). For liberal democratic members of the UN Security Council, the choice to create international courts was less a function of principled ethics than it was a means to deflect public pressure to act in locations with little strategic value. For the illiberal members of the Security Council, support for the creation of the ad hoc tribunals was a product of diffuse reciprocity.[19] Russia and China both sought to use support for tribunals strategically as a means to advance a broader grand strategy of engagement with the liberal West.

Drawing on the historical evidence from the origins of the Nuremberg tribunal through the creation of the ad hoc international criminal tribunals established for the former Yugoslavia and Rwanda, this chapter presents a very different narrative from the one that dominates the literature. It is one where the process of institutionalization is shaped by the intersection of interests defined in terms of power with principles of human rights. Rather than the product of the inevitable momentum of a "river of justice" or a "justice cascade," realpolitik provided the opportunities norm entrepreneurs needed to build a more principle-based legal regime.

The Postwar Tribunals

The International Military Tribunal at Nuremberg is often cited as a cornerstone of international humanitarian law. Through the IMT, norms regarding treatment of civilians during conflict were more precisely defined, and the accused were held individually accountable for violation of these principles. Among the crimes prosecuted at Nuremberg, those pertaining to genocide tend to dominate public perception of the court's historical legacy.[20] Yet, as Bass has argued, "One of the great ironies of Nuremberg's legacy is that the tribunal is remembered as a product of Allied horror at the Holocaust, when in fact America and Britain, the liberal countries that played major roles in deciding what Nuremberg would be, actually focused far more on the criminality of Nazi aggression than on the Holocaust."[21] Understanding this irony requires that we unpack the politics that surrounded the origins of the IMT and the role that power played in the development of international humanitarian law.

How did power shape the pursuit of justice at Nuremberg after World War II? First and foremost, realpolitik determined whether a court would be created at all, and subsequently, who would face trial. Military leadership on both sides of the war recognized that whether you would stand trial was entirely dependent on your relative power at the conclusion of the war. Those lacking power—the defeated forces—must face judgment by those holding power—the victorious. Hermann Goering, the highest-ranking Nazi prosecuted during the Nuremberg trials, pointed out that "the victor will always be the judge, and the vanquished the accused."[22] On the American side, General Curtis LeMay famously remarked, "I suppose if I had lost the war, I would have been tried as a war criminal. Fortunately, we were on the winning side."[23] It was the Allied leadership that would determine the type of justice their defeated foes would face. In other words, justice was first and foremost a function of power.

Leaders of the Allied powers met several times in the latter stages of World War II to discuss an endgame strategy for the war and the postwar international order.[24] An important part of these discussions involved the question of what to do about their defeated enemies at the conclusion of the war. Initially, discussions reflected a notion of justice in terms of "eye-for-an-eye" retribution against the defeated Axis powers.[25] Still in the heat of battle, conversations about the Axis powers tended to be more about victory and vengeance rather than justice in the way that term is used in contemporary international humanitarian law. At the conclusion of the Moscow Conference in November 1943, participants drafted the Moscow Declaration, which stated that the Nazis would be "judged and punished" for their actions during the war. However, the form and process of judgment and punishment remained ambiguous.[26] A similar statement was issued by FDR, Churchill, and Chiang Kai-shek in what became known at the Potsdam Declaration, issued in July 1945. In the Potsdam Declaration, Allied leaders promised the Japanese that "stern justice shall be meted out to all war criminals."

While there was consensus among the Allied leaders that the Nazis should face judgment for their actions, there were differing views on the purpose of justice as well as what role a court should play in the process of producing justice. At the subsequent meeting held in Tehran from November 28 through December 1, 1943, Stalin argued that justice should take the form of mass executions from which few should be spared. Stalin's proposal would entail the execution of 50,000 to 100,000 Germans.[27] Though taken aback by the severity of Soviet sentiment, both FDR and Churchill were subject to public demands that defined justice along similar lines. As noted by Gary Bass, calls for justice largely came in the form of a hue and cry for revenge "of the swift and certain kind."[28] In Britain, public opinion polls showed that a majority of respondents preferred execution of Nazi leadership, reflecting that Britons showed a far greater interest in punishment than due process.[29] Neither the British nor the Soviets initially showed much interest in pursuing formal trials. Ultimately, it was U.S. president Franklin Delano Roosevelt who saw the appeal of creating a court and who convinced British prime minister Winston Churchill and Soviet Union leader Joseph Stalin to support the idea.

Particularly for the Americans and the Soviets, the appeal of creating a court was rooted in a desire to hold the Nazis accountable for the war itself.

For FDR, this view was documented in a correspondence to Secretary of State Edward Stettinius, in which FDR expressed his desire to put the Nazis on trial for waging war.[30] In the letter, Roosevelt made no mention of the Holocaust, crimes against humanity, or war crimes. "Waging war" in the context of the laws of war involves aggression, and the interest in trying the Nazis for waging a war of aggression was also central to FDR's successor, Harry Truman, who was president at the time the IMT was established. At the conclusion of the Nuremberg trials, Truman remarked that the IMT succeeded in placing "international law on the side of peace as against aggressive war."[31] The American emphasis on the crime of aggression as a principal motivation for creating the court was further supported by Allied observers. The British prosecutor at Nuremberg observed that "the Americans are primarily concerned with establishing that the prisoners conspired together to wage a war of aggression—a very vital part of the case."[32] This emphasis on aggression also resonated with the Soviets, whose views were influenced by Aron Trainin, the Soviets' chief international law expert. In his 1944 book, *The Criminal Responsibility of the Hitlerites*, Trainin argued that the gravest offense of Nazi Germany was committing a fundamental "crime against peace" by waging a war of aggression.[33] Moreover, the Soviets were on record in their criticism that the League of Nations did not go far enough in condemning and criminalizing "aggressive war."[34] Trainin's work was circulated among the British before the London Conference, and D. Maxwell Fife, head of the British delegation, "reportedly declared it 'a godsend' for clarifying the important issues of the day."[35] Ultimately, it was this notion of aggression as a "crime against peace" that found its place among the crimes tried under the London Charter.

Why was aggression the primary concern of the Allied leaders with respect to postwar justice? The laws of war are constituted by two distinct dimensions: the *jus ad bellum* and the *jus in bello*. The former term refers to acceptable justifications for the use of armed force (i.e., distinguishing between "just" and "unjust" wars), whereas the latter term refers to conduct during conflict (i.e., war crimes).[36] Summarizing this crucial distinction, Michael Walzer notes, "War is always judged twice, first with reference to the reasons states have for fighting, secondly with reference to the means they adopt."[37] The initial basis for the criminal proceedings at Nuremberg hinged on questions of the *jus ad bellum*, even as specific charges of war crimes by individuals were adjudicated in the proceedings. For the Allies, a primary political goal of the Nuremberg trials was to establish the legal and moral culpability of the Nazi regime in waging a war of aggression. By establishing culpability on the part of the conquered, the Allies would be able to legitimize not only their participation in the war but also their execution of it. This notion of absolution of violations of the *jus in bello* as a function of whether participants waged a "just" war is commonplace in the historical record of conflict and war.[38] For example, Clausewitz, in his famous treatise on war, suggested that it is the aggressor that bears responsibility for the consequences of the fighting he initiates.[39] This does not mean that Allied leaders were concerned that they might somehow face prosecution for their actions taken during the war. After all, this process was consciously designed to be victor's justice. Rather, the quest for legitimacy appeared to be rooted more in an interest to gain soft power during a period of global transformation where international order was being reconstituted.[40]

This desire to legitimize their own actions during the war was manifest in a meeting of the Allied Chief Prosecutors for the Nuremberg Tribunal held in November 1945, eleven days before the start of the trials. At that meeting, a "gentlemen's agreement" was reached to maintain a united front among the prosecution teams and to prevent the tribunal from being utilized as a forum for discussion of potential Allied breaches of international law.[41] It was also agreed that each would draft and circulate a memorandum identifying their country's wartime transgressions so that preparations could be made to keep these from becoming tools for the defense.[42] The British memorandum suggested that the German defense team might raise the issue of "so-called British imperialism" conducted before World War II.[43] The Soviets delivered a list of topics they wished to keep out of the tribunal proceedings, including questions about the Soviet-German Non-Aggression Pact of 1939, Soviet-Polish relations, and "the Baltic question."[44] For the Americans, the firebombing of German cities and the nuclear destruction of Hiroshima and Nagasaki were sensitive issues. Truman wrestled with the weighty issues of what should be done in the interest of securing military victory and protecting the lives of American servicemen when he made the decision to use atomic weapons against the Japanese. Indeed, he suggested that the use of atomic weapons "is far worse than gas and biological warfare because it affects the civilian populations and murders them by wholesale."[45] Documentary evidence suggests that his decision to drop the bomb was based substantially on the notion that the Japanese had brought the horrors of war unto themselves by waging a war of aggression. In a letter to Samuel Cavert, Truman writes, "Nobody is more disturbed over the use of Atomic bombs than I am but I was greatly disturbed over the unwarranted attack by the Japanese on Pearl Harbor and their murder of our prisoners of war."[46] Prosecutors agreed before the trials that these sensitive issues would be kept out of the proceedings and were largely successful in doing so.

Some may question whether seeking legitimacy is consistent with a realist explanation, one that emphasizes interests defined in terms of power. After all, realpolitik is in large part based on the notion that "might makes right." It could be argued that the desire to legitimize their actions during the war implies that there was an underlying normative order for the use of force. Such normative principles might be seen as a means to moderate the effects of power. In this case, however, Allied concern over legitimacy did not seem to have any such moderating effect on the use of force. Civilians in Germany and Japan were not spared from acts now widely considered to be barbarous—the purposeful targeting of the civilian population and the application of weapons of mass destruction. Instead, it is more likely that Allied pursuit of legitimacy reflected interests to develop their soft power.[47] Because realism is commonly characterized in terms of an emphasis on hard power, this pursuit of legitimacy may seem more consistent with a constructivist rather than a realist perspective. However, classical realist scholars argued forcefully that the "power over opinion" is an essential element of politics. In fact, E. H. Carr, one of the fathers of classical realist thought, argued that "power over opinion is therefore not less essential for political purposes than military or economic power, and has always been closely associated with them."[48]

Transcripts of the wartime conferences make it clear that for the Soviets the appeal of creating a tribunal was primarily rooted in their interest to generate propaganda rather than justice. Jackson noted that the Soviets viewed the court as "one of the organs of government power, a weapon in the hands of the ruling class for the purpose of safeguarding its interests."[49] Similarly, historian Francine Hirsch writes, "The Soviets . . . agreed to participate in an international tribunal of major Nazi leaders . . . for the sake of catharsis, and with the faith that a public trial and conviction of the 'Hitlerites' would serve positive political goals—demonstrating the evils of fascism and the valor of the peace-loving Soviet people."[50] However, the Soviets were not alone in the view that international legal mechanisms offered an opportunity for advancing their political agendas.[51] For the Americans, it was the court's design and jurisprudence that had significant implications for soft power. This process was strongly influenced by the particular views of several key individuals.

U.S. Secretary of War Henry Stimson was among the first advocates of shaping the process of postwar justice to conform to American interests in generating soft power. In discussions with FDR about the design of the Nuremberg tribunal, it was Stimson who successful argued for adjudication and due process over those who sought summary executions of Nazi leadership.[52] Although FDR was initially torn between the "rough justice" advocated by his fellow Allied leaders and Stimson's more legalistic approach to dealing with the Nazis, Stimson's views were more congruent with those of FDR's successor, Harry Truman. Truman was a man for whom the cultivation of soft power was integral to his foreign policy. This view was most evident in his articulation of the Truman Doctrine, which would define the Cold War as an epic struggle between "free peoples" and "totalitarian regimes."[53] Truman was also a man with strong personal convictions about due process in law.[54] In the case of the Nuremberg tribunal, the jurisprudence employed in the proceedings mattered a great deal in terms of setting precedent—both in a strictly legal sense and in terms of influencing subsequent discourse. Drawing on basic premises of due process as practiced in the American judiciary, Stimson's insistence that the war crimes trials conform to the domestic standard of jurisprudence introduced the principle of justice as fairness in an environment that was largely dominated by notions of justice as terms of power. In selecting Justice Robert Jackson to serve as the chief U.S. prosecutor for the Nuremberg tribunals on May 2, 1945, Truman ensured that this view would have influence both on the design of the court and its legal process of adjudication. Like Truman, Jackson held strong convictions about procedural fairness, and he believed that due process was essential to protect the public from government overreach. In an address to the American Society of International Law, Jackson declared, "The ultimate principle is that you must put no man on trial under the form of judicial proceedings if you are not willing to see him freed if not proved guilty. If you are determined to execute a man in any case, there is no occasion for a trial. *The world yields no respect to courts that are merely organized to convict.*"[55]

Although the London Charter left specific procedural issues to the discretion of the tribunal, Article 16 expressly stipulated that the court provide a "fair trial for defendants."[56] The charter identified several rights to be afforded to the accused: (a) the right to a detailed specification of the charges being brought against him, translated into his native language; (b) the right to provide explanatory testimony during any preliminary examination or during the trial; (c) the right to have court proceedings conducted in or translated into his native language; (d) the right to conduct his own defense or to have the assistance of counsel; and (e) the right to present evidence in his defense, and to cross-examine witnesses testifying against him. These rights were to be showcased for international consumption. Each of the Allied countries invited a substantial number of journalists, photographers, filmmakers, writers, artists, and political cartoonists to bring the trials to the widest international audience in addition to the population back home. This was also true of the proceedings in Tokyo that would follow, which some likened to a show trial.[57] As described by a correspondent for *Time* magazine, the Tokyo tribunal "looked . . . like a third-string road company of the Nuremberg show."[58] These arrangements indicate that the Allied powers recognized the trials as political events with significant consequences for international relations in the emerging postwar order.[59]

These basic characteristics and causal patterns were also evident in the Tokyo trials, which began on May 3, 1946. Over a period of two and one-half years, the International Military Tribunal for the Far East (IMTFE) prosecuted twenty-eight defendants who held the highest government and military positions in Japan from 1928 to 1945. As was the case with Nuremberg, power shaped the origins of the court. Like its immediate predecessor in Germany, the IMTFE was an instrument of victors' justice. The tribunal was established by the victorious powers, and only crimes committed by the defeated would be adjudicated during the proceedings. The IMTFE was established through the Tokyo Charter, drafted under the direction of the supreme commander of the Allied powers (SCAP), General Douglas MacArthur. Under the charter, the SCAP was granted the sole power to appoint the members of the tribunal, including the president, and to determine its basic structure and rules.[60] Moreover, although the membership in the tribunal was broader than was the case at Nuremberg, encompassing a number of Asian and South Asian countries who fought against the Japanese, the proceedings were largely under the control of the Americans.[61]

As was the case with Nuremberg, prosecuting the crime of aggression was the principle motivation for the Americans' interest in forming the tribunal. In his Proclamation by the Supreme Commander for the Allied Powers, issued on January 19, 1946, General MacArthur opened with the following statement: "Whereas, the United States and the Nations allied therewith in opposing the illegal wars of aggression of the Axis Nations, have from time to time made declarations of their intentions that war criminals should be brought to justice."[62] This statement not only seems to equate the notion of "war criminal" in relation to the crime of aggression, but its prominence at the opening of MacArthur's proclamation suggests the importance placed on aggression as the primary motivating factor for the IMTFE. As noted by one of the tribunal's judges, the object of America's interest in creating the Tokyo tribunal "was not the atrocities which occurred during the war, but the original attack on Pearl Harbor alone."[63] This was most certainly the case for General MacArthur and Chief Prosecutor Joseph Keenan, both of whom initially desired to limit the charges filed against the Japanese to this one offense. Keenan explained, "It was our purpose in the beginning to base the prosecution solely on the Pearl Harbor episode and the events immediately contributing thereto. We concluded, and I think correctly so, that it would be necessary at some stage of the trial to develop fully the entire Japanese plan for military aggression, for only by a correct analysis of its origin and purposes could the Japanese situation be pictured in its true light."[64] For the Americans, the attack on Pearl Harbor represented aggression in its purest form.

The relative importance of the crime of aggression is also evidenced by the tiered nature in which the crimes covered under the Tokyo Charter were prosecuted. Under Article 5 of the Charter, "crimes against peace" (aggression) were listed as a "class A" offense, whereas "war crimes" and "crimes against humanity" were listed as "class B" and "C" offenses, respectively. Not only did the order suggest a hierarchy, but so too did the manner in which these were adjudicated. Defendants charged with aggression were tried at the central venue in Tokyo, whereas those charged of class B and C offenses were tried in the locales where the crimes were committed.[65] This would suggest an effort to make the crime of aggression even more central to the tribunal, if that was indeed possible, than was the case for the Nuremberg court. Anticipating a potential attempt by the defense to challenge the notion that aggression constituted an accepted principle under international law, Chief Prosecutor Keenan argued in his opening remarks that "the question of aggressive war has been considered by so many nations and deliberately outlawed by them that their unanimous verdict rises to the dignity of a general principle of international law."[66]

As was the case at Nuremberg, justifying its participation in the war by prosecuting the crime of aggression also served to justify its behavior during the war. Anticipating potential backlash against its use of the atomic bomb, "the Allies felt in need of vindication, not only for the justness of their cause in the war, but also a vindication of their conduct of the war."[67] Like the IMT at Nuremberg, the dropping of atomic weapons on Hiroshima and Nagasaki were kept out of the proceedings altogether. The IMTFE judges ruled that evidence regarding the use of atomic weapons was inadmissible, arguing that "if a means is justified by an end, the use of the atomic bomb was justified."[68]

Interests defined in terms of soft power figured prominently for the IMTFE as they had for the Nuremberg tribunal. For the Americans, soft power was not just tied to the issue of aggression, but also to the structure of the court and its jurisprudence. This interest regarding soft power manifests itself in several forms during the Tokyo proceedings. First, it was reflected in the decision to design a more diverse court, both in terms of its membership and the national origins of its judges. In addition to the four powers represented at Nuremberg, judges at the IMTFE came from Australia, Canada, China, India, the Netherlands, New Zealand, and the Philippines. Second, interests defined in terms of soft power were reflected in American concerns regarding due process rights for the accused. As was the case with the Nuremberg tribunal, due process rights were considered essential for the Japanese and the international community to view the trials as just. Although the proceedings of the IMTFE have received substantial criticism in the more recent scholarly literature, many scholars have pointed out that "by comparison to prevailing standards at the time, the procedure at both Nuremberg and Tokyo Tribunals was notably cognizant of the rights of the accused."[69] Section III, Article 9 of the Tokyo Charter specifies numerous rights afforded to the accused, including those pertaining to the process of indictment, language used in the proceedings, counsel for the accused, evidence, and trial motions.[70] Charges brought against defendants were drafted in their native tongue, and the trial proceedings were contemporaneously translated for them and the rest of their defense team. Defendants were allowed to choose their own defense counsel, participate in their defense strategy, call their own witnesses, and cross-examine prosecutions witnesses. Lastly, defendants had the right to appeal tribunal verdicts to the supreme commander of Allied powers.[71]

Consideration of soft power and its role in American postwar foreign policy were also reflected in the choices made regarding who would stand trial. Specifically, this involved the decision to exempt Emperor Hirohito from culpability and prosecution. At the close of the war, MacArthur had originally stated that Japan's punishment would be "long and bitter" and that it would never again be a world power.[72] However, as concern over the emerging Communist threat increased among U.S. policymakers, American views shifted. The American foreign policy priority became one that sought to stabilize Japan both politically and economically. General MacArthur would later take credit for the decision to exclude the Japanese emperor based on a strategic assessment of America's interests in postwar Japan. He stated, "I believed that if the emperor was indicted, and perhaps hanged, as a war criminal, military government would have to be instituted throughout all Japan, and guerrilla warfare would probably break out."[73] Although calls for Hirohito's indictment as a war criminal were heard across the Allied nations at the end of the war, ultimately, the American position ruled the day. By the start of the trials in 1946, all eleven of the Allied nations had agreed to exempt the emperor from tribunal prosecution.[74] As noted by Richard Minear, "the decision to exclude the emperor was a political decision, not a decision based upon the merits of the case."[75] In this case, the decision involved strategic interests and the need to cultivate soft power in order to facilitate stability in Japan.

The empirical evidence from both the Nuremberg and the Tokyo tribunals makes clear that power was instrumental to the creation of the courts. Power largely determined whether the courts would be created in the first place, who would pass judgment on whom, and the manner in which justice would be established. However, the evidence also shows how principles are woven within the process of realpolitik. In addition to shaping decisions regarding the form and function of the court, the proceedings themselves provided a venue for norm entrepreneurs to shape the legacy of the Nuremberg tribunal. Once the decision to establish a court was made, the discourse began to shift from one based solely on the issue of "just" versus "unjust" wars to one based on the actions during conflict and the rights to be afforded to defendants in the legal process.

Although the Holocaust was not the primary impetus for the creation of the IMT at Nuremberg, it later emerged as the central focus of the proceedings once they were initiated and ultimately served to shape its historical legacy. In particular, it was the American and British prosecutors that brought extensive evidence of the Holocaust to bear on the proceedings, and this evidence was "overwhelming and horrifying."[76] Indeed, though the media had been providing information about the Nazi program to exterminate European Jewry for years, the evidence provided during the Nuremberg trials provided a stark look at what many had failed to see. Even Telford Taylor, U.S. chief counsel for war crimes, remarked, "But like so many others, I remained ignorant of the mass extermination camps in Poland, and the full scope of the Holocaust did not dawn on me until several months later, at Nuremberg."[77] The human impact of the testimony and evidence had a transformative effect on how the tribunal was viewed and how it has been remembered ever since. This evidence gave relative precedence to the issues of war crimes and crimes against humanity (under which the Holocaust fell) over the broader questions of the *jus ad bellum*.

This discourse about what constitutes violations of the *jus in bello* was not only a central part of the Nuremberg trials but was a formative step toward a broader discussion about conduct in conflict, accountability, and due process. In 1947, the UN General Assembly passed Resolution 177 (II) to form an International Law Commission (ILC) charged with the task of promoting the development of international law and facilitating its codification. During its second session in 1950, the ILC adopted the Nuremberg Principles, which codified crimes against the peace and security of mankind.[78] In addition, it was also asked to consider the creation of an international criminal court. Many, including Telford Taylor, have lauded the contribution the Nuremberg Principles have had in the quest to protect human rights and hold accountable those who commit atrocities during conflict: "As a moral and legal statement, clothed with judicial precedent and United Nations recognition, the Nuremberg principles are an international legal force to be reckoned with."[79] One element that has gone unnoticed in the literature is how the principles fused the two aspects of the laws of war. The *jus ad bellum* and the *jus in bello* are two dimensions of one set of de jure laws and norms; however, de facto the two have operated quite separately. More precisely, they have acted sequentially. In practice, violations of the *jus ad bellum* serves as a trigger for prosecution of the *jus in bello*, and initial "judgments" are a function of whether one was the victor or the loser in the conflict. Victors could assert that the loser was guilty of waging aggressive war, not vice versa (at least in any functional sense). Once such judgment is passed by the victors in battle, the loser can then be tried for their conduct during the conflict. This is largely what we see in the events leading into the Nuremberg trials. Interest among the Big Three (Churchill, Roosevelt, and Stalin) for trying the Germans (and later the Japanese) for war crimes (*jus in bello*) stemmed from their common belief that both were guilty of committing the crime of aggression. Of course, the crime of aggression was part of the judicial process at Nuremberg, but only one party (those who lost the war) could possibly be found guilty. Guilt or innocence on this count was largely determined politically, not juridically, by the victors before the courts martial was formed in the first place.

The trials and the Nuremberg Principles that followed serve as the foundation on which the sequential relationship between the *jus ad bellum* and the *jus in bello* began to be challenged. As the Holocaust came to define the primary issue during the course of the proceedings, this sequential relationship between waging an "unjust" war and war crimes broke down. The Holocaust was qualitatively different than other atrocities and war crimes committed during conflict: it cannot be justified as a function of war because its victims were not defined by their citizenship or allegiance along the lines of the political conflict. The Holocaust was, in part, an atrocity committed by the Germans against their own people. Thus, although aggression was the principal concern of those who established the Nuremberg trials, the process of adjudication altered this perception. In other words, the Holocaust was a "game changer."

The Holocaust not only changed the game in shifting the emphasis of the Nuremberg trials toward the issue of war crimes and crimes against humanity but also was the impetus for generating a new international movement for human rights following World War II. In the span of only two days in 1948, two landmark agreements were created in the United Nations: the Genocide Convention and the Universal Declaration of Human Rights. It is not a coincidence that the Genocide Convention was the first human-rights treaty adopted by the UN General Assembly. As Richard Falk notes, "The Genocide Convention would not exist but for the Holocaust."[80] The convention defined genocide as "the intentional destruction of a national, ethnic, racial and religious group, in whole or in part."[81] Moreover, the convention expanded the scope of crimes beyond the *jus in bello* by declaring that genocide was a crime that could be committed "in time of peace or in time of war."[82] The Genocide Convention was quickly followed by the adoption of the Universal Declaration of Human Rights on December 10, 1948.[83] Though not specifically designed to address the Holocaust as the Genocide Convention was, the Universal Declaration can also be seen as a direct response to the Nazi barbarism evident during World War II. The Holocaust gave a stark look at a world where pure tyranny was given free rein to exploit natural human cruelty.[84] There can be little doubt about what the drafters of the declaration were referring to in the preamble when they spoke of "barbarous acts which have outraged the conscience of mankind."[85] As such, it is difficult to refute the argument that, without the Holocaust, there would be no Universal Declaration of Human Rights.[86]

It was within the context of this new framing that the ILC was created and the Nuremberg Principles were codified. De jure, the three classes of crimes covered under Principle VI—war crimes, crimes against humanity, and crimes against peace (i.e., aggression)—are consistent with the laws of war. However, in also requesting the ILC to consider the creation of an international criminal court to adjudicate violations under Principle VI, the de facto practice reinforces this break from the sequential logic of the laws of war in their political sense. There was nothing in the Nuremberg Principles that took into account special prerogatives (or responsibilities) for great powers or for the victorious over the defeated. In other words, the ILC, beginning with the Nuremberg Principles, moved the discourse regarding the laws of war and the creation of a regime governing atrocities from the domain of the political, where power is largely determinative, to the domain of the legal, where principle establishes order and guides action.

The Nuremberg tribunal and the Nuremberg Principles that followed are seminal moments in the development of the contemporary regime governing atrocities committed in war. Once the IMT was established, prominent jurists served as norm entrepreneurs who defined the institutional narrative as one squarely based on the notion of the protection of human rights and one that supported individual accountability for gross violations of those rights. The creation of the ILC provided a forum in which these principles could be further explored and developed, and it served as a foundation on which human rights activists could press states to act to afford justice for the victims of atrocities. Often lost in this narrative, however, is the fact that neither the Holocaust nor concerns regarding gross violations of human rights more generally served as the initial impetus for the formation of the IMT. Rather, the tribunal existed initially in response to the desire of the architects of the Allied war effort to legitimize their own actions during the war by delegitimizing the actions of their now defeated enemies. Put differently, human rights principles and norms may be important factors in explaining why the Nuremberg trials were conducted as they were, but they are not sufficient to explain the creation of the IMT in the first place. Interests defined in terms of power played a key role in creating the court.

Unfortunately for those seeking to use the IMT and the Nuremberg Principles as a springboard for the creation of a permanent international criminal court modeled on them, power politics would also play a key role in the decades that followed—a role that served to create an immovable obstacle in the path of institutional development.

International Humanitarian Law and the Cold War

The Nuremberg Principles set forth by the ILC in 1950 specified individual culpability for violations and stipulated three major classes of crimes against the peace and security of mankind. As shown in table 1.1, Principle VI defines these crimes as (1) crimes against peace, (2) war crimes, and (3) crimes against humanity. Crimes against peace are largely defined in terms of wars of aggression, whereas war crimes are defined as violations of the laws or customs of war. These include "murder, ill-treatment or deportation to slave labour or for any other purpose of civilian population of or in occupied territory, murder or ill-treatment of prisoners of war, of persons on the seas, killing of hostages, plunder of public or private property, wanton destruction of cities, towns, or villages, or devastation not justified by military necessity."[87] The third class of crime specified under the Nuremberg Principles, crimes against humanity, would appear to include genocide, though it is not specifically defined under the terms of the 1950 draft. Under the draft, crimes against humanity include "murder, extermination, enslavement, deportation and other inhumane acts done against any civilian population, or persecutions

Table 1.1. The Nuremberg Principles

Principle I	Any person who commits an act which constitutes a crime under international law is responsible therefore and liable for punishment.
Principle II	The fact that internal law does not impose a penalty for an act which constitutes a crime under international law does not relieve the person who committed the crime from responsibility under international law.
Principle III	The fact that a person who committed an act which constitutes a crime under international law acted as Head of State or responsible Government official does not relieve him from responsibility under international law.
Principle IV	The fact that a person acted pursuant to order of his Government or of a superior does not relieve him from responsibility under international law, provided a moral choice was in fact possible to him.
Principle V	Any person charged with a crime under international law has the right to a fair trial on the facts and the law.
Principle VI	The crimes hereinafter set out are punishable as crimes under international law: (a) Crimes against peace (aggression) (b) War Crimes (c) Crimes against Humanity (including genocide)
Principle VII	Complicity in the commission of a crime against peace, a war crime, or a crime against humanity as set forth in Principle VI is a crime under international law.

on political, racial or religious grounds, when such acts are done or such persecutions are carried on in execution of or in connection with any crime against peace or any war crime."[88]

With the Nuremberg Principles in place and institutional precedent on which to draw, a constructivist should expect that emergent norms regarding prosecution of atrocities would play a more active role in international politics. Moreover, global civil society saw a dramatic rise in the number of human-rights nongovernmental organizations (NGOs) in the decades following World War II, a development one would expect to have a positive impact on state behavior. Given these conditions, we should expect three trends if principles and norms of human rights were the dominant influence on state behavior. First, we might expect that states would be more hesitant to violate the principles in the execution of their foreign policies. Second, we should see significant progress on the creation of a permanent international court to adjudicate violations. Third, where violations of the Nuremberg Principles have been documented, we should see prosecution of those responsible. A quick overview of the available evidence shows that none of these expectations would come to pass in the forty years following the creation of the Nuremberg Principles.

The Cold War era offers evidence of state-sponsored, gross human-rights violations, including those crimes specified under the Nuremberg Principles. Table 1.2 lists alleged violations of the crimes specified under the principles. Across all categories of crimes punishable under international law, we see numerous situations that call for the administration of justice. A compelling case can be made that U.S. military actions in Vietnam (1956–75), Cuba (1961), Cambodia (1970), Laos (1970), Grenada (1983), and Panama (1989) all constitute acts of aggression in violation of Principle VI.[89] The invasion and annexation of Tibet by the People's Republic of China (PRC) in October

Table 1.2. Some possible violations of the Nuremberg Principles during the Cold War

War Crimes	Crimes against Humanity	Genocide	Aggression
Netherlands (Indonesia 1945–49)	South Africa 1948–90	PRC (Tibet 1950–)	PRC (Tibet 1950)
UK (Malaya 1948–60)	Korea 1950–53	Nigerian Civil War (1967–70)	USSR (Hungary 1956)
UK (Kenya 1952–60)	Algeria 1954–62	Indonesia (1965–66)	US (Vietnam 1956)
US (Korea 1950)	Vietnam 1956–75	Guatemala (1962–96)	US (Cuba 1961)
US (Vietnam 1968)	Cambodia 1970–75	Khmer Rouge (Cambodia 1970–75)	USSR (Czechoslovakia 1968)
Pakistan (Bangladesh 1971)	Bangladesh 1971	Pakistan (Bangladesh 1971)	US (Cambodia/ Laos 1970)
	Chile 1973–90	Burundi (1972)	USSR (Afghanistan 1979)
			US (Grenada 1983)
			US (Panama 1989)

1950 was also seen by many as an act of aggression.[90] Similarly, the Soviet invasion of Hungary on November 4, 1956, not only suggested a violation of the draft Code of Offenses against the Peace and Security of Mankind in terms of waging a war of aggression but also inflicted substantial civilian casualties that could constitute a war crime.[91] The Soviets would engage in a similar incursion in Czechoslovakia in August 1968, as well as a larger invasion of Afghanistan in 1979.

In addition to aggression, the Cold War era saw many other possible crimes specified in the Nuremberg Principles. In addition to a possible violation of a crime against peace, the PRC's annexation of Tibet was accompanied by accusations of genocide in 1959 by the International Commission of Jurists.[92] Ethnic cleansing associated with the civil war in Nigeria (Biafran War, 1967–70) has also been categorized as constituting a program of attempted genocide. Other prominent cases of genocide during the Cold War stem from atrocities committed by the Khmer Rouge in Cambodia, the Pakistani military against the Bangladeshi, and the Tutsi government in Burundi (1972). War crimes and crimes against humanity were also all too common during the "proxy wars" of the Cold War, as well as during the violence that accompanied the independence movements during the process of decolonization. Some prominent violations were brought to trial in military courts, such as the trial of William Calley Jr. and twenty-five other U.S. servicemen stemming from the civilian massacre at My Lai during the Vietnam War.[93] Most incidents, however, never had their day in court, domestic or international.[94]

Though it is difficult to ascertain whether the emerging norms stemming from the Nuremberg Principles reduced the likelihood of gross human-rights violations, the evidence strongly suggests that they had little effect on state behavior. The expectation that newly emergent norms and recent institutional precedent would facilitate the creation of a permanent international criminal court was also not realized in the decades following World War II. As a result, violators did not face the international justice one might have expected given the circumstances following the Nuremberg trial.[95] The reason for this lack of institutionalization was that geopolitical interests trumped human rights principles and norms.

Cold War power politics were characterized by several key features: (1) the ideological basis for conflict, (2) competition for alliance partners, and (3) tit-for-tat reciprocity between the superpowers. Each of these played an important role in confounding the growth of international justice during the Cold War. First, both the American and the Soviets framed the Cold War in the context of competing ideological narratives. The American view was articulated in the Truman Doctrine, which defined the Cold War as a conflict between two "ways of life": "One way of life is based upon the will of the majority, and is distinguished by free institutions, representative government, free elections, guarantees of individual liberty, freedom of speech and religion, and freedom from political oppression. The second way of life is based upon the will of a minority forcibly imposed upon the majority. It relies upon terror and oppression, a controlled press and radio, fixed elections, and the suppression of personal freedoms."[96] Similarly, the Cold War narrative from the Soviet perspective was one of Communist emancipation from capitalist domination and imperialist oppression. On their own, one might expect that such ideological narratives would help the movement toward respect for human rights rather than hinder it. However, it is the connection between ideological narratives and the strategic interest to expand their relative sphere of influence through alliance relationships that presents the problem. On both sides of the Cold War divide, realpolitik prompted both the Americans and the Soviets to support authoritarian and repressive regimes in exchange for their allegiance.[97] Clearly, such practices were at odds with their stated ideology, and not surprisingly, neither was inclined to acknowledge these rather glaring incongruities. Moreover, such support could be seen as acts of complicity should these governments engage in violations of human rights under international law. Thus, it stands to reason that neither would seek to promote any process—including trials in an international criminal court—that would bring these hypocrisies to light.

Another characteristic of Cold War realpolitik was the use of tit-for-tat reciprocity. Each sought to maximize their soft power through the use of propaganda, including that which was generated from actions that might constitute violations of the Nuremberg Principles. Using an example from the Korean War, Geoffrey Robertson describes this type of reciprocity: "They [North Korea] maintain to this day . . . that US planes dropped poison gas and biological bombs that spread illness and death: captured USAF pilots confessed to this before (and probably as condition of) their release, but on return to the US they retracted their confession, widely attributed at the time to 'brainwashing.' . . . This was how human rights issues played out in the Cold War, as propaganda claim and counter-claim."[98] Thus, the unfortunate by-products of power politics that increased human suffering were consistently "packaged" to conform to the broader narrative of the Cold War. Robertson adds, "The best that can be said for Cold War law was that the superpowers felt obliged to resort to such fictions, covering up as best they could the atrocities committed by their own allies in order to accuse more loudly the other side."[99] Schiff offers a similar account: "At the interstate and interbloc level, human rights concerns suffered from politicization, as Western critics of East bloc violations could too easily be criticized for using the subject as a political tool rather than being genuinely concerned about victims of abuse, particularly given Westerners' acceptance of similar depredations by their authoritarian allies."[100]

These points illustrate why the world's Cold War superpowers considered the development of an international criminal court based on the Nuremberg Principles to be in conflict with their broader geopolitical interests. Given this outlook, it should not be surprising that these countries not only made no effort to promote further institutionalization of the Principles but actively sought to use their influence to keep this process from moving forward. Both the UN Commission on Human Rights' and the General Assembly's response to the work of the ILC offer evidence of this derailment. In the decades that followed the creation of the UN Universal Declaration of Human Rights, the Commission on Human Rights met annually, but did not engage in investigating or condemning potential violators. Instead, the commission's work was often characterized by bloc-voting and an unwillingness of member states to endure criticisms of their conduct or that of their allies.[101] Similarly, the ILC continued to work on developing the Code of Offenses against the Peace and Security of Mankind, to be used in the creation of an international criminal court. It presented a draft to the General Assembly in 1954.[102] However, the General Assembly chose to postpone consideration of the draft until the Special Committee on the Definition of Aggression completed its work.[103] Ultimately, the draft remained in limbo until 1981 when the General Assembly called on the ILC to resume its work. The 1954 Draft Code remained in a deep freeze for twenty-seven years, and this process had only begun to thaw in the 1980s.[104] Cold War realpolitik served as an insurmountable obstacle to the development of an international court to adjudicate violations of the Nuremberg Principles.

At this point, power politics can be seen to have had a significant impact on the move toward international justice at two key junctures. In addition to providing the original motive for the creation of the Nuremberg tribunal, power politics then served to stifle the development of a regime based on the Nuremberg Principles. Both developments can be seen as fundamental to the process of legalization, yet principled politics do not seem to be the primary driver of outcomes at these points. Moreover, even with institutional precedent, human rights principles were insufficient to overcome political resistance from the two Cold War superpowers.

The Ad Hoc UN Tribunals

The conventional wisdom in the literature on international criminal courts is that creation and timing of the ad hoc international criminal tribunals in the mid-1990s was primarily a function of a combination of three things: (1) the continued development of international humanitarian law, (2) the growth in political activism in global civil society, and (3) the end of the Cold War. The standard account suggests that the end of the Cold War served to break the political obstacles impeding those who sought to bring international justice to violations of the Nuremberg Principles. For example, using the metaphor of the "river of justice" to characterize the normative development of international law in the area of human rights, Schiff writes, "Describing the gathering stream of ideas about international criminal law as the progress of a river enables the use of linked metaphors with some apt characteristics. Obstructions, for instance the Cold War, temporarily hindered the flow, but as time went on, the current was restored."[105] Indeed, it is difficult to account for the creation of the ad hoc UN tribunals (and subsequently, the ICC) without acknowledging the role that principles, norms, and political activism played in the process. However, it is important to recognize that institutional outcomes were shaped by the interplay between idealpolitik and realpolitik. The end of the Cold War did indeed break an impasse of tit-for-tat reciprocity that stifled institutional development for decades; however, the argument that this event simply cleared the way for the triumph of principled politics has difficulty responding to several questions. The principled "river of justice" or "norm cascade" argument is rooted in the notion that these ideas are elements of a broader liberal ideology. Indeed, scholars have made it clear that liberal democratic states are the primary supporters of the creation of international criminal courts.[106] Both the ICTY and the

International Criminal Tribunal for Rwanda (ICTR) were created under the authority of the UN Security Council. Was the support of the liberal members of the UNSC, particularly the United States, Britain, and France, solely an expression of commitment to principles of human rights and the rule of law? Moreover, if support was primarily a function of liberal principles and values, why would Russia and China support (or refrain from vetoing) the Security Council resolutions creating the tribunals? A closer look at the empirical evidence suggests that power politics still played an instrumental role in the timing, creation, and design of the courts.

Liberal States and International Criminal Tribunals

The end of the Cold War was a transformative event in world politics. Among the most conspicuous developments was the sudden and rapid rise in the number of internal conflicts worldwide. In the decade following the end of the Cold War, state-to-state wars were vastly outnumbered by the rising number of civil wars and ethnic conflicts.[107] The troubles began almost immediately after the Cold War ended in 1991. In Somalia, the fall of the Barre government initiated a subsequent civil war, as various rebel groups fought to gain power. The conflict and famine that accompanied it killed hundreds of thousands of Somalis and also displaced up to two million more. At the same time, Yugoslavia began its slide into civil war as breakaway republics claimed their independence while Belgrade sought to maintain control over the country. As violence erupted and escalated, growing media coverage brought the carnage to people's attention across the globe. A pivotal moment came on August 2, 1992, when *New York Newsday* reported that Bosnian Muslims held captive at the Omarska prison camp near Prijedor were being slaughtered by their Serbian guards. Subsequent reports likened conditions in the camp and another like it at Trnopolje to those of Nazi concentration camps during World War II.[108] Shocking photos and video of prisoners were published that recalled similar catastrophes during the Nazi era Holocaust.[109] Given the reports and images, it appeared that genocide had once again reared its ugly head in international society.

In Europe and North America, reports and images of these events caused widespread concern and sparked public demands that something be done to stabilize these situations and alleviate the human suffering on display in places like Somalia and Yugoslavia.[110] For policymakers, responding assertively to public opinion can reap political gains, at least in the short run, as they will appear attentive to the wishes of the polity that elected them to office. Moreover, gains to national soft power—at home and abroad—are often achieved when a government lives up to its professed political values.[111] The human tragedies unfolding abroad gave policymakers in liberal democracies the opportunity to back up their professed commitment to human rights with concrete action. Moreover, policymakers in liberal democratic states also face potential audience costs should they ignore the will of the people expressed in opinion poll data. Numerous studies have shown that public opinion can influence state behavior in democratic states, as policymakers are hesitant to face the political consequences of raising the ire of the electorate.[112]

There are political incentives to being responsive to public opinion and potential audience costs for ignoring it. But what action should be taken to respond to this rash of human tragedy taking place around the world? The most direct and assertive response would be to utilize military power to stabilize conflict zones through humanitarian intervention. Indeed, in liberal democratic states on both sides of the Atlantic, public opinion suggested support for just such assertive action. In the United States, opinion polls taken in 1992 showed strong public support for military intervention in Somalia—some as high as 84%.[113] Similarly, a 1993 *Los Angeles Times* poll found 58% of respondents supported using military force to address the violence in the former Yugoslavia. The following year, another poll showed that support for military intervention had grown to 69%.[114] In Britain, public opinion showed widespread support to "do something" about the situation in the former Yugoslavia, including consistent majority support for sending British troops.[115]

Policymakers in the United States decided to follow the public's preferred course of action to apply a military solution in Somalia. It did so by first seeking UN approval. On December 3, 1992, the UNSC passed Resolution 794 that authorized the formation of a coalition of UN peacekeepers (UNITAF), led by the United States, to provide security and assist humanitarian efforts in Somalia. Operation Restore Hope, as the American military operation was called, began with high ideals and high optimism. Unfortunately, "mission creep" slowly altered the aims of the intervention, from one based primarily on the goal of providing humanitarian assistance to one that sought to capture the warlord Mohamed Farah Aidid.[116] Aidid's forces increasingly engaged U.S.-led peacekeeping forces until a fateful day in October 1993. On that day, a raid in Mogadishu resulted in the deaths of over a thousand civilians and militia, as well as eighteen American servicemen. After the battle, the corpses of several of the slain American servicemen were dragged through the streets of Mogadishu, and media images of these atrocities stunned the American public.[117] Public support for Operation Restore Hope plummeted immediately, creating potentially significant audience costs to continue the operation.[118] Soon after, President Bill Clinton withdrew American troops from Somalia.

As the Somalia intervention came to a sudden and inglorious close, the war in Yugoslavia continued to escalate.[119] Soon after, chaos erupted in Rwanda in April 1994 when the plane carrying President Juvénal Habyarimana was shot down over Kigali. Ethnic Hutus hunted down and killed Tutsis en masse in a genocidal rampage.[120] In a period of only a few months, more than 75% of the Tutsi population in Rwanda was slaughtered.[121] Though public concern remained high and human rights activists pressed for action in these situations, the recent experience in Somalia served as a powerful deterrent to the use of military intervention in the Balkans.[122] It offered two types of lessons—operational and political. Operationally, the experience in Somalia made clear the high costs of military intervention and the risk that objectives will not be achieved because of mission creep. The total operational cost of the Somali intervention amounted to over $7 billion, and mission success proved to be elusive.[123] The Somali intervention also offered political lessons. First, military intervention invariably produces collateral damage, and humanitarian actions often contribute to civilian casualties.[124] Thus, not only was the intervention largely unsuccessful in contributing to U.S. soft power abroad, but it actually served to strain the country's foreign relations.[125] Second, the experience in Somalia underscored the volatility of domestic public opinion. Though public opinion for intervention was initially strong, it turned quickly negative as the costs of the operation mounted. The Somali intervention clearly showed that public opinion is likely to erode when military casualties rise, particularly in cases where such casualties cannot be rationalized in terms of national security priorities. Thus, the potential political gains of responding assertively to public demands for military action in cases of humanitarian crises can quickly turn negative for policymakers who now find themselves dealing with audience cost.

The lessons of the Somali intervention presented a quandary for policymakers in liberal democratic states: How could they respond to public demands for action, yet insulate themselves from the vagaries of foreign interventions, particularly for situations where losses cannot be rationalized in terms of national interests or strategic value? Given the political implications involved, establishing international criminal tribunals offered an appealing means to square the circle. Creating courts offers definitive political advantages over a military response to humanitarian crisis. First, its operational cost is substantially lower. In contrast to the $7 billion price tag for the Somalia intervention, the first budget set for the ICTY in 1993 was only $5.5 million.[126] International criminal tribunals are certainly not cheap, but when compared with military alternatives, they appear quite economical. Second, adjudication does not present the kinds of political risks that military intervention does. They do not produce military casualties nor collateral damage. As such, they are unlikely to generate the kinds of domestic audience cost associated with military intervention. Aryeh Neier, cofounder of Human Rights Watch, noted that "it was a way to do *something* about Bosnia that would have no political cost domestically."[127]

How do we know that support for the tribunals was more a function of political calculus than principled action among the liberal democratic members of the UNSC? Though the literature on tribunals often points to the role of public opinion, such domestic political pressure was not focused on creating courts. Rather, it was focused on taking action to address human suffering. Most polls either focused on the military option, or left the particular policy mechanism ambiguous. In other words, the general public was not necessarily clamoring for courts. Given a choice between (1) doing nothing, (2) taking military intervention, or (3) creating a tribunal, the last option likely offered the most net gains for the liberal democratic members of the P5.[128] The pressure to take action in the face of humanitarian crisis is a reflection of principles and norms. However, the empirical evidence shows that state behavior in response to such public outcry was shaped by interests defined in terms of power. These states sought to maintain material power by pursuing a response with lower operational costs. They also sought to maintain domestic political power by pursuing the less risky option. Moreover, the choice of creating international tribunals also enabled policymakers to apply an idealistic response to a moral imperative.

A New Russia

Russia's interests regarding the creation of ad hoc international criminal tribunals were shaped by its emerging post–Cold War grand strategy and the political leadership navigating it through its early years. The end of the Cold War marked a structural shift from bipolarity to a new multipolar world order. For Russia, the transition from the Soviet era to the new Russian Federation was one characterized by a significant loss in relative power, a development that increased insecurity in the new global environment. As shown in figure 1.1, Russia's gross domestic product (GDP) fell from $2.233 trillion in 1989 to $1.297 trillion in 1996. In response to this changing security context, the early post-Soviet grand strategy in Russia was one based on realignment with the West. In particular, this involved a strategy of Europeanization.[129] The end of the Soviet Union created something of an identity crisis within Russia, and it opened up a space to reimagine national identity. It was in this new space that the post-Soviet Russian leadership formulated a pro-Western notion of Russian identity that would strongly influence their

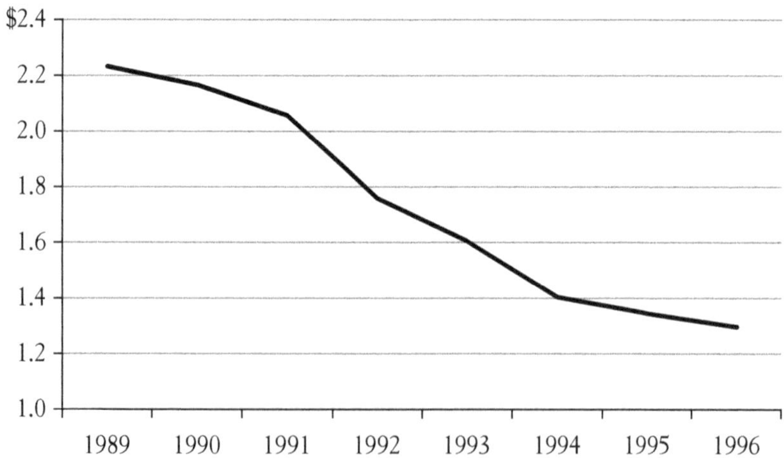

Figure 1.1. Russian gross domestic product (PPP), 1989–96 (in US$ trillions).
***Source:* International Monetary Fund.**

foreign policy by creating new linkages with the West, and in particular, with Europe.[130] Foreign Minister Andrei Kozyrev stated, "The United States and other Western democracies are as natural friends and eventual allies of the democratic Russia as they are foes of the totalitarian USSR."[131]

Realignment with the liberal West involved creating links to both the North Atlantic Treaty Organization (NATO) and the European Union (EU), as well as supporting its international security agenda. The Russian government of Boris Yeltsin sought to make progress toward gaining full membership in all European security institutions, including NATO.[132] In January 1994, NATO established the Partnership for Peace (PfP), a program that created a pathway for membership in the organization without extending the security commitment of the alliance. Russia joined the program in June 1994, but also sought a more expansive and deeper relationship with NATO, both within and outside the PfP.[133] Russia received a special 16+1 status in the North Atlantic Council and Political Committee (1995), something no other PfP member received.[134] Moreover, Russia also signed a Partnership and Cooperation Agreement (PCA) with the EU in 1994, another measure intended to draw Russia into the European sphere. Good relations with the United States were also integral to Russia, as Yeltsin's government received assistance from the United States to support economic development and liberalization, as well as democratic reforms. When Russia joined the Group of Eight (or G8, a governmental political forum) in 1997, it represented the culmination of a profound tectonic shift in post-Soviet geopolitics. This process of Westernization linked Russian interests with those of the Europeans and Americans, making the Russians more responsive to their interests across a wide spectrum of policies issues, including the creation of international criminal tribunals through the United Nations.

This development does not suggest that Russia would lead the drive for the creation of tribunals in the Security Council. It was politically problematic for the Yeltsin government that Yugoslavia was the first situation for which a tribunal came under consideration. The Serbians were a close ally of the Russians, sharing a deep cultural history of common bonds. Thus, when the liberal democratic members of the Security Council showed an interest in involvement in the war in Yugoslavia, Russian interests were divided. On the one hand, their deep history of support for the Serbs pressed Yeltsin to come to their defense. On the other hand, the post-Soviet Russian grand strategy sought opportunities to develop closer ties with the EU and

United States and also to increase Russian soft power among them by backing up the liberal democratic discourse emanating from Moscow. The Russians squared this circle by supporting policy options that attempted to spare the Serbs of the most aggressive response—UN or NATO military intervention. Instead, the Russians supported a series of Security Council resolutions that represented more lenient alternatives to military action, including UNSC Resolution 724 (December 1991) that established an arms embargo against Yugoslavia and UNSC Resolution 757 (May 1992) that put economic sanctions in place. Russia initially preferred diplomacy over sanctions, but ultimately was willing to compromise in the face of Western pressure.

Although this strategy of Westernization/Europeanization was relatively short-lived, ending with the rise of the Putin regime in December 1999, the timing perfectly aligned with Western support for the creation of international criminal tribunals. Similar to the rationale underlying liberal democratic support for their creation, Russian support was a product of policy compromise in the interest of maximizing power.

China after Tiananmen

Like Russia, China's actions concerning the creation of the ad hoc tribunals were influenced by events and their broader foreign policy grand strategy. Specifically, this involved damage repair to Chinese soft power in the wake of the Tiananmen massacre in 1989.

When Deng Xiaoping assumed power in China in 1978, he initiated a new economic development program referred to as the "open-door policy."[135] Deng's strategy was to spur development and growth by opening the economy to the outside world. Over the next decade, China opened its doors to trade with nearly every country in the world. In addition to trade, technological inflows into China increased rapidly, and inflows of foreign capital reached unprecedented levels. The profound shift in economic strategy produced striking results. Figure 1.2 illustrates the dramatic rise in Chinese GDP during the 1980s. Over a ten-year span, Chinese GDP increased over 240%, rising from $249 billion to $845 billion.[136]

Although the open-door policy provided significant economic gains, it also had far-reaching implications for Chinese foreign policy. Wu Xinbo

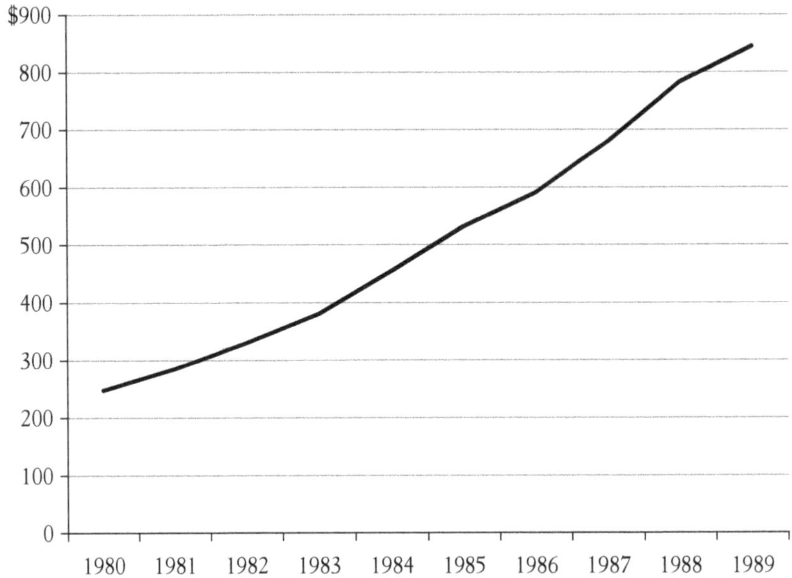

Figure 1.2. Gross domestic product of the People's Republic of China, 1980–89 (PPP, in US$ billions). ***Source:*** **International Monetary Fund and World Bank, https://docs.google.com/spreadsheet/ccc?key=0AonYZs4MzlZbdFNNUGVrVEJOWVls VVB5Y0QyTURBNkE#gid=0 (accessed February 21, 2015).**

points out that "the open-door policy initiated in 1979 has rendered China access to the markets, technology, and capital of the developed countries and has greatly augmented China's comprehensive national capability. In return, it requires China to maintain good political and economic relations with the developed countries, which means that China has to be responsive to their concerns and effectively cooperative with them in international affairs."[137] This need for good relations, particularly with the United States and the more powerful members of the European Community (EC), was particularly important because China sought increased engagement with multilateral organizations in which these countries maintained considerable influence. As part of this new economic grand strategy, China sought to gain access to development assistance by joining the World Bank and the International Monetary Fund.[138] China also announced in 1986 that it wished to join the General Agreement on Tariffs and Trade (GATT) as a full member.

This emerging grand strategy of global engagement faced a tremendous political challenge in 1989. In the spring of 1989, more than one million

Chinese students and workers gathered in Beijing's Tiananmen Square and began the largest public protest in the history of the People's Republic.[139] Beginning in mid-April, the protests grew steadily over the coming weeks, as more and more protestors flocked to Beijing. On the evening of June 3, military forces were ordered to put down the "counter-revolutionary riot" by force and opened fire on the throng of unarmed civilians. Hundreds were slaughtered, though there is disagreement over the exact number of casualties. The impact of the Tiananmen massacre on China's foreign relations was felt immediately. The United States and its allies quickly imposed a series of economic and diplomatic sanctions against the PRC. These included the suspension of official development assistance and export credits, sales of military and police equipment, and high-level official visits. Moreover, the World Bank and the Asian Development Bank halted lending to China under pressure from the United States and members of the EC.[140] In addition, talks regarding possible Chinese membership in the GATT were put on hold indefinitely.[141]

The PRC's immediate response was largely to lash out in self-defense against the international rebuke for the actions taken at Tiananmen Square. However, in the early 1990s, this approach gave way to a concerted effort to repair its damaged diplomatic and economic relationships with the international community.[142] It was during this time that discussions concerning the creation of international criminal tribunals took place in the UN Security Council. Using their veto power to block the proposals to create the tribunals would have come at a significant cost to Chinese soft power and would have run contrary to their interests to repair their damaged relations, particularly with the United States and EC member states. Moreover, given their actions at Tiananmen Square, opposing tribunal justice would likely have been seen as evidence that the PRC condoned grave violations of international humanitarian law, both at home and abroad. Doing so would have incurred a tremendous cost, both politically and economically. Even so, the Chinese were reluctant to support the resolutions, given their consistent emphasis on respecting Westphalian sovereignty in their foreign policy.[143]

The Chinese resolved this conundrum by charting what they perceived to be a pragmatic course. They voted in favor of UN Security Council Resolution 827 that established the ICTY, a move that provided them an opportunity to show the United States, Britain, and France tangible evidence of their support for human rights. The design of the tribunal was also instrumental in their support. As noted by Wu Chengqui, retaining control of tribunal creation and application through the council on an ad hoc basis was essential to their support for the resolution to create the tribunal.[144] In terms of the issue of sovereignty, creating a tribunal for Rwanda was more problematic for the Chinese. Because several of the breakaway republics had already gained international recognition as sovereign states, the conflict in the former Yugoslavia could be in some respects considered an interstate war. In contrast, this was not the case in Rwanda, where bloodshed was the product of a civil conflict. Enforcing international law in cases of internal conflicts raised significant sovereignty concerns for the Chinese. As was the case with UNSC Resolution 827, using their veto would come with a political cost that they preferred to avoid. The Chinese chose to abstain rather than oppose the proposal, a strategy that enabled them to avoid being the sole obstacle to American and European interests without sacrificing closely held principles—in this case, sovereignty. It is a strategy the Chinese have used in the past. Wu Xinbo notes, "If, for instance, China finds a proposal brought to the UN Security Council incompatible with its principles while actually not mattering much to its national interests, Beijing does not often veto the proposal; instead, it usually chooses to abstain from voting. By so doing, it avoids unnecessarily offending the United States or being the only country standing in the way. Beijing understands that if it abuses the veto power in the United Nations just out of concern for its principles, it may hurt China's own interests and have a negative impact on its international image."[145]

It is interesting to note that relations between China and the United States began to improve around this same time. In 1994, President Bill Clinton announced his decision to delink the issue of human rights from the question of renewing China's most-favored nation status.[146] This was a significant marker of a gradual warming of relations between Beijing and Washington.[147]

The empirical evidence strongly suggests that Russian and Chinese support for the ad hoc tribunals—whether in the form of an affirmative vote or an abstention in Security Council voting—was primarily the product of strategic behavior rather than reflective of human rights concerns. Because of the strategic importance of improved relations with the liberal-democratic permanent members of the UN Security Council, both were reluctant to use their veto power to stop the creation of the tribunals. As was the case with the Nuremberg tribunal, once these courts were established, they gave norm entrepreneurs another opportunity to further develop the river of justice in international humanitarian law.

Lessons Learned

The International Criminal Tribunal for the Former Yugoslavia was established on May 25, 1993, by unanimous approval of Security Council Resolution 827.[148] The institutional design, rules, and procedures drew on the experience of the Nuremberg trials. Yet, the new tribunals faced formidable obstacles to developing a functioning court. To establish legitimacy for the process and rulings of the tribunal, the designers placed emphasis on making the court a truly international body and giving the appearance of independence from the UNSC.[149] Thus, they selected judges from a diverse array of nations around the world. Moreover, none of those chosen for the crucial role of the chief prosecutor came from countries that were permanent members of the Security Council.[150] The designers thought that constructing the court to represent truly international diversity would increase the legitimacy of the tribunal in two ways. First, distancing it from the Security Council would provide cover from accusations that the tribunal was administering "victor's justice." In its first annual report, the ICTY declared, "First, unlike the Nürnberg and Tokyo Tribunals, the Tribunal is truly international. It has rightly been stated that the Nürnberg and Tokyo Tribunals were 'multinational tribunals, but not international tribunals in the strict Sense,' in that they represented only one segment of the world community: the victors."[151] Second, the designers of the ICTY thought that local populations would find "international justice" to be more independent and objective: "The Tribunal is not the organ of a group of States; it is an organ of the whole international community."[152]

This emphasis on due process and diversity may have facilitated perceptions of fairness; however, it also significantly complicated the process of institutional development. Utilizing judges with different legal backgrounds made resolution of substantive legal issues more complex and time-consuming. One prosecutor noted, "In a context where there is no particular authority and where no jurisdiction necessarily carries more weight than any other, we have found no better way than to consider each issue as it comes up, debate it, and try to find a sensible consensus."[153] As noted in the tribunal's first annual report:

> In addition to all of the steps usually required to establish a new international institution, the Tribunal has been required to turn its attentions both to the quasi-legislative task of preparing a code of criminal procedure (its rules of procedure and evidence) and to the administrative and regulatory aspects of its activities. These include tasks as diverse as the provision of legal aid, assignment of counsel, an entire international process service, the design and construction of both a courtroom and a detention unit, rules and regulations governing the treatment of detainees, witness safeguards, arrangements for the transportation of witnesses to The Hague and the overall safety and security of judges, to name but a few. . . . The practical problems facing the Tribunal at its inception seemed endless.[154]

Building a unified conceptual legal framework and institutional standard operating procedures was thus cumbersome and slow.

Although the subsequent tribunal created to prosecute crimes committed during the Rwandan genocide of 1994 was able to build on the institutional structure created by its predecessor in The Hague, it too faced substantial obstacles. Among the most significant were complications in obtaining cooperation from the government of Rwanda.[155] Though the Rwandan government initially requested that a tribunal be established, it objected to several elements of the ICTR's institutional design. First, the Rwandan government objected to the very limited *ratione temporis* (temporal jurisdiction) established for the court. The Rwandan ambassador to the United States explained, "the government of Rwanda regarded the dates set for the *ratione temporis* competence of the international tribunal for Rwanda . . . as inadequate. The genocide which the world witnessed in April 1994 had been the result of a long period of planning during which pilot projects for extermination had been successfully tested before this date."[156] The Rwandan government proposed that the tribunal's jurisdiction be extended to consider actions committed since October 1, 1990. The Security Council rejected the proposal in order to expedite the process of litigation and to limit the magnitude of the court's potential docket. There was already substantial concern that the magnitude of the crimes committed in Rwanda threatened to overwhelm the system.[157] Some have suggested that the jurisdictional limits were also a function of political interests among members of the Security Council: "Those limits were the product of a highly political process within the Security Council and reflect diplomatic concerns. Broader jurisdiction for the ICTR could well have led to inquiries that would have either embarrassed the UN as a whole or particular permanent members of the Security Council."[158] Another stumbling block to cooperation between the tribunal and the Rwandan government involved punishment. The rules of the ICTR specified that capital punishment is not permitted. The maximum penalty that could be given to a defendant found guilty of crimes was a sentence of life in prison. In contrast, Rwandan legal norms permit capital punishment. As such, Rwandan officials were concerned that individuals tried through the ICTR "would get off more lightly than ordinary Rwandans who faced the death penalty in local courts."[159] Because the tribunal was aimed at trying those leaders with command and control authority, this incongruity in sentencing provisions seemed likely to provide lesser penalties for those who held the most accountability for the genocide. Not surprisingly, the early relationship between the Rwandan government and the ICTR was described as "frosty."[160] Unfortunately, difficulties in obtaining cooperation crucial to the court simply added to the obstacles obstructing progress.

In addition to retarding the speed in which the tribunals could begin investigating and prosecuting crimes, these institutional and political obstacles contributed to another problem for the tribunals: cost. Although the initial budget for the ICTY was quite modest (just under $11 million for the first year of operation), organizational costs quickly skyrocketed. Figure 1.3 illustrates the rapid growth in tribunal expenditures. In its first five years of operation, the ICTY's budget increased from $11 million to over $103 million, an increase of over 900%. The costs incurred by the ICTR also grew quickly. In its first four years of operation, the ICTR's budget increased from $40.2 million (1996) to $66.2 million (1999). Between 1995 and 1999, actual expenditures totaled nearly $180 million.[161]

The experience of the ad hoc tribunals offered important lessons. The relevant lessons, however, depend on the perspective taken—realist or idealist. Permanent members of the Security Council have drawn lessons from a more realist perspective. On the one hand, the establishment of tribunals provided an alternative to more risky or expensive (both materially and politically) solutions to internal conflicts. Although creating courts through UNSC resolutions on an ad hoc basis provided Security Council members

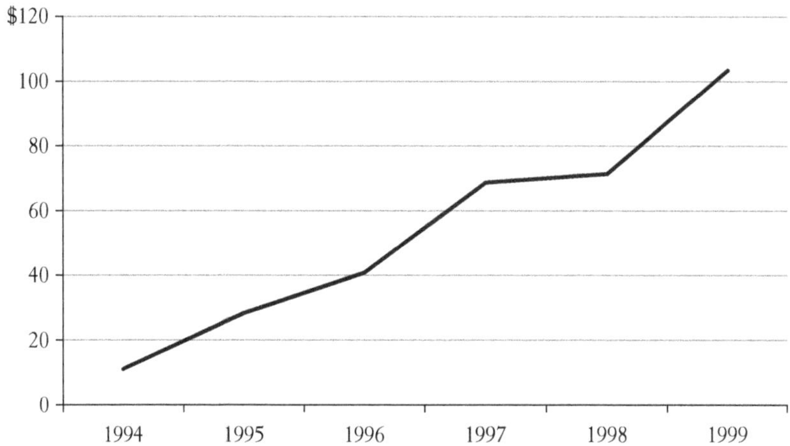

Figure 1.3. Budget of the International Criminal Tribunal for the former Yugoslavia, 1994–99 (in US$ millions). *Source:* UN Advisory Committee on Administrative and Budgetary Questions, UN Doc. A/48/915 (1994); UN Doc. A/49/790 (1995); UN Doc. A/50/925 (1996); UN Doc. A/51/7/Add. 7 (1997); UN Doc. A/54/645 (1999).

with tremendous latitude and flexibility, this came at a cost—in terms of expense, speed, and efficiency. Moreover, the experience of the ICTR revealed that creating tribunals that catered to specific cases opened the door to contestation over institutional design. In that case, the local government sought to influence the rules of the court to reflect its particular interests, and a failure to realize those design goals hindered the tribunal's ability to garner cooperation so essential to a well-functioning court.[162] It is from this point of view that members of the Security Council would consider the appeal of developing a permanent international criminal court.

Idealists, on the other hand, were less concerned with the more pragmatic challenges faced by the ad hoc tribunals. This group includes international lawyers and jurists, human rights scholars and activists, and human rights NGOs. For them, the primary lesson to be drawn from both the ICTY and ICTR was that international justice still had not yet replaced "victor's justice."[163] William Schabas writes, "But while this independence of the ICTY seemed a significant development compared with Nuremberg, the institution was in fact an emanation of the Security Council. As such, its political agenda was set by what at Nuremberg were still referred to as the 'great powers' but by 1993 were labeled with the perhaps less pejorative term of the 'permanent five.' In substance, nevertheless, the creators of the ICTY were not all that different than those who established the Nuremberg Tribunal, although the institution was not destined for whom they had vanquished."[164] For idealists, international criminal justice continued to have an essential flaw: while the ad hoc tribunals may have moved beyond victor's justice in the strictest sense, they still did not establish a system of equality under the law, regardless of the differences in power of those involved. Antonio Cassese remarked that the ad hoc tribunals were "marred by various failings, chiefly that of dispensing selective justice."[165] The ad hoc tribunals offered important lessons to both realists and idealists alike, creating an interest in moving beyond the ad hoc system to a permanent international criminal court. The lessons—and the rationales that they engendered—offered very different views of what the future of international criminal justice should look like. These differences formed the fault lines in the politics that would lead to the creation of the International Criminal Court.

The establishment of international courts to hold perpetrators of atrocities individually accountable for their actions is a profound achievement in the continued evolution of the human rights movement: "The work of these tribunals has cast a light by which the International Criminal Court (ICC) and future tribunals can be guided in their efforts to achieve the noble and lofty goals of ending the era of impunity and enforcing basic human rights."[166] From Nuremberg to The Hague, tribunals have pronounced sentence on individuals whose thirst for power prompted often unspeakable acts of brutality and cruelty. Human rights advocates are right in exalting the rise of international criminal courts and the important role played by countless individuals and organizations to bring these institutions into being.

Although it is difficult to imagine the creation of international criminal courts (distinct from postwar "show trials") absent growing human-rights norms, the evidence presented in this chapter makes clear that this process has been shaped by interests defined in terms of power at nearly every step. This includes the motivation behind the creation of the post–World War II international military tribunals, the role of geopolitics in halting the development of a permanent court to adjudicate violations of the Nuremberg Principles, and the timing and design of the ad hoc UN tribunals. Although the effect of power politics appears frequently in the expansive literature on international criminal courts, it is often underspecified or applied to very specific outcomes or issues.[167] Drawing on the realist tradition in international relations theory provides a framework that makes clear how interests defined in terms of power drove the behavior of the states throughout the process of institutionalization. It provides a compelling framework to understand the creation, design, and timing of international criminal courts.

Bringing the role of power into sharper relief is also helpful in making clear some important normative aspects of creating an effective atrocities regime. First, though the evidence strongly suggests that power politics were often central to the decision to create international criminal courts, once established, these can become effective vehicles for providing justice and can contribute to the promotion of human rights principles. In other words, regardless of the reasons behind their creation, international courts provide moments of opportunity to advance principles of justice. Though the Nuremberg trials may have been motivated by realpolitik, those involved in prosecuting cases in the court were successful in making it a cornerstone of a broader movement of criminal accountability. One lesson to be drawn from the evidence presented here is that norm entrepreneurs need to identify opportunity when it presents itself and make the most of it.

A second important policy lesson involves the rationale that motivates international criminal law. On the one hand, the international justice movement is aimed squarely at restraining the application of power and holding accountable those who abuse it. However, the experience of the tribunals also makes clear that achieving international justice is dependent on power. Jack Snyder and Leslie Vinjamuri argue that "justice does not lead; it follows."[168] In contrast to those that argue that legitimacy is the principle agent of compliance to international law, a realist perspective (or what some might prefer to call the "pragmatist" perspective) emphasizes the necessity of power in order to facilitate the process of justice.[169] Richard Goldstone, the first chief prosecutor of the ICTY, gives credence to the latter: "International courts, like other international bodies, depend for their success on the cooperation of governments. No international court is likely ever to have its own police officers, able to enforce its orders. Much of the cooperation from relevant governments received by the ICTY was the direct or indirect consequence of pressure from Washington, DC."[170] International criminal tribunals depend on powerful states willing to provide the necessary muscle to stabilize conflict situations, facilitate the cooperation of reluctant governments, aid in the apprehension of those indicted by the court, and lastly, shoulder the heavy financial burden international criminal justice requires. For these reasons one might temper a highly idealistic pursuit of international justice with one that acknowledges the crucial role power plays and seeks to navigate a prudent and pragmatic course aimed at providing justice for those who fall victim to the most serious international crimes. Indeed, some have sharply criticized the ICC for prosecuting crimes drawn only from smaller countries (all African) while remaining passive against allegations brought against the actions of the world's most powerful states.[171] Understanding the significant and often complex ways that power politics affects the process of providing justice might temper such criticisms by showing that pragmatism taken in the short term may be necessary in order to ultimately achieve the lofty idealistic aims of the International Criminal Court over the long haul.

In the wake of the experience of the ad hoc UN tribunals, both idealists and realists sensed that international justice was an unfinished project. Thus a new (or more accurately, renewed) discourse on the creation of a permanent international criminal court gained momentum. Among the most central issues underlying this debate was the one involving this tension between power and principle: Should legal principle be compromised in acknowledgment of the practical dependence international criminal courts have on powerful states? This debate would play out during the Rome Statute negotiations to create the International Criminal Court.

Chapter 2

Nested Interests and the Institutional Design of the International Criminal Court

> Demands for justice in world politics are . . . demands for the removal of privilege or discrimination, for equality in the distribution or in the application of rights as between the strong and the weak, the large and the small.
>
> —Hedley Bull

The Rome Statute of the International Criminal Court (ICC) was passed on July 17, 1998, amid an outpouring of emotion and raucous applause.[1] David Scheffer, head of the U.S. delegation recalls, "There was enormous applause and glee throughout the large room. Almost everyone stood and applauded and yelped, with civil society delegates in the room congratulating government delegates and the Italian delegation literally jumping up and down."[2] Many consider the ICC to be among the most significant new international institutions of the past century. For them, the ICC represents the apex of international humanitarian law—the first comprehensive international criminal court with truly global reach to try cases involving genocide, crimes against humanity, and war crimes. Among them, UN secretary general Kofi Annan declared, "this Court will be a gift of hope to future generations. Its creation represents a giant step forward in the march towards universal human rights and the rule of law."[3] Scholars have echoed these views: "The International Criminal Court . . . soars with the loftiest of ideals as it grapples with the basest of human acts."[4]

The emerging conventional wisdom in the scholarship on the ICC echoes some of these views in the explanations offered for why the court was created and how it was designed. Broadly speaking, the story of the formation of the ICC is often told as the triumph of principles over power politics. Constructivist scholars point to the importance of the growth of human rights norms and the role played by human rights activists and nongovernmental organizations (NGOs) in convincing states to support the Rome Statute that established the ICC.[5] For example, Beth Simmons and Allison Danner argue that the court finds its strongest support from a coalition of "principled, highly accountable, non-violent states."[6] There is a common theme in the literature of a politics largely driven by a divide between principled and nonprincipled (or less principled) actors. Support or opposition to the court commonly has been explained largely in terms of a state's support (or opposition) to evolving principles of international humanitarian law and the principle of equality under the law.

This view of state interests is far too simplified to accurately reflect the complex politics surrounding the formation and design of the ICC. In contrast, this chapter shows that many states had other interests in play during the Rome Statute negotiations. These interests involved more than simply issues of human rights—they involved interests defined in terms of power. Moreover, interests defined in terms of power were for many states not an inconsequential matter. In fact, concerns over the effect the creation of the ICC might have on a state's relative power called to question the very basis of international order. In the creation of the court, the struggle to supplant the current Westphalian system with a more Kantian order based on respect for law and principled norms was not the only contest. This chapter shows that, beneath the surface of the Rome Conference negotiations, a battle was also waged between states seeking to maintain their relative position in the global hierarchy and those who sought to restructure that hierarchy in part by creating a specific type of international criminal court. Although this struggle did not involve all those who participated in the Rome Conference, it did involve several of the world's most powerful states and a coalition of states who have waged a broader struggle to close the gap between the privileged and the marginalized in international society.

This chapter brings together two different strands of theoretical international relations (IR) research to explicate these dynamics. One shows how power is vested in the creation and design of international institutions, whereas the other reveals the importance of interinstitutional linkages (i.e., regime complexes).[7] This chapter synthesizes elements drawn from each to explain state interests regarding a subset of Rome Conference participants and why the issue of Security Council control was so central to the negotiations regarding the design of the ICC. Hypotheses generated from this analytical framework are then tested empirically by combining nonlinear regression analysis with careful textual analysis of archival records and legal documents. These cover three separate phases of the process of institutional design, including the Preparatory Committee (PrepCom) meetings (1996–98), the Rome Conference (1998), and the Kampala Review Conference (2010).

The Conventional Wisdom

Most of the theoretical research addressing the question of what factors explain the creation of the ICC begin by considering the likely political motives underlying potential support or opposition to the court. Many prominent works quickly dismiss power as a driving interest, and subsequently, cast doubt on both realist and rationalist frameworks.[8] For example, Allison Danner and Erik Voeten argue that international criminal tribunals "present an apparent problem to realist theorists as they regulate what should be the ultimate prerogative of states: their conduct in war."[9] Many fail to see how commitment to the Rome Statute could possibly contribute to a state's material power or its strategic interests. Political scientist Judith Kelley writes, "It is not very clear what concrete gains any one state can anticipate from supporting the ICC."[10] In another example of this skepticism toward rationalist or realist frameworks, Nicole Deitelhoff writes, "The establishment of the ICC is not easily accommodated within international relations theories that rely either on the existing power structure . . . or on current neoliberal rational-choice-based theories of legalization and institutional design, which hinge on the strategic choices of self-interested actors."[11] Thus the creation of the ICC "cannot be explained in terms of power and states' initial interests."[12] Similarly, Benjamin Schiff states that realists "have no explanation for its [the ICC's] creation in the first place."[13] Kathryn Sikkink adds that power "cannot explain how and why the idea of individual criminal accountability came to be applied in a world where many perpetrators still hold the monopoly on violence."[14]

This widespread skepticism about the potential of the ICC to produce gains for a state's material power pointed both legal scholars and political scientists toward a logical alternative: interests defined in terms of principles. For example, legal scholar William Schabas emphatically states that the creation of the ICC is "without a doubt . . . the result of the human rights agenda that has steadily taken center stage within the United Nations."[15] Similarly, Kelley argues that affinity for the ICC is primarily a function of three variables: democracy, human rights, and membership in the Like-Minded Group (LMG).[16] The initial strand of principles-based scholarship focused primarily on the normative power of human rights principles and the norm entrepreneurs seeking to promote the diffusion of these principles in international society. These norm entrepreneurs came in three forms: (1) states, (2) human rights NGOs, and (3) independent political activists and international lawyers. State norm entrepreneurs are commonly represented by membership in the Like-Minded Group. The name itself, "like-minded group," points to the centrality of a commitment to liberal principles of human rights and the rule of law. Antonio Franceschet notes that the LMG "framed its agenda in terms of the high moral ground of legalism."[17] To be "like-minded" in this sense suggests that there is more at stake than simply a congruity of material interests among members. Several prominent works forward arguments grounded in this assumption. Some arguments emphasize that the success of the LMG was due to having the stronger normative argument; others emphasize the role of the norm entrepreneurs in making those arguments.[18] Although it is difficult to imagine the creation of the ICC without such principled actors, such accounts have difficulty in accounting for specific preferences in institutional design.[19] There is considerable disagreement on which type of institutional form provides the strongest vehicle for the protection of human rights—a comprehensive and independent international court, an ad hoc court established within the specific parameters of a given situation, a hybrid court that mixes international and domestic rules and judges, or a truth commission similar to the one created in South Africa.[20]

A subsequent strand of scholarship sought to supplement existing explanations for court support by showing how other factors may contribute to the formation of a consensus regarding the Rome Statute. Jay Goodliffe, Darren Hawkins, Christine Horne, and Daniel L. Nielsen suggest that a state's willingness to join (or to oppose) international institutions like the ICC is affected by its "dependence network."[21] The central idea supporting this framework is that states are sensitive to reactions by their network partners regarding their position on the Rome Statute. They write, "Leaders observe how other governments behave within their dependence network and alter their own actions to be more consistent with those of their partners."[22] One obvious limitation is that this view does not offer a theory of interest; it does not tell us what a state's initial preference might be—only that it will feel pressure to conform to the behavior of its dependence-network partners. Presumably, for many states this involved conforming to the emerging consensus of the principled LMG. An important advantage of this framework is that it opens the door to understanding potential linkages between principled interests and material interests. Some states may join the LMG not because of shared principles, but rather because of concerns of a potential backlash by their network partners. However, the framework raises questions about who leads and who follows. Goodliffe and Hawkins suggest that, within a network, larger (more powerful) states are more likely to exert influence than smaller ones.[23] If that is the case, why did the smaller European Union (EU) nations not follow Britain and France in opposing the Rome Statute? Moreover, why did the United States not follow the EU's lead in supporting the statute, given that it is its primary dependence-network partner? Lastly, if we treat the European Union as an integrated economic (and to a lesser degree, political) actor, why did the EU not follow the behavior of its top three trade partners—the United States, China, and Russia?

Most scholars who emphasize the role of norms and ideas do not suggest that these factors can explain all the variation in reasons for state interests to commit to human rights institutions but, for the most part, have been unable to identify how material interests may directly affect the calculation of interests.[24] One reason much of the existing literature has difficulty in recognizing the role of power in the creation of the court is because the relationship between design and support (or opposition) to its creation is often conflated. For example, Sikkink suggests that "powerful states did not lead the trend toward . . . accountability," pointing to the fact that the United States "unsigned" the Rome Statute and was a major opponent of the ICC during the George W. Bush administration.[25] However, strong support from the United States was instrumental in the creation of the ad hoc tribunals that preceded the ICC. Indeed, Schabas notes that "the most enthusiastic—and ultimately decisive—support for the idea of the tribunal was coming from the United States of America."[26] Moreover, the United States was also supportive of the 1994 Draft Statute for the ICC created by the International Law Commission (ILC). Thus, it seems questionable to infer U.S. opposition to international courts in general based on its specific opposition to the Rome Statute. Rather, it instead points to the importance of institutional design changes made between the ILC Draft and the Rome Conference. Where a state stands regarding joining the court is a direct function of the process of institutional design, for that determines what exactly it is supporting or opposing. Thus, theorizing interests regarding the court must begin by considering them in the context of preferences in institutional design.

Theorizing Design Preferences

The theoretical framework utilized in this chapter is built on two insights—that institutions are a form of power and that institutional linkages may have significant impact on interests and outcomes. Drawing on the existing works that developed these ideas, I synthesize a theoretical framework that identifies a principal political fault line in deliberations over the design of the ICC. This involved whether or not the court should be firmly nested within the broader institutional structure of the United Nations and the Security Council.

Institutions as a Form of Power

Randall Stone points out that international institutions are increasingly significant elements of state power.[27] Focusing on international economic institutions, Stone documents how such entities are increasingly important tools for states seeking to maximize their economic power. Institutions are a form of power, not just a product of it. Moreover, given the rising stakes involved, states are keenly interested in realizing egoistic preferences during negotiations about institutional design.[28] The process of institutional design is an integral component of state power as well, for as Alex Wendt has noted, "Institutional design creates and reproduces political *power*."[29] Institutional rules can enable—or empower—some actors while constraining others.[30]

John Ikenberry has shown that powerful states utilize institutions in such a way to lock in the advantages that existing power hierarchies afford them. He notes that great powers often use a postwar moment to entrench their powers with new institutional and military orders.[31]

The institution of the United Nations Security Council (UNSC) is a conspicuous example of these dynamics in practice, as both a product of great power interests and a means by which their relative dominance in international politics is reaffirmed and maintained. The process of designing a system of great power cooperation that characterizes contemporary international society was begun at the Moscow Conference in 1943 and continued at the conference held at Dumbarton Oaks in Washington, DC, in 1944, and at the Yalta Conference in 1945.[32] This notion of great power leadership would be legitimized internationally through the creation of the United Nations.[33] At the San Francisco Conference in 1945, the great powers were able to gain broad support for a design of the UN that entrenched privileges for the P5 in the form of permanent membership on the Security Council that included veto powers.[34] As Ian Hurd notes, "The importance of the conference lies in its attempt to legitimize a universal system among all countries that would entrench a system of Great Power dominance through the Security Council."[35] Although obtaining the consent of the world's smaller powers required political maneuvering, concessions, and coercion, the United Nations entrenched an international norm of great power dominance once the original forty-six countries signed on. Specifically, the veto powers afforded to the five permanent members of the Security Council by the UN Charter "remains the icon of inequality in the UN system," an inequality determined solely by power at this unique moment in history.[36] Ultimately, the great powers were able to entrench their relative power through the form and function of the Security Council regime: "When the Council is united, its members can wage war, impose blockades, unseat governments, and levy sanctions, all in the name of the international community. There are almost no limits to the body's authority."[37]

The UNSC, as an institution, legitimizes great power exceptionalism in international society.[38] Through the rules of the United Nations, permanent members of the Security Council (P5) are afforded special prerogatives in exchange for accepting the added responsibility of managing global peace and security articulated in Chapter VII of the UN Charter. These special prerogatives can be seen to increase the relative power of the P5 in two ways.

First, it subordinates non-P5 members to obey the mandates of the Security Council. As noted by Bruce Cronin and Ian Hurd, "The United Nations Charter invests considerable political and legal authority in the Security Council, and the requirements of UN membership impose a substantial level of obligation on the states to follow the Security Council mandates."[39] Second, the UNSC conveys a "hyper-sovereignty" on its permanent members. Their power is constrained only by the veto power vested in their fellow Security Council members.

The institutional design of the United Nations—of which the Security Council is an integral part—does more than simply provide unequal gains for permanent members of the UNSC relative to all other UN member nations. It establishes a particular form of international order, one that creates a distinct hierarchy among its constituent units.[40] Moreover, the rules established in the UN Charter entrench this hierarchy even as the global balance of power has changed over time.

Regime Complexes and Institutional Nesting

The second element of the theoretical framework used in this chapter is from the literature on regime complexes.[41] Theories of regime complexes consider the potential effects of relationships that exist between institutions. These relationships may take several distinct forms: embedded, nested, overlapping, or clustered (figure 2.1).[42] "Embedded" and "nested" regimes appear identical, but are distinguished by the scope of the linkage. Embedded

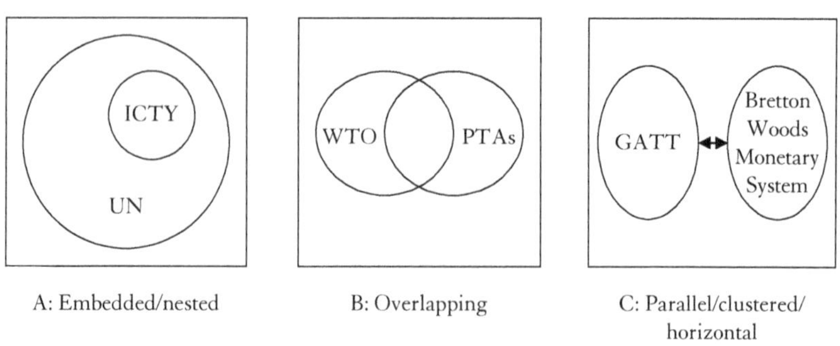

Figure 2.1. Typology of regime complexity

institutions refer to those that draw on broad, overarching institutional arrangements,[43] whereas nested institutions are those that "are folded into broader institutional frameworks that concern the same general issue area but are less detailed in their application to specific problems."[44] Nesting thus reflects a narrower conceptualization of a similar linkage. One example of a nested relationship is the ICTY, which is nested within the authority of the UN Security Council under Chapter VII of the UN Charter. Institutional linkages may also display an overlapping characteristic, where two independent regimes impact each other, though such interaction was not necessarily a product of institutional design. A good example of overlapping institutions is the World Trade Organization (WTO) and the array of regional preferential trade agreements (PTAs) used to manage international trade. Similarly, interaction effects may also be the product of conscious "clustering" of institutional arrangements into "institutional packages" as a strategy to achieve functional objectives.[45] The General Agreement on Tariffs and Trade (GATT) and the Bretton Woods monetary regime serve as a prime example. Such arrangements do not necessarily lead to overlap between institutions, but can create effects between and among parallel institutions. Generally speaking, embedded, nested, and overlapping frameworks suggest a hierarchical arrangement at play, whereas clustered, parallel, and horizontal frameworks do not necessarily convey a sense of hierarchical structure, but instead reflect an institutionalized division of labor.[46]

Much of the initial work on regime complexes has focused on the effect of overlapping relationships. This framework reveals how actors can exploit overlapping institutional jurisdictions when deciding where to adjudicate a dispute in order to gain a tactical advantage.[47] Rather than focus on potential overlapping arrangements (because the ICC reserves the authority to initiate proceedings rather than litigants), I turn instead to potential embedded or nested relationships because these suggest potential influence on both the form and function of the subsidiary institution. Two such relationships come quickly to mind when considering international criminal courts: the broad institution of Westphalian sovereignty that has defined international society since 1648, and the narrower relationship with the institutional structure and rules of the United Nations regime. Which nest is the most consequential regarding the design of the ICC?

Defense of the institution of Westphalian sovereignty is often explicitly stated as the primary reason to oppose the ICC.[48] As summarized by Charles

Smith, "Those opposed to the creation and institutionalization of a standing criminal tribunal argue such an institution threatens and undermines the sovereignty of nations."[49] A commonly held presumption is that principled states will be willing to bear the costs, while the less principled will defer to their defense of sovereignty, often viewed by human rights activists as the last refuge of a scoundrel.[50] However, delegating sovereignty on a specific issue to an international institution does not constitute relinquishing sovereignty in general, nor does it necessarily suggest that those nations seek to weaken the institution of Westphalian sovereignty.[51] Thus it is difficult to utilize this embedded relationship between the ICC and the Westphalian order as a means of explaining state interests regarding the formation of the court.

This chapter turns instead to the institution of the United Nations and the Security Council. While contemporary international criminal courts can be seen to be "nested" within a broader regime governing atrocities committed during conflict, the most direct and important nest involves the United Nations.[52] Those knowledgeable about the structure of the ICC may quickly object, noting that the court is not a subsidiary organ of the UN but an independent organization created by treaty. By focusing on outcomes already determined (i.e., Rome Statute), some miss the point that the ICC *could have been*, and some would argue *should have been*, largely under the direct control of the UN Security Council (UNSC).[53] The immediate precursors to the ICC were the ad hoc courts created for the conflict in the former Yugoslavia and Kosovo (ICTY) and the genocide in Rwanda (ICTR). Both of these international criminal courts were created by and nested within the authority of the UNSC.[54] Moreover, in the initial Preparatory Committee (PrepCom) deliberations, the institutional design of the ICC was based in large part on those used for both the ICTY and ICTR. Whether or not the ICC would also be placed in this nest formed a—perhaps *the*—crucial political fault line in the process of the institutional design of the court. In the language of regime complexes, the choice was between a court "nested" within the UN/UNSC or one that operated "parallel" to it. The outcome of this process of institutional design would in many instances determine who would ultimately favor joining the court and who would oppose it.

Theorizing Design Preferences

When one recognizes how power is vested within institutional frameworks, it is not difficult to appreciate how interests can be shaped by them. Taking this framework of nested institutions within the context of interests defined in terms of power prompts the following general expectation: states whose participation in an institution provides them with an advantage in terms of relative power over other states will favor the creation of subsidiary institutions that, at minimum, do not threaten this advantage. From this, we can also assume that states would favor the creation of subsidiary institutions that serve to strengthen the degree of advantage derived from the status quo. The creation of the ad hoc tribunals for Yugoslavia and Rwanda offers some initial support for this hypothesis. Since the ad hoc tribunals were established by the Security Council under the auspices of the UN, it should come as no surprise that nothing within the jurisdictional competencies afforded to the tribunals compromised the privileges afforded to the UNSC under the UN Charter. In fact, the tribunals might be seen as contributing to the relative power of the P5 by expanding the jurisdictional authority of the UNSC. The punishment of crime has traditionally fallen within the core competencies of states under the umbrella of Westphalian sovereignty. The creation of the ICTY and ICTR expanded the jurisdictional reach of the UNSC to punish nationals convicted of crimes in the name of international society. By increasing the scope of its authority, the tribunals served to increase the power of the UNSC.[55]

In contrast to the ad hoc tribunals that were designed largely at the discretion of the UNSC, the design of the ICC was open to negotiation. Thus, state support (or opposition) to the court must be seen as a direct function of the process of institutional design. The general theory developed here can be applied to institutional design using the same logic applied to formation. It prompts us to expect that states would prefer an institutional design that complements their existing institutional memberships and the advantages vested in them. Conversely, if a proposed design challenges these existing advantages, they should be more likely to oppose the creation of the court under that design structure. For the ICC, one of the most significant debates about institutional design was whether the new Court would be nested within the UN (and thus, nested within the authority of the UNSC). Who would we expect to support such a nested design? The answer to this question is relatively intuitive: the P5 should have strong preferences to nest the ICC within the authority of the Security Council as was the case with the ad hoc tribunals that preceded the ICC. Although the predicted preferences of P5 members under the "nested interests" framework are not particularly counterintuitive, the framework can help us answer a more challenging question. Who would be the strongest opponents of such a nested design? Put differently, who would have the strongest preferences for a strong and independent court free from Security Council control?

Reasons for opposing nesting the ICC in the UNSC could include two broad rationales—one principled, the other power based. First, this preference might be a function of adherence to legal principles—particularly the principle of equality under the law. This is the rationale put forth publicly by the Like-Minded Group whose members believed that this principle was essential in the continued evolution of the atrocities regime away from the practice of "victor's justice." However, there is more counterintuitive rationale that may underlie a state's preference to ensure that the new court would remain outside of the UN nest. If nesting provides for an increase in the relative power of the P5, should states disadvantaged by these institutional prerogatives not seek to utilize the design of new institutions to weaken the power imbalances supported by the status quo? Moreover, they might also see such an act as a significant first step in the process of weakening the great-power exceptionalism at the foundation of the institution of the UNSC. If weaker states were able to create an ICC with the power to hold the P5 accountable for the consequences of exerting their military force, this would certainly constitute a major reduction of their relative power. Thus, the nested interests framework would lead us to expect that states that are dissatisfied with institutions that promote great-power exceptionalism or contribute to increasing global inequality would be more likely to prefer an institutional design that wrests international criminal courts from the UNSC nest.

Research Design

This nesting framework highlights a political tension between two groups of states: those empowered by the great-power exceptionalism entrenched within the existing institutional structure and those dissatisfied with a system that institutionalizes privilege based on power. The nesting framework makes it easy to identify those who are empowered (P5), but which states can be considered "dissatisfied powers"? The first step in the process of research design is to identify this group.

The literature on power-transition theory is extremely helpful in defining "dissatisfied power." As described by Organski and Kugler, dissatisfied powers will be aggrieved as to their relative power status in the system and will seek to mitigate perceived power differentials.[56] Rather than interpreting relative dissatisfaction subjectively and then classifying countries accordingly, I seek to find objective proxies that can capture perceptions of dissatisfaction with relative power balances. I utilize two alternative proxies to operationalize dissatisfied powers. The first captures those countries that are dissatisfied specifically with the special prerogatives afforded to the permanent members of the Security Council. I operationalize this variable by combining two proxies: membership in the group Uniting for Consensus and membership in the G4, both of which were organized to push for reform of the Security Council. Uniting for Consensus (commonly referred to as the Coffee Club) was formed in 1995 by Italy, Mexico, Pakistan, and Egypt, and quickly grew to roughly fifty members. The G4 includes Germany, India, Japan, and Brazil. Each of the G4 countries fits the description of great (and rising) powers reflected in the power-transition theory model, and as the model expects, each is likely to see the status quo of international political order as unsatisfactory: "The challengers, for their part, are seeking to establish a new place for themselves in international society, a place to which they feel their increasing power entitles them. Often these nations have grown rapidly in power and expect to continue to grow . . . and they are unwilling to accept a subordinate position in international affairs when dominance would give them much greater benefits and privileges."[57] The interest of each group in reform of the UNSC stemmed from opposing points of view. Members of the G4 sought to close power disparities by gaining permanent member status on the council, whereas members of the Coffee Club sought to dismantle the relative power of the P5 by expanding membership in the council. Although it would be rational for aspiring states (such as the G4) to seek to maintain the institutional status quo granting exceptional status to permanent members of the council, one would predict that dissatisfaction with their status quo power would turn to institutional reform should it become evident that their quest for membership would fail. The timing of the negotiations over the design of the ICC may have coincided with this realization for G4 members. This first proxy provides a means to gauge how dissatisfaction focused on a related institution might affect its design preferences for subsequent institution building.

But what about states whose dissatisfaction stems from a general frustration over their place in the hierarchy of international society? Would such dissatisfaction influence preferences regarding a specific institutional design as well? At first glance, it is not entirely clear what the most suitable proxy for such a broader conceptualization of "dissatisfied" countries would be. However, two possibilities come to mind: (1) countries of the Non-Aligned Movement (NAM), and (2) BRICs (Brazil, Russia, India, China, and other countries such as South Africa). Although NAM countries have often expressed concern regarding power balances, it is not the central motivating principle of the group. Instead, the group's raison d'etre is rooted in Cold War politics and has had difficulty in finding coherence in its mission since the end of the Cold War. The BRIC countries certainly represent ascendant (and potential challenger) status in the post–Cold War era that would make them likely candidates for dissatisfied power status. However, because two of the four (Russia and China) benefit from their membership in the P5, it would be irrational to expect them to mobilize their "dissatisfaction" in opposition to an institution that affords it special powers and privileges. In contrast, we should expect them to strongly defend their powers vested in the P5 and to oppose new institutions that might constrain that strategic advantage. Therefore, using BRIC membership is not the most suitable proxy for dissatisfied power.

I suggest that membership in the G20-DN (Group of Twenty Developing Nations) serves as a suitable alternative to operationalize this broader sense of dissatisfaction.[58] The G20-DN has its roots in trilateral discussions by India, Brazil, and South Africa (IBSA Dialogue Forum) resulting in the Brasilia Declaration.[59] In this document, the three nations make a specific call for reform of the UN—specifically the Security Council.[60] It also referred to the distorting effects of globalization and the role that the trade regime played in this process: they agreed that "globalization . . . must benefit the largest number of countries" to make the system more "equitable."[61] At the Fifth Ministerial Meeting in Cancun, the group grew to twenty members and was instrumental in derailing the Doha trade round in 2003—the so-called "development round." Consistent with the Brasilia Declaration, the members of the G20-DN agreed that the GATT/WTO trade regime contributed to the growing economic disparity between economically powerful countries and the developing world. For this reason, the trade regime was seen as an instrument for the creation and maintenance of the hierarchical international order—an order in which they found their relative position weakening.[62] Though egoistic trade preferences were varied within the G20-DN, the group specifically "talked of *rebalancing inequities*, not proportionate and reciprocal concessions" as the great powers tended to frame trade negotiations during the round.[63] In other words, the goal of continued talks would be to redefine the mission of the WTO as an international institution from one based on the principle of egoistic gains to one based on the principle of equalizing global power (im)balances. The organizational coherence of the group around this issue of rebalancing global inequities make it a logical choice to measure whether a state should be considered a "dissatisfied power" under the definitions put forward by Organski and Kugler.[64]

Thus, the key independent variables are defined by membership in one of three groups: (1) the P5, (2) Uniting for Consensus and the G4, and (3) the G20-DN (plus Uniting for Consensus and the G4). The next challenge is to operationalize design preferences. During the course of informal discussions and formal negotiations, state representatives may offer statements that give us a sense of design preferences. However, representatives generally do not come to the table with a specific "ideal design" in hand, and design proposals are fluid during the course of negotiations. Therefore, getting a sense of where a country stands is best measured by its response to a concrete design proposal. Fortunately, two concrete designs were put forward during the process of ICC negotiations that vary in terms of the areas of interest put forth here: the 1994 Draft Statute created by the International Law Commission (ILC Draft) for consideration at the PrepCom meetings (1996–98), and the 1998 Rome Statute put up for a vote at the conclusion of the Rome Conference negotiations. Although there are numerous differences in design between the two, among the most critical (and contentious) involved the role of the UNSC in the operation of the court. As noted by Schabas, the ILC Draft functionally nested the court within the operational authority of the UNSC: "When the draft statute of the ICC [ILC Draft] was submitted to the United Nations General Assembly by the International Law Commission in 1994, the concept was very much that of a permanent counterpart to the ICTY, to act more or less on stand-by waiting for specific assignments from the Security Council."[65] The relationship between the court and the Security Council was spelled out in Article 23:

1. Notwithstanding Article 21, the Court has jurisdiction in accordance with this Statute with respect to crimes referred to in Article 20 as a consequence of the referral of a matter to the Court by the Security Council acting under Chapter VII of the Charter of the United Nations.
2. A complaint of or directly related to an act of aggression may not be brought under this Statute unless the Security Council has first determined that a State has committed the act of aggression which is the subject of the complaint.
3. No prosecution may be commenced under this Statute arising from a situation which is being dealt with by the Security Council as a threat to or breach of the peace or an act of aggression under Chapter VII of the Charter, unless the Security Council otherwise decides.

Article 23 gave the UNSC the authority to refer cases for investigation and trial, authority to determine if acts of aggression had occurred that warranted referral to the court, and afforded the council the power to halt a case.[66] In an important sense, the latter provided each council member with a veto on proceedings and did so in language that afforded the council sole discretion in determining whether it should assume control over the decision to move forward or halt proceedings. In contrast, the Rome Statute emphasized a design that was much more independent of the UNSC and therefore removed it from the institutional nesting that marks its ad hoc precursors, the ICTY and ICTR. Thus, we can get a sense of design preferences by comparing the significance of institutional membership on support or opposition to each of these design proposals.

The hypotheses proposed in this chapter are tested using a mixed-methods approach. Because no formal votes were conducted at the PrepCom meetings, state preferences on the ILC Draft must be analyzed using a qualitative methodology. Primary data analyzed are minutes and summaries of PrepCom meetings, statements made by members of delegations participating in the PrepCom meetings, official statements released by state delegations and state missions to the UN, and observations of independent personnel present during the meetings. To access this information, I draw on archival records of the PrepCom meetings available through the ICC's Legal Tools database, author interviews with key personnel, statements made through the media, and policy statements and press releases issued by the permanent missions to the UN.[67] Analysis of state preferences for a court independent of the UNSC institutional nest uses a combination of quantitative and qualitative techniques. The vote held on the Rome Statute makes it possible to measure the significance of institutional membership on state support or opposition to this design for the court. Because the dependent variable is dichotomous, a nonlinear estimator is required. Probit analysis of state signature of the Rome Statute is used to test the statistical significance of the various causal variables included in the analysis. It enables us to answer the question: Is membership in the group of dissatisfied powers a significant predictor of state support for the proposed design? Signature is chosen as the dependent variable rather than ratification because it is better suited to the political dynamics hypothesized here, particularly that related to the motivation and strategy of dissatisfied powers. In this chapter I test a theory of institutional design preferences, not state commitment, so issues of ratification are largely irrelevant unless a lack of ratifications forces states back to the negotiating table to hash out a new design proposal. The hypothesis forwarded in this chapter would suggest that some signers pushed the statute (in part) to put pressure on the P5 to join the court under this design structure. This political pressure involves the pressure to sign, not to ratify, because such dissatisfied powers have no control over whether P5 members will ratify the treaty. They can, however, put pressure on states to follow through on the commitments signaled by their signature of the statute, for failing to do so could weaken that country's international soft power.[68] So what should we see in terms of design preferences under this framework? Table 2.1 summarizes the predicted preferences of the various groups of interest in this analysis.

These power-based variables are then combined in the analysis with those representing two major alternatives present in the existing literature: liberal principles and sensitivity to exposure to prosecution. Liberal principles are operationalized through the use of two measures: (1) the level of democracy as measured by the Freedom House Index,[69] and (2) the level of human rights NGO activity in a given state.[70] Another explanation found in the literature on international criminal courts is that state reluctance to join the ICC is

Table 2.1. Predicted design preferences for an International Criminal Court

Group	ILC Draft Statute	Rome Statute
P5	Favor	Oppose
Uniting for Consensus+G4	Oppose	Favor
G20-DN	Oppose	Favor

largely a function of a state's military exposure to prosecution.[71] The logic of the argument is that states whose troops are deployed abroad—particularly for missions that are not in defense of their homeland (such as humanitarian interventions or peacekeeping operations)—should be less willing to expose them to potential prosecution for their actions during combat missions.[72] To test this argument, I include the number of peacekeepers (logged) that countries contributed to international humanitarian intervention missions at the time of the Rome Conference negotiations.[73]

The PrepCom Meetings and the ILC Draft Statute

A close review of the archival records from the PrepCom deliberations makes clear the strong and unanimous support P5 members had for an ICC nested largely within the authority of the UNSC, consistent with the predictions offered here. Preferences among P5 members for the ILC design conform to expectations in the context of how interests are nested within existing institutional arrangements. For the Security Council, interest in creating a permanent court was more pragmatic than principled. As shown in chapter 1, the need for a permanent court and any subsequent change of institutional design was not the product of a sense that existing tribunals were somehow deficient in the justice they meted. Instead, the motivation to pursue a new court was primarily based on a desire to reduce institutional costs and to increase efficiency. The functional obstacles to setting up ad hoc tribunals in times of crisis were so formidable that they potentially threatened the efficacy of the adjudication process.[74] There was also the issue of operational costs. Jamison Borek, deputy legal adviser at the State Department, made clear the American conception behind the proposed court: "A primary purpose in establishing a permanent international criminal court is to avoid the necessity of the Security Council establishing ad hoc tribunals to deal with crimes arising under international humanitarian law."[75] In other words, for the P5 creating a permanent court would be largely an issue of efficiency and cost savings over continuing to create tribunals on an ad hoc basis. This position was also articulated by the British delegation who expressed their "desire to obviate the necessity for the Council to establish new Ad Hoc Tribunals."[76] For the U.S. and British delegations, the ICC was conceived as a permanent form of the ad hoc tribunals.[77]

Discussion regarding the relationship between the court and the council centered largely on Article 23 of the ILC Draft Statute that specified the council's authority and control over the initiation of legal proceedings. The P5 members were consistent in their support for the ILC Draft, particularly the inclusion of Article 23 in the final design of the ICC. For example, the Russian representative stated, "Our delegation believes that the [ILC] Draft Statute provisions on the Security Council powers in relation to the future Court are well founded. In our view they reflect a quite important aspect: the provision of the Statute should in no way prejudice those provisions of the UN Charter which are related to the powers of the main UN bodies and, first of all, that of the Security Council. . . . In this connection we consider the provisions of Art. 23 of the Draft Statute to be of utmost importance."[78] This position was further articulated in the minutes of the PrepCom meeting in 1996, which stated that "the representative of the Russian Federation said that the court statute should not, *in any way*, limit the powers of the Security Council."[79] France also strongly favored a design that maintained a high degree of institutional nesting, and the French delegation "argued that the Security Council should screen all state complaints to see if they involve a situation of threat to or breach of international peace and security."[80] In essence, this provision would serve as an extension of UNSC veto powers wielded by the P5. The U.S. delegation articulated a preference for an even higher level of Security Council control than that which was articulated in the language of the ILC Draft. David Scheffer, head of the U.S. delegation recalled, "The draft statute also provided for state party referrals to the court, while we still preferred only Security Council referrals."[81] Although such control over the "trigger mechanisms" does not constitute a design that strictly nests the ICC in the UN/UNSC as a subsidiary organization, it does nest its operational control within this existing institutional authority structure. In essence, this constitutes de facto nesting if not de jure.

In terms of the hypotheses proposed here, the available evidence is most convincing in terms of the interests of P5 members for a nested design. Cherif Bassiouni, vice chairman of the PrepCom, noted that no non-P5 country representatives voiced support for the ILC Draft Statute's stated role for the council.[82] In particular, David Scheffer recalled that the design that afforded the Security Council sole referral power found no favor outside of the P5.[83] Thus, although the empirical evidence makes clear the P5 preferences with regard to nesting, the specific preferences of other participants are more opaque. Nevertheless, documentary evidence does show that the dissatisfied powers defined here were often quite outspoken in expressing their opposition to the degree of control nested within the UNSC as articulated in the ILC Draft Statute. Some of the objections were relatively limited and focused on specific provisions within Article 23. For example, Hans-Peter Kaul, head of the German delegation (and member of the G4), emphasized their objection to council control over trigger mechanisms as well as extension of veto powers. He stated, "It would be in our view quite inappropriate if the Security Council could submit individual cases or prevent the investigation and prosecution of cases involving such situations."[84] The delegation from Chile also offered specific objections to parts of Article 23, stating that paragraph 3 "implied an improper subordination of the Court to the Security Council." In this case, such subordination would be a function of the nested design reflected in the ILC Draft.

Other members of delegations defined here as dissatisfied powers offered broader objections to functionally nesting the court within the authority of the UNSC. For example, Lorenzo Ferrarnin of the Italian delegation stated that "the relationship between the court and the Security Council should preserve the independence of the court."[85] The Indonesian delegation was also skeptical of a role for the Security Council. In a meeting summary, the rapporteur noted that "the representative of Indonesia said that since, in many instances, Security Council deliberations had been political, the court should not be affected by its considerations."[86] Similarly, the Mexican delegation "saw no reason to involve the Security Council in the work of the international criminal court." The delegation added, "The court should be based on the principle of universality. That could only be achieved by leaving the Security Council out of its structure. Article 23 should be deleted from the Statute."[87] This statement was consistent with Mexico's earlier opposition to the creation of the ICTY. At the time, Mexico issued an official report questioning the Security Council's authority to create the ICTY under its Chapter VII powers.[88]

Some delegations from dissatisfied powers hinted that their objections were based at least in part on considerations of how a nested design would affect relative power balances. As noted in the official PrepCom proceedings, "Some delegations found article 23 either completely unacceptable or in need of substantial revision precisely because it conferred more authority on the Security Council than did the [UN] Charter or than was necessary in contemporary international relations."[89] The Argentinian representative asked, "How could a government be party to a treaty that would apply to all States parties, except for the permanent members of the Security Council?"[90] This would seem to suggest that the Argentinian delegation associated the nested design with reinforcing a tiered international system based on power afforded to the Security Council. The Venezuelan delegation, a member of the G20-DN, showed sensitivity to the realization that a nested design would increase the relative powers of the P5. Its representative stated that affording the UNSC the sole power to refer and defer cases would violate the "equality of states."[91] The delegation later added, "It would not be appropriate to confer new functions on the Security Council beyond what was provided for in the Charter."[92] Libya's position was among the most provocative in terms of opposition to the Security Council. In calling for the complete deletion of Article 23, the Libyan delegation said that "the Security Council had been used as a 'sword in the hand' of hegemonic great powers." It added, "The great powers should not be allowed to extend their vetoes to the international criminal court."[93]

Ultimately, deleting Article 23 would largely remove the ICC from the UNSC nest. At the conclusion of the sixth PrepCom meeting held from March 16 to April 3, 1998, a consensus began to form behind the idea of an ICC fully removed from the UN nest, setting up the dividing line for the negotiations held in Rome in summer of 1998. At this point, the P5 were unified in their design preferences, though the United States, Russia, and China were probably the staunchest advocates for strict control of the court by the UNSC. On the other side were the beginnings of the Like-Minded Group, seeking a more independent institution free of the UNSC nest. The nested interests framework begs the question—Is membership in the group of dissatisfied countries a significant predictor of whether or not it would support the institutional design articulated in the Rome Statute?

Removing the ICC from the UNSC Nest

During the course of the Rome Conference, delegations from the group of dissatisfied powers expressed preferences similar to those that they had stated during the PrepCom meetings. Among the Coffee Club members, Canada assumed a leadership position in organizing support for a strong and independent design for the ICC. Canada is widely regarded as the leader of the Like-Minded Group, and Canadian diplomat Philippe Kirsch was instrumental in managing the Rome Conference negotiations as conference chair. Likewise, other Coffee Club members took assertive positions vis-à-vis the relationship between the court and the Security Council. At the Rome Conference, the delegation representing Pakistan argued that "the role assigned to the Security Council in activating the trigger mechanism should be the exclusive realm of States parties, as Security Council decisions were based on political considerations and not on legal principles." The delegation added that Pakistan "therefore opposed any Security Council role in relation to the Court."[94]

G4 countries—those who advocated vigorously for reform of the Security Council—expressed similar preferences regarding institutional design of the ICC. Though their positions were similar, the origins and context of their dissatisfaction with the structure of the contemporary world order were different than that of the Coffee Club countries.[95] In the case of the G4, each had sought to find a seat at the table with the existing P5 members. Japan expected to be welcomed to the club in 1995 when the UN celebrated its fiftieth anniversary. Germany let it be known that it expected to follow Japan.[96] India also had been lobbying for a seat at the table as they continued to develop their nuclear weapons program. However, in the time leading into the Rome Conference, they all found decreasing prospects of attaining their goals.[97] India's chances for joining virtually disappeared in the fallout from the nuclear tests it conducted in May before the Rome Conference.[98] With prospects for inclusion waning, changing strategies to one that sought to whittle away the advantages afforded by permanent membership makes sense, and supporting a strong and independent ICC served as a means to accomplish this agenda.[99] The representative of the Indian delegation, Dilip Lahiri, stated that a preeminent role for the Security Council in design of the court, "constitutes a violation of sovereign equality, as well as equality before the law, because it contains an assumption that the five veto-wielding States do not by definition commit the crimes covered by the ICC Statute, or in case they so commit, they are above the law and thus possess de jure impunity from prosecution, while individuals in all other States are presumed to be prone to committing such international crimes."[100] Germany's position also hardened against a design that retained the ICC within the UNSC nest. Before the PrepCom meetings, Germany was largely supportive of the notion of a criminal court nested within the authority of the council, as the ad hoc courts had been. However, by the time the Rome Conference began, it had become one of the staunchest advocates of an institutional design that freed the court from Security Council control. When the delegation from Singapore offered a compromise design that offered the UNSC limited control over the court, the German delegation spoke out against it. They argued that "the institutional design of the ICC should not give *any* chance to the UN Security Council to create obstacles for the Prosecutor."[101] Moreover, the German delegation actively sought to prevent the P5 from mobilizing support for its design preference. For example, members of the German delegation attended a meeting of francophone countries organized by France and addressed the representatives from smaller states in attendance, arguing that "the important decisions at hand should not be left to the powerful P5."[102] The Germans sought to bolster support for their design preferences by offering support to delegations from developing states attending the francophone meeting.

Though the rhetoric drawn from archival records itself makes a compelling case, I have employed probit regression analysis to test whether classification as a "dissatisfied power" is a significant predictor of state support for a design that creates a court independent of the UNSC nest. The dependent variable used in the probit analysis is support for an "unnested" design, defined either by signature of the Rome Statute (which establishes a high degree of institutional independence from the Security Council) or by specific statements regarding state design preference if they were available. Some countries—most notably India—supported the "unnested" design, but did not sign the Rome Statute because its representatives felt that the proposed design did not go far enough in insulating the court from the Security Council.

Thus they were coded as "supporting" because support here denotes a design preference, not just support for the Statute as written. Two primary models are tested—one using the narrower definition of dissatisfied power, the other using a more general measure of dissatisfaction. The first model tests the significance of state membership in groups seeking reform of the UN Security Council (UfC+G4) on whether they support an "unnested" design for the ICC. The results for UfC+G4 were omitted by the statistical software program used (Stata) because the variable perfectly predicts the outcome. In other words, *all of the members of the UfC and G4 supported the unnested design* as predicted by the hypotheses forwarded in this chapter.

What about countries representing a broader, more general dissatisfaction with the unequal distribution of power evident in contemporary international society? The second model tested the effect and significance of "dissatisfied powers" when the variable includes the G20 group of developing countries (G20-DN). The results of the probit analysis reveals that dissatisfied power status is statistically significant in explaining support for the unnested design at nearly the .05 level ($p = .064$). Although this result may raise questions for some scholars regarding the level of significance, it is crucial to note that Guatemala is the lone outlier in this group (and has since joined the court through accession).[103] This outlier is discussed in detail in chapter 3. Moreover, when marginal effects are calculated, not only is the level of significance high, but the impact of membership in the group of dissatisfied powers has a considerable effect on design preferences. As shown in table 2.2, membership in the group of dissatisfied powers increases the probability of support for an unnested design by 17% ($dy/dx = .168$). For a few of these states, this preference was so strong that they opted not to sign the Statute because this design did not go far enough in removing the court from the UNSC nest and ensuring its independence from the council. Among this group of countries was Indonesia, whose representative "emphasized how important it was for the Court to be impartial and devoid of political influence of any kind, including the Security Council."[104] Cuba was another G20-DN member that supported an institutional design that reflected a parallel rather than nested relationship between the court and the council. However, it too opted not to sign the statute because "the Statute did not meet the aspirations of the great majority of humankind, particularly the peoples of the South."[105] Manuel de Jesus Pirez Perez, legal adviser for the Cuban Ministry of Foreign Affairs, would later clarify this objection: "The International Criminal Court's

Table 2.2. Factors affecting support for ICC design independent of UNSC nest (marginal effects after probit model 2)

	(Model 2) Support for RS
Membership	
g20_dn (d)	0.168**
	(0.0591)
logngo	0.0707*
	(0.0298)
logpk	0.0299
	(0.0170)
libdem	−0.0467**
	(0.0155)
cinc	−6.326[a]
	(2.525)
N	187

Note: Marginal effects; standard errors in parentheses (d) for discrete change of dummy variable from 0 to 1: * $p < 0.05$, ** $p < 0.01$.

lack of independence is concerning, considering the way in which its relations with the Security Council have been defined. Article 16 of the Rome Statute grants power to the Council to suspend the Court's investigations or indictments, and Article 5 purports to regulate in the future the Criminal Court's jurisdiction to the ruling that the Security Council could make on the existence of an aggression act committed by a State. These two elements question the true efficiency and independence of the Court."[106]

The evidence regarding dissatisfied power status on state interests does not refute that principled norms and human rights activism play a strong role in preferences, but rather suggests that their influence is not sufficient to explain design preferences. Initial probit results reveal that the level of democratic freedom (Libdem) is indeed a statistically significant predictor of preferences, whereas the number of human rights NGOs (LogNGO) present in a country does not quite reach the .05 threshold.[107] It is likely that the two are highly interrelated, as one might expect both (1) a higher level of NGOs present in liberal democracies that support them, and (2) a higher level of influence since these NGOs are likely to be more successful in mobilizing liberal polities than nonliberal ones.[108] However, when converted into their marginal effects, it is clear that the degree of influence these factors have on predicting design preference is considerably less than is the case for dissatisfied power status. As shown in table 2.2, the marginal effects reveal that as the level of democracy decreases (i.e., gets higher on the Freedom House Index), the probability that a country will support the unnested design decreases by 5%.

Consistent with expectations, the quantitative and qualitative empirical evidence make clear that dissatisfied powers strongly preferred an institutional design that would create a court free from the UNSC nest. The picture for the states "privileged" by the institutional status quo is more complicated during the latter stages of negotiations. Among the P5, the United States, Russia, and China held fast to their preference for a nested design; however, both Britain and France ultimately broke ranks from the P5 consensus and signed the statute (and later ratified it). Although this does not refute the fact that both strongly preferred the nested design model, it does raise the question of why they changed their position. This question is addressed in chapter 3.

The Kampala Review Conference

The first review conference held from May 31 to June 10, 2010, at Kampala, Uganda, offers another opportunity to gauge state interests with respect to the institutional design of the ICC. As stipulated in Article 123 of the statute, the United Nations was to convene a review conference seven years after the statute entered into force. The statute specified that the purpose of the review conference was to consider any amendments to the statute. In a sense, the Kampala Review Conference represents another iteration of the politics of institutional design, though this time involves design modifications rather than institutional creation. Amid the many issues that were addressed, one issue dominated negotiations at Kampala: whether to activate court jurisdiction over the crime of aggression and the process by which jurisdiction would be exercised.

The inclusion of aggression under the competencies of the ICC was by no means a new development in the process of the court's institutional design. Aggression was included in both the ILC Draft Statute in 1994 as well as the Rome Statute in 1998. Article 5(1) of the Rome Statute lists the crime of aggression as falling within the jurisdiction of the court. However, under Article 5(2), jurisdiction was to be exercised only after provisions were established that defined the crime and set out the conditions under which jurisdiction would be exercised by the court. Though there was much debate over the issue of definition, the most contentious aspect of the negotiations over ICC jurisdiction regarding aggression concerned the role of the Security Council. The design hypotheses forwarded earlier would lead us to expect that P5 members would demand that the council retain control over the trigger mechanism with regard to aggression (if they would support its inclusion in the statute at all), whereas dissatisfied powers would seek to further weaken P5 power by strongly advocating for the inclusion of aggression under crimes covered by the court and ensuring that authority for exercising this jurisdiction rested firmly with the Office of the Prosecutor rather than with the Security Council.

It is difficult to perform a precise test of these hypotheses, at least with regard to the dissatisfied-powers hypothesis, because no formal vote was taken during the Kampala Conference. However, the available evidence certainly appears consistent with these expectations, particularly with regard to the behavior of the P5. One might expect that the British and French defection from the P5 consensus against a strong ICC independent of Security Council control signaled a dramatic shift in interests for both. However, positions taken during the Kampala Review Conference suggest that P5 interests remained quite homogeneous. On the issue of aggression, the position of the P5 has remained consistent since the PreCom discussions of the ILC Draft Statute. The P5 consistently interpreted Article 39 of the UN Charter to confer on them exclusive powers to determine whether an act of aggression has taken place. From this interpretation, all five members remained adamant that a Security Council determination was an essential precondition to the ICC's jurisdiction over aggression.[109] Article 23(2) of the ILC Draft suggested that ICC jurisdiction over aggression would be controlled by a prior determination by the UNSC that aggression had occurred in a given situation. In other words, the council would have a monopoly of control over the trigger mechanism for court jurisdiction over the crime of aggression. The P5 were unified in their support of this design and held fast to this position throughout the Rome Conference negotiations. As noted by Claus Kress and Leonie von Holtzendorff, "The permanent members of the

Security Council adopted the ILC proposal and defended it with the greatest possible vigour until the last minutes of the negotiations."[110] Unable to break the unity of the P5, supporters of the Rome Statute ultimately decided to punt on the issue of aggression in order to seal the deal on the remaining aspects of the court's design. Thus, the exercise of jurisdiction was put off until design issues could be resolved during the review conference. Aggression was the unfinished business left over from Rome.

In preparation for the upcoming review conference, the Assembly of States Parties (ASP) created the Special Working Group on the Crime of Aggression (SWGCA) in 2002. Its purpose was to create working proposals for possible amendments to the statute involving adopting a specific definition of aggression as well as rules pertaining to the court's jurisdiction over this issue. Led first by Tuvako Manongi from Tanzania and then Silvia Fernandez de Gurmendi from Argentina (both countries classified as "dissatisfied powers" under the broader definition previously given), the SWGCA proposed that the court could exercise jurisdiction after the Security Council had determined that an act of aggression had taken place. However, in situations where the Security Council does not act to provide a determination regarding aggression, the proposal also listed several options that would grant the Office of the Prosecutor (OTP) the authority to move ahead with prosecution without it. These could either be a function of a specific amount of time passing or an alternative body making the determination that aggression had taken place. The latter could be the Pre-Trial Chamber, the General Assembly, or the International Court of Justice. This notion of wresting control of jurisdiction from the UNSC to the court also figured prominently in a series of proposals circulated during the conference. These included proposals submitted by Argentina, Brazil, and Switzerland (commonly referred to as the ABS Proposal), a proposal by the Canadian delegation, and a synthesis of the two, referred to as the ABCS nonpaper. Delegations of countries identified here as "dissatisfied powers" played key roles in the development of these design proposals, and each sought to retain the power of the court to exercise jurisdiction when the Security Council was unable or unwilling to act. In particular, Brazil was among the most assertive in seeking to constrain the P5 in its design proposals. Beth van Schaack recounted that coalition members such as Brazil and South Africa (another dissatisfied power as defined here) "seemed to approach the negotiations primarily as an opportunity to score points on a larger Security Council reform agenda."[111]

She added, "Brazil in particular was clearly endeavoring to play a big power role in opposition to the P-5."[112] Although there was some disagreement among the states parties on different aspects of the design proposals, a strong consensus was built among the dissatisfied powers in favor of limiting the role of the UNSC in the process of prosecuting aggression.[113]

Not surprisingly, members of the P5 did not support such design proposals and were indeed both adamant and outspoken in their preference for council control over aggression. In a prior statement to the ASP, Stephen Rapp, U.S. ambassador at large for war crimes issues, stated, "Our view has been and remains that, should the Rome Statute be amended to include a defined crime of aggression, jurisdiction should follow a Security Council determination that aggression has occurred."[114] This view is consistent with the consensus shown by all P5 members during the Kampala Review Conference. France and Britain showed no sign of defecting from this consensus as they had seven years prior at the Rome Conference. Neither could be persuaded to join the consensus behind the ABCS proposal because it rejected the idea of a Security Council monopoly on the exercise of ICC jurisdiction over aggression.[115]

As had been the case at Rome, the fault lines were clearly demarcated between the court and the Security Council. In contrast to the outcome in Rome, however, at Kampala it was the unified P5 that prevailed: "There was simply not the political will in Kampala to overcome the concerns of the permanent members of the UN Security Council (the P-5), who unanimously expressed the view that the Security Council must be given the right to act as the sole filter as to whether the ICC may proceed with investigations into the crime of aggression."[116] The result of the conference was a political compromise between the P5 and their allies and those who sought to address systemic power imbalances by enabling ICC jurisdiction over the crime of aggression. The inclusion of aggression in the statute at all certainly must be seen as a victory of the coalition of principled states and those states who consider its addition as a positive step in rebalancing the system. Explaining its rationale for supporting the addition of aggression to the court's mission, the Mexican delegation declared, "The counterbalance of political and military asymmetries is given by Law. That is the most powerful weapon of the Court and the international system."[117]

On the other hand, numerous concessions were made that afforded the Security Council considerable control over the extension of the court's jurisdiction. In cases where primary investigations are established from either referral by a member of the ASP or through the *proprio motu* powers of the Office of the Prosecutor, the Kampala compromise retains significant power to the council to halt further investigations. First, the OTP can only move forward with an investigation if the Security Council has not acted in at least six months to make a determination whether aggression has taken place. In such an event, the prosecutor would still have to request authorization to proceed from the Pre-Trial Chamber before moving ahead with an investigation regarding aggression. Moreover, the Security Council still retains the power to defer ICC action through its Article 16 authority, even if it has not made an active determination regarding aggression.[118]

Although the Kampala resolutions reserve a significant degree of control over the exercise of jurisdiction over crimes of aggression for the P5, these were achieved with further concessions. These include the exclusion of nonmember states to ICC jurisdiction, as well as provisions that allowed states the right to opt out of court jurisdiction over aggression. The nonmember exclusion shields the P5 members who were not party to the Rome Statute from any possibility of prosecution by the court regarding aggression. Moreover, it vests the power to extend jurisdiction to nonmember states only through a Security Council referral, a power it may exercise to apply jurisdiction to nonmember states over other crimes covered under the statute. Lastly, the final resolutions agreed to at Kampala delayed the implementation of jurisdiction over crimes of aggression until at least 2017 and were subject to subsequent action by the Assembly of States Parties. For these reasons, Beth van Schaack anticipates that "in light of the circuitous and cumbersome jurisdictional regime created by the new amendments combined with the existing jurisdictional obstacles in the ICC Statute, aggression prosecutions will likely be few and far between."[119]

Theories of regime complexes can help us understand how state interests regarding international institutions can be affected by existing institutional arrangements. This framework highlights how the institutional status quo can (and often does) have significant implications for state power by empowering some while constraining others under its rule structures. The advantages (and disadvantages) ensconced in existing institutional arrangements can figure prominently in both state interests involving the creation of new institutions as well as the evolution of existing ones. As the evidence presented in this chapter makes clear, state preferences regarding support or opposition to the creation of a new international institution (or change to an existing one) hinge on the process of institutional design. Thus, understanding how state interests can be nested within existing institutional structure helps us to understand the design preferences of states engaged in the process of negotiation.

The findings drawn from this theoretical approach are significant to our general understanding of the politics of international institutions. As international institutions continue to proliferate, states will likely seek to use institutions strategically, using design as a means to forward their own relative power or constrain the power of others. Navigating this increasingly dense web of interconnected institutions to forward a "national interest" will become increasingly challenging. As the cases of Britain and France make clear, interests nested in a country's membership in a given institution (UNSC) may clash with interests accrued from membership in another (the EU). In addition, not only are states left to find an option that provides the greatest net effect, but they may at times be inclined to include domestic political factors in the calculus. Not all institutions are nested in existing institutions and the nature of nested relationships varies both in character and potential impact. However, as the number of international institutions continues to grow, it stands to reason that the regime complex framework will be not only increasingly helpful but very likely necessary for understanding institutionalization and state behavior. As Oran Young notes, "this sort of institutional interplay is destined to loom larger in the future, as interdependencies among functionally distinct activities rise in international society and the density of international regimes increases."[120] Therefore, the utility of this approach across issue areas is likely to be increasingly necessary to understand why international institutions are formed and why they take the form that they do.

The case of the creation of the ICC offers an ideal situation to illustrate how these dynamics play out in practice. It has been said that "the leaders of the Rome conference faced a trade-off between legal principles and power realities, which they resolved in favor of legal principles."[121] A closer look at the evidence using the nested-interests framework suggests that this view is not entirely true. Instead, the theory yields a counterintuitive insight that challenges the conventional wisdom: state interests regarding the ICC were in many cases influenced by concerns over relative power. Although proponents of a court free of the UNSC nest couched their arguments in principled terms—of equality under the law irrespective of power—ultimately in the process of creating the ICC, we see struggle between those empowered by existing institutional arrangements and a group of dissatisfied powers seeking to dismantle the advantages of the privileged. Some scholars have hinted about these geopolitical dynamics. Among them, Schabas writes, "The Rome Statute was an attempt to effect indirectly what could not be done directly, namely reform of the United Nations and amendment of the Charter."[122] Similarly, Ruth Wedgwood described the process of creating the ICC as something of a "palace revolution" against the UNSC and the competencies assigned to it by the UN Charter.[123] And yet, none has offered a theoretical framework or rigorous empirical testing to explain the geopolitical dynamics involved in the creation of the court.

Understanding the geopolitics involved in the design and creation of the court helps us see that the ICC is one of the exceptional cases among international institutions. Unlike the many regimes and organizations created to overcome coordination problems, the potential gains and losses offered by the court involved more than just short-term advantages to relative power. Moreover, the court involved more than just the articulation of rules to guide and govern such transactions and interactions. Though an international legal institution, the court represented more than law. The theoretical framework and empirical findings presented here make it clear that what was at stake during the Rome Conference in 1998 was much more than the design of an international criminal court—it was the organization of international order itself.

Chapter 3

Explaining the Outliers

Domestic Politics and National Interests

> Labour's foreign policy can be characterized as a kind of two-level game in which international concerns must be linked with a domestic agenda, in this case essentially a party political one.
>
> —Mark Wickham-Jones

The theory of institutional design preferences forwarded in chapter 2 provides a lens for identifying how a country's preferences can be influenced by its interests regarding relative power and its satisfaction or dissatisfaction with its relative place in the hierarchy of international society. This certainly applied to the case of the International Criminal Court (ICC) because its design had such potentially dramatic implications for international order. In particular, this involved the system of great-power privilege ensconced in the institution of the UN Security Council (UNSC). However, as pointed out in chapter 2, key outliers emerged in the groups that were analyzed—among both the privileged and dissatisfied powers. Their unexpected behavior raises several important questions. Given their solidarity going into the Rome Conference, why did Britain and France break ranks with their fellow P5 members and ultimately support the design favored by the Like-Minded Group (LMG)? Among the dissatisfied powers, Guatemala was the only one that did not support the Rome Statute design that took control of the ICC away from UNSC and the P5 (five permanent members).[1] Why did

Guatemala not follow suit of the other dissatisfied powers? Certainly no theory can account for all outcomes. However, the significance of these outliers warrants a closer look to explain their behavior. Understanding why these states did not behave as expected is important to bolster confidence in the power of the theoretical framework proposed in chapter 2. Did these countries act contrary to their interests regarding relative power?

A closer examination of the available empirical evidence shows these outliers do not really refute the broader arguments about the role that interests defined in terms of power have on institutional design preferences so much as they provide examples that illustrate how they shape preferences differently at different levels of analysis. In the cases examined in this chapter, power considerations were not limited to the international level. Rather, political leadership in each country gave priority to domestic power interests over concerns about relative power at the international level. To capture the effect of this trade-off between domestic and international interests, this chapter draws insights from the literature on two-level games to show how the actions of these outliers were influenced by interests concerning domestic political power.[2]

The chapter begins with a critique of existing explanations evident in the literature on the International Criminal Court. I then draw on Robert Putnam's two-level game framework to generate expectations regarding state preferences for each of the outliers.[3] Although it has been noted that domestic politics played a role in the decisions made by the representatives of Britain and France at the Rome Conference, this chapter analyzes the available evidence to reach a fundamentally different conclusion than is commonly reflected in the literature. It explains the British shift as primarily a function of New Labour's electoral tactics to unseat the Conservatives and assume control over the government. In other words, New Labour utilized principles of idealpolitik to forward a realpolitik agenda. However, this chapter shows that this use of principled rhetoric did not signal a fundamental shift in British attitudes, nor was it the product of organized domestic political mobilization; rather it was a relatively short-term political tactic that was later discarded in the late 1990s. Unlike the cases of Britain and France, Guatemala's behavior regarding the court has not garnered scholarly attention. Instead, the literature largely focuses on the Like-Minded Group, reflecting perhaps an assumption among scholars that this group represented largely homogeneous interests in institutional design. Like the other two outliers examined here, domestic politics are equally important to explain Guatemala's behavior regarding the ICC. In this case, reluctance to join the LMG in favor of a strong and independent court was a product of individual and party survival—an attempt to remain in power.

Institutional Design and Domestic Politics

Constructivist scholarship argues that shifting preferences during the design negotiations at the Rome Conference were largely a function of the persuasiveness of the principled argument for an independent court put forward by the LMG.[4] This perspective would suggest that representatives from Britain and France were convinced of the legitimacy of an institutional design that placed a priority on principle over power. If this was in fact the case, then both did more than just defect from the P5 consensus to accept the LMG design proposal. Rather, they too became "like-minded" in giving priority to principle over power in their design preferences. In other words, consistent with constructivist theory, the internalization of norms produced a change of identity, and this new identity redefined their interests vis-à-vis the ICC.[5] As shown in the previous chapter, however, it seems that they were not as "like-minded" as some might have guessed (or hoped). At the Kampala Review Conference, the British and French were once again fully engaged in a consensus among P5 member states in the new round of negotiations on the institutional design of the court. In particular, this group jealously guarded UNSC control over ICC jurisdiction for cases of aggression. Thus, it would seem that the British and French shift during the Rome Conference hinged less on the power of the principled argument than it did other factors particular to that specific historical context. The question then becomes, What other factors made them more amenable to the LMG design preference at the time of the Rome Conference?

Alternative realist and neoliberal explanations would likely be based on the notion that any change in preferences would be the product of a recalculation of the relative gains available afforded by an alternative design. Consistent with these perspectives, Jay Goodliffe and Darren Hawkins suggest that states' preferences are influenced by the actions of other states within their dependence networks.[6] These networks may revolve around separate issues areas, including security, economics, and institutional memberships.

Such states may seek consensus with network partners in hope that this might either yield material gains (such as trade concessions) or avoid potential punishments resulting from clashing interests.[7] Goodliffe and Hawkins add, "We do not wish to imply that states are always clearly and explicitly rewarded or punished for their behavior by their network partners," but that expected returns reflect a condition of "diffuse reciprocity."[8] This notion of dependence networks is certainly useful in identifying possible incentives for states to change their preferences on an issue. However, when considering its utility in explaining the behavior of both Britain and France at the Rome Conference, important questions arise. Why would dependence network dynamics have a stronger effect on Britain and France to conform to the European Union (EU) consensus instead of the other way around? At the time, the United Kingdom (UK) and France represented over one-third of the GDP of the EU even though they represented only 13% of the membership.[9] Moreover, considering that the top three trading partners of the EU as a whole are (1) the United States, (2) China, and (3) Russia, one would expect that there would be more—indeed, much more—to gain or lose for EU states by not conforming to the preferences of these states, all of which expressed a strong initial preference to nest the ICC within the authority of the UNSC.[10] It is also unclear why the UK, in particular, was willing to break with its primary dependence partner, the United States. Not only is the United States the top destination for UK exports and the second-highest source of imports to Britain, but the strategic alliance between the two has historically been characterized as constituting a "special relationship."[11] It is difficult to "net out" the potential costs and benefits for Britain and France to change their design preference (or at least their willingness to accept a suboptimal design), but the available evidence would cast serious doubt that the costs are offset by potential gains of conforming to the EU consensus on the Rome Statute.

A second significant question arising from the dependence network model is that it holds design constant. As specified in chapter 2, a state's position of support or opposition to an international institution depends largely on its design elements. The design of the ICC, as with all major international institutions, involves myriad design elements. These include key factors such as level of obligation, precision, and delegation.[12] Therefore, it is highly unlikely that a group of states would have identical design preferences, even where there may be congruity of interests, as was the case with the P5. Linking preferences to design is better characterized by actor "win sets"—a range of design elements that encompass all possibilities from the ideal model to the least acceptable. Thus, whether a country will accept a given design proposal depends largely on whether it fits within its design win set. As with all negotiations pertaining to the creation of new international institutions, the Rome Conference was marked by numerous design concessions offered by parties in order to build consensus for support. This suggests that the win sets of participating states are not fixed but to some degree fluid, as are the specific design preferences.

The notion of dependence networks and diffuse reciprocity is helpful and the predicted outcomes are consistent with the aggregated data, but the explanation for causal inference is problematic given actual circumstances surrounding the Rome Conference.[13] To address these limitations, I draw on the logic of two-level game frameworks to explain the deviations from the expected behavior under the general theory forwarded in chapter 2.[14] In contrast with liberal theories that suggest all foreign policy behavior is a function of domestic interest-group politics, the two-level game framework acknowledges that foreign policy interests are Janus-faced, simultaneously having both international and domestic dimensions.[15] The nested-design theory has been offered here to explain the international interests of actors whose relative position in international society can be significantly affected by the outcome of the institutional design negotiations. To explain deviations in expected behavior under the two-level game framework, we must ask, "What are the relevant domestic actors that might affect a state's system-level preferences during the negotiating process?" Moving down from the structural (system) level, we might then take a closer look at the behavior of those who vie for control of the state—individual politicians and the political parties they belong to.

A Machiavellian perspective would argue that at this lower level of analysis an actor's primary interest would be the acquisition of power (or maintaining power they already have).[16] As is the case at the international level of analysis, power is necessary for political survival. As will be shown in the following sections, these domestic sources of power politics provide significant insight into the behavior of the UK, France, and Guatemala at the Rome Conference and beyond. The analysis in this chapter begins by exploring the electoral politics of the 1997 election in the UK that brought the Labour government of Tony Blair to power. This outcome not only contributed to the shift in the British position on the ICC during the Rome Conference but also to France's shift by making it the sole outlier among EU nations who were supportive of the Rome Statute. The cases of Britain and France are followed in the chapter with a section that focuses on how Guatemala's position at Rome was influenced by party politics and fears that joining the ICC would be disastrous for the ruling party, the Frente Republicano Guatemalteco (FRG). Party leadership was leery of exposing itself to international prosecution, and this desire to maintain its domestic power ultimately trumped its desire for international balancing. Once these domestic political conditions changed, Guatemala's position vis-à-vis the ICC changed as well. In this case, Guatemala's accession to the Rome Statute is consistent with the hypotheses offered in chapter 2 regarding the dissatisfied powers.

New Labour's "Ethical Foreign Policy"

On March 17, 1997, Britain's Prime Minister John Major announced that the next election would be held on May 1 of that year. At the time, the Labour Party faced a daunting task: the Tories held power in Britain for nearly two decades since Margaret Thatcher became prime minister in 1979. When Tony Blair became leader of the Labour Party in 1994, he looked to Labour's victory in 1945 for guidance in how to change the party's electoral fortunes.[17] Blair came to the conclusion that he needed to move the political discourse beyond the simple dichotomy that characterized party rhetoric in years past. Party politics were defined in terms of the left versus the right. Blair proposed a "Third Way" for British politics, beyond the left and right, and began a program to rebrand the identity of the Labour Party. Reflecting on his election strategy for the Labour Party, Blair writes, "To win the trust of the British people, we must do more than just defeat the Conservatives on the grounds of competence, integrity and fitness to govern. We must change the tide of ideas. Our challenge is show that in our policies, in our commitment and in our optimism we are ready to meet the country's call for change and its hopes for national renewal. Britain stands at a crossroads, and Labour stands ready. Our challenge is to forge a new and radical politics for a new and changing world."[18]

The specific dimensions of this idea of "New Labour" were articulated in a 1997 Labour Party manifesto that laid out the party's platform and road map for success in the election.[19] Most of the document focused on domestic affairs, signaling its relative priority in electoral strategy. As Blair recounted, "The 1997 campaign was fought almost exclusively on a domestic policy basis."[20] This sentiment would suggest that public opinion, or Labour's perception of it, was not driven by foreign policy issues. More specifically, it would suggest that there was little political pressure on members of either party to support the creation of an international criminal court. Rather, Blair and the Labour Party focused on the public's sensitivity to domestic issues, and these were reflected in the emphasis of the Labour Party manifesto. Labour's five primary campaign pledges in the manifesto were (1) welfare to work proposals, (2) speedy punishment of young offenders, (3) reduction of National Health Service (NHS) waiting lists, (4) reduction in class sizes in schools, and (5) nursery care facilities for three- to four-year-olds.

Nevertheless, the New Labour's election manifesto did include some foreign policy elements. Two key elements stood out: (1) higher priority placed on human rights, and (2) more active engagement with the EU. Although neither of these foreign policy priorities signaled any commitment to design preferences for the formation of a new international criminal court, both would figure prominently in Britain's actions during the Rome Conference. Blair's Labour Party platform promised that "we will make protection and promotion of human rights a central part of our foreign policy," a move that was intended to distinguish itself from the realpolitik that marked Conservative governments from Margaret Thatcher to John Major.[21] This was the genesis of the notion of an "ethical foreign policy" under the Blair government. British Foreign Secretary Robin Cook declared, "Our foreign policy must have an ethical dimension. . . . The Labour government will put human rights at the heart of our foreign policy."[22] This emphasis on an "ethical dimension" for foreign policy enabled Labour to characterize its foreign policy as a radical departure from that of the Tories. Scholars of British electoral politics have argued that this emphasis on charting a starker contrast with the Conservatives was an essential element of Labour's election strategy. As one scholar put it, "New Labour calculated that there was an electoral incentive to bring ethical considerations to the forefront of the foreign policy debate."[23] Some critics argued that the lack of specifics articulated in Labour's manifesto render it more of a list of aspirations than concrete policy.[24] Moreover, this led some to question whether the high principles on which policy would be based amounted to little more than political spin devised for electoral gain. Paul Williams remarked that "New Labour has created more foreign policy slogans than even its most clairvoyant spin doctors could have envisaged during its 1997 election campaign."[25]

Though short on foreign policy specifics, the 1997 Labour Party manifesto included a specific campaign promise regarding the ICC that was based on the notion of an ethical foreign policy and the promotion of human rights. The manifesto clearly states, "We will work for the creation of an International Criminal Court to investigate genocide, war crimes, and crimes against humanity."[26] Like most campaign promises, this statement was vague regarding the specifics of this commitment. It was, however, among the only specific elements of Labour's notion of an ethical foreign policy articulated in the manifesto. Thus this position statement gained significance as a key part of the broader ethical foreign policy agenda.[27] But what type of International Criminal Court was it committed to supporting? The manifesto provided no details about institutional design preferences.

Several scholars have pointed to the 1997 election and change in government in Britain as the source of changing preferences regarding the ICC.[28] There seems to be an assumption, however, that the new Labour government represented a fundamental shift in how British national interests were defined. If this was truly a shift in British ideology brought in under new leadership, one could argue that ideals triumphed over realpolitik. But was this really the case? If so, we should see (1) consistency in the new government's commitment to, and application of, an ethical foreign policy; and (2) the UK's adoption of the LMG position in subsequent design negotiations regarding the ICC. In fact, we see neither outcome in the time following the rise of the Blair government. Critics contend that "despite an undoubted shift in elite discourse, evidence of continuity in foreign and defense policy is much more compelling."[29] They point to a series of foreign policy decisions that would seem to be at odds with a commitment to an ethical foreign policy. For example, even though Britain supported humanitarian intervention in Kosovo, asylum policy in the UK remained highly restrictive. One journalist remarked, "The Kosovar Albanians are the victims of the greatest crime of postwar Europe, but as soon as they cross the Channel, they grow horns and become scrounging frauds."[30] Another controversial foreign policy decision involved the sale of arms to Indonesia as political unrest in East Timor grew. These weapons were ultimately used to suppress the East Timorese. Tim Dunne and Nicholas Wheeler suggest that the case of arms sales to Indonesia "poses the question of whether Britain has sacrificed its commitment to human rights on the altar of trade."[31] A similar issue involved what became known as the arms-for-Africa affair. The UK had exported weapons and supplied mercenaries in Sierra Leone in violation of UN arms restrictions.[32] Later in the tenure of Blair's Labour government, British support for military actions in Iraq and Afghanistan also faced substantial criticism among human rights activists.[33] Probably the most obvious example of the lack of consistency in the government's commitment to basing its foreign policy decisions on an "ethical dimension" is that this notion did not appear in the party manifesto created for the election in 2001.[34] Some have argued that the "ethical dimension" was dropped from the manifesto "because of the significant gaps emerging between New Labour's statement of intent and its actual practices."[35] Instead of an ethical dimension, the emphasis of foreign policy was placed on maintaining active engagement with the EU—a position consistent with the party's 1997 manifesto.

These developments call to question whether or not Britain had undergone a fundamental transformation, one that redefined both its national identity and its foreign policy. If the "ethical foreign policy" of the Labour government had truly proselytized the British to be more "like-minded" with the LMG than with its fellow P5 members, one would expect to see evidence of this shift in later negotiations regarding the ICC. The Kampala Review Conference held in 2010 was the first forum for negotiations concerning the ICC following the Rome Conference. As shown in chapter 2, there is little evidence to support the idea that a newly "principled" Britain now found more common ground with the LMG than with its fellow P5 members. Instead, the Kampala Review Conference showed a renewed and reinvigorated sense of cohesion among the members of the P5, particularly on questions of institutional design regarding ICC control over the crime of aggression.

So how exactly did the rise of New Labour affect British behavior on institutional design at the Rome Conference? The pronouncement of a new "ethical foreign policy" certainly mattered, but not necessarily because it reflected a fundamental shift in how interests would be defined. Instead, the evidence seems to suggest that interests defined in terms of power had a more prominent effect on outcomes than is generally assumed in the existing literature. Two elements figure prominently in reaching this conclusion. First, the statement regarding the ICC, its links to the broader notion of an "ethical foreign policy," and the way it was perceived by both the public and the media significantly constrained the British position during the Rome Conference. Second, Labour's commitment to strengthening its relationship with the EU—another key party platform—altered the balance of power between the British delegation at Rome and the LMG. Taken together, these domestic political factors served to expand the British win set regarding the institutional design that pushed it closer to that of the LMG. At the same time, design concessions offered to entice P5 support broadened the LMG's win set to a point where agreement could be reached with the UK delegation.

As discussed earlier, much of the intent behind the rhetoric of a new "ethical dimension" centered on political strategy—in other words, as a means to political power. Once articulated in party documents and public statements by both Tony Blair and Robin Cook, the notion of an ethical foreign policy gained political traction among the electorate and garnered significant attention by the media in the UK. But what exactly would such a foreign policy look like? Only the brief statement regarding Labour's support for the creation of an international criminal court offered tangible evidence of how this would manifest itself in policy under New Labour. Although the statement is concrete in its statement of support for a court, it did not articulate any particular design preference for such an institution. Subsequent public statements made after the election but before the Rome Conference give a clearer idea of what type of court Labour leadership had in mind when it professed its support. In a speech given on August 17, 1997, Robin Cook briefly outlined why the ICC was needed: "The current tribunals on Rwanda and on the former Yugoslavia have demonstrated the need for the legal mechanism to bring to justice those who brutally break international law. A permanent international criminal court would enable that work to begin more speedily when it is next required; would remove the need for an ad hoc decision that authorized legal processes with respect to a particular country; and would enable its lawyers to retain expertise and authority in this specialized field."[36] These sentiments suggest that the need for a permanent international criminal court is largely a functional one and stemmed from the inefficiencies evident in the ad hoc tribunals created under UNSC authority. This view was largely consistent with the stated positions of other P5 members before the Rome Conference. It is also consistent with prior UK statements made during the PrepCom meetings. It is likely, therefore, that when the statement was included in the 1997 Labour manifesto, that drafters had in mind a design consistent with the 1994 ILC Draft Statute. In prior statements, the British delegation stated explicitly that the ILC Draft "adopts the right approach" to the establishment of an international criminal court.[37] There is no indication that this attitude changed with the Labour victory in 1997.

However, what the drafters of the manifesto had in mind regarding the ICC seemed to be interpreted quite differently by the British media, and in turn, the electorate. One significant drawback of the notion of the "ethical dimension" was that it was largely taken to represent a dichotomous character to foreign policy. In other words, in the public eye, this concept largely framed foreign policy elements as either "ethical" or "unethical."[38] This conceptualization placed substantial constraints on the foreign secretary's office because successful diplomacy and negotiations depend on flexibility and compromise among a range of possible options. Indeed, party insiders suggested that even Robin Cook eventually considered the concept to be something of a millstone around his neck when engaged in diplomatic exchanges.[39] Entering the Rome Conference, the British delegation sought to follow through on the pledge made by the Blair government. However, during the conference, the LMG gained the upper hand in framing the terms of the debates around a design proposal sharply at odds with the 1994 ILC Draft Statute (over the role of the Security Council). They were able to do so because representatives from their members had assumed key roles in the proceedings, including chairing most of the working groups and the bureau, the executive body that managed the day-to-day operations of the conference.[40] In this emerging environment, the ethical foreign policy concept put British negotiators in a difficult position. Opposing the emerging consensus on the institutional design of the court would likely be viewed by the British media and public as going against their stated commitment to support the ICC and would likely incur significant domestic political costs. Reneging on its promise would certainly affect public trust of the new Labour government. For Blair, securing and maintain public trust "really matters."[41] The significance of Britain's actions during the Rome Conference loomed exceptionally large because (1) support of the ICC was one of very few specific foreign policy elements identified by New Labour, and (2) the timing of the conference ensured that action regarding the ICC would be among the first major foreign policy actions of the new government. These potential domestic political costs created pressure to expand the British win set toward the LMG design win set.

This was not the only domestic political factor pushing for a larger British design win set. The 1997 Labour manifesto also promised a stronger British role in the European Union. In contrast to the Conservatives, Labour sought to become the "party of Europe" by increasing its engagement with the EU. Labour also promised that it not only supported remaining in the EU, but that it intended to "lead from the front" when it assumed the EU presidency in 1998.[42] What did this mean for British bargaining interests during the Rome Conference? The LMG membership included all EU member nations at the time, with the exception of Britain and France.[43] As such, Britain and France stood as obstacles to garnering a united European consensus on institutional design. Opposing the Rome Statute design would incur audience costs for the British at two levels. First, it would strain British relations with the EU at a time when it sought to assume a position of strong leadership within the institution. Second, opposing an EU consensus on the ICC and straining relations with the other member states would likely incur additional domestic political costs among the British electorate. Thus, failing to sign the Rome Statute would be politically catastrophic for New Labour, as two of its key platforms would be violated within the first year of the government.

Figure 3.1 illustrates the negotiating process during the Rome Conference in terms of two win sets—those of the UK and the LMG. As noted in chapter 2, one of the key design features contested by members of the P5 and members of the group of dissatisfied states involves the degree of independence the ICC would have in relation to the UNSC. At this point, the question does not specifically involve the interaction between satisfied or dissatisfied powers, but rather simply why the UK defected from the P5 consensus on the issue. Because the original (i.e., pre-conference) design win sets of the UK and the LMG did not overlap (UK_1 and LMG_1), there was little probability of an agreement. Domestic and EU-level audience costs pressed the UK to expand its win set to UK_2. Although negotiations were rather fluid and it is difficult to make a highly precise estimate of when the win sets overlapped, the archival records suggest that potential domestic political costs alone were insufficient to push the UK win set to the right of LMG_1. This must be seen as a necessary but insufficient explanation for British support of the Rome Statute design. Here we see that the LMG also

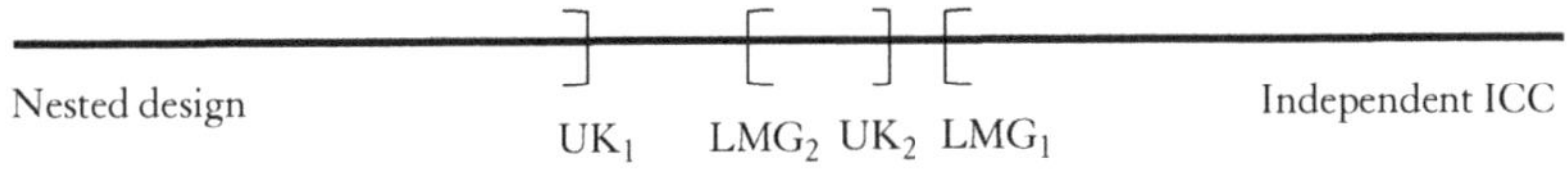

Figure 3.1. UK and LMG design win sets at the Rome Conference

shifted its win set in order to attract British (and other P5 member) support. For the more idealistic members of the LMG, the design concessions put forward by the broader win set was seen as regrettable; however, pragmatists in the group knew the importance of gaining great-power support.[44] One significant design concession came in the form of what later became Article 16 of the Rome Statute, which afforded a measure of control to the UNSC. Article 16 states, "No investigation or prosecution may be commenced or proceeded with under this Statute for a period for 12 months after the Security Council, in a resolution adopted under Chapter VII of the Charter of the United Nations, has requested the Court to that effect; that request may be renewed by the Council under the same conditions."[45]

The Singapore delegation also put forward a version of this language during the PrepCom meetings in 1997. At the time, the British delegation viewed the proposal favorably.[46] However, its support for what became known as the Singapore Compromise wavered during the Rome Conference proceedings, signaling how reluctant the British delegation was to support the LMG design.[47] In fact, at a private meeting of the P5 held at the Russian ambassador's residence, the group sought to draft a compromise design that afforded a broad opt-out provision. Although there was consensus among the members of the group, the proposal met little support with members of the LMG, and European representatives were particularly opposed.[48] Facing the rebuke of their fellow EU members, the British reconsidered their position.

Ultimately, the combination of sensitivity to potential domestic audience costs and the design concession regarding Security Council deferral authority served as the final impetus to garner British support for the Rome Statute at the eleventh hour. The compromise reached during Rome Conference deliberations offered the UK a means to retain a role for the UNSC in the operation of the court, provide a concrete means to back up the Blair government's campaign rhetoric on foreign policy, and make a meaningful gesture toward the EU consensus within the LMG. What we see in the case of the UK are the unanticipated effects of New Labour's strategic use of principled rhetoric during a pivotal election. It is tempting to explain Labour's decision to commit to an ethical foreign policy and subsequently to the creation of the International Criminal Court as responsiveness to real political pressure put upon them by human rights activism in Britain. Yet, closer examination reveals little to back up this claim. Rather, the evidence shows that Blair's New Labour focused on domestic policy issues and placed little emphasis on foreign policy. Instead of responding affirmatively to political pressure, the creation of a new "ethical foreign policy" was largely aimed at distinguishing New Labour's brand in contrast to that of the Conservative Party. Moreover, there is no evidence to suggest that New Labour had a strong and independent ICC in mind when they made their commitment to support the court. The statements of the British delegation during the Rome Conference suggested that, as was the case with the United States, their support was based on the notion that the design of the court would be largely consistent with the 1994 ILC Draft Statute. As such, commitment to the court did not represent a threat to Britain's strategic interests nor the power it derives as a permanent member of the UN Security Council.

Yet, the evidence also raises an important question: If commitment to the ICC as part of this new ethical foreign policy was not in response to significant public pressure, why would Blair's government be wary of potential domestic political cost had they decided not to sign the Rome Statute? In truth, significant domestic blowback was unlikely had the Blair government decided not to sign the Rome Statute at the conclusion of the Rome Conference. Yet, as Blair made clear in his memoirs, public trust was important to him. Although there was much public euphoria in Labour's 1997 victory, Blair expressed concerns about how he would handle the situation should public opinion turn against him. Likening the early days of his government to a "honeymoon" between New Labour and the British electorate, he wondered, "What would happen if we became estranged?"[49] Reneging on a specific, concrete campaign promise so early in his government's tenure would certainly have been considered risky for one who was reluctant to break the trust granted to him by the British electorate.

France: The Last Domino Falls

Like Britain, France had consistently and ardently pushed for a design for the court that nested it within the authority of the UNSC as was the case with the ad hoc tribunals. In fact, some have argued that "France may have been the most adamant . . . in adhering to a vision of a weaker court without too many powers to act independently."[50] In 1996, France created a draft statute that largely mirrored the 1994 ILC Draft, particularly in terms of Security Council control over initiation of Court proceedings. Moreover, throughout the Rome Conference, the French delegation showed little interest in compromise on its key design positions. This included the Singapore Compromise, which the British ultimately accepted and was instrumental in their acceptance of the Rome Statute design. For the French, the Singapore Compromise was insufficient to bridge the gap between their design win set and that of the LMG. Once the UK defected from the P5 consensus, however, it significantly altered France's position and decision calculus in the final days of the conference.

The nature and timing of French behavior does not lend itself to a principle-centric explanation. It is unlikely that French representatives were convinced at the eleventh hour that a more independent ICC was the best design model for the court. And yet, ultimately, they too broke with the P5 consensus regarding a nested design. As was the case with Britain, French design preferences were strongly influenced by interests concerning power at multiple levels. In contrast to those of Britain, these preferences had less to do with concerns regarding possible domestic political cost and party politics than it did with intra-EU politics. Although an election held in 1997 saw a shift in the distribution of power among France's political parties, the French delegation was not as vulnerable as the British to domestic political cost arising from the outcome of the Rome Conference. Commitment to the ICC was not a significant issue for any of the parties during the campaign. However, the French were just as vulnerable to intra-EU audience costs as the British, and this vulnerability had potentially significant implications for French power.

Like the British, French power interests were nested in two institutions that figured prominently in the Rome Conference negotiations: the UNSC and the EU. Their relative power is increased by the privileged position permanent membership on the Security Council affords. However, they also derive significant power from their membership in the European Union, and the French were not only among the first members but were key players in its institutional design. In May 1950, two prominent Frenchmen, Robert Schuman and Jean Monnet, drafted the internationally renowned Schuman

Plan. This proposal is widely considered to be the initial blueprint for the project of European integration after World War II.[51] The political dilemma faced by France (and Britain) during the Rome Conference was that the other members of each of these institutions had contrasting preferences regarding the institutional design of the court. As a result, France's power interests were being pulled in opposite directions simultaneously. For the most part, the French gave priority to their interests nested in the UNSC. Unlike the British, who were constrained by the specificity of their 1997 campaign pledge regarding the ICC and the way that this pledge was perceived by the British public, the French had more latitude in seeking a court design favorable to the UNSC. A reluctance to accept a strong and independent court did not necessarily cast them in the role of being anti-ICC as it did for the British. In both the PrepCom meetings and the Rome Conference, the French maintained that they supported the creation of an international criminal court. Moreover, because the British design win set largely conformed to theirs, they were not alone among EU nations in seeking a court whose design did not challenge the authority of the UNSC.

As soon as Britain changed positions, the game changed significantly. France now faced the prospect of emerging from the conference as lone holdout among EU nations against the Rome Statute design. Moreover, as shown in chapter 2, Germany's active lobbying and tactics foiled French attempts to garner support for its design preference.[52] This came when members of the German delegation crashed a meeting of francophone countries organized by France to rally support for its position. Though they previously had not supported the Singapore Compromise, they soon began to signal a changing perspective after the British defected from the P5 consensus. In a meeting with NGO representatives, French foreign minister Hubert Vedrine suggested that that it was still early and that patience was needed as France considered the proposals on the table, including variants of the Singapore Compromise. Human rights activists were initially unsure of what to make of the comments. Following Vedrine's remarks, Richard Dicker of Human Rights Watch said, "France's statement on Singapore could mean absolutely nothing, or it could really be a move away from rigidity."[53] The UK shift was prompting the French delegation to reconsider the parameters of its design win set, yet at this point it still was not enough to bring it within range of the LMG win set. The French signaled that additional design concessions were needed, and additional comments made by the foreign minister provided some direction. Vedrine remarked that France did not have a problem with granting the ICC automatic jurisdiction in situations involving genocide or crimes against humanity. However, he said, war crimes require "a different formulation."[54] The French were not concerned that they might face possible court action involving either genocide or crimes against humanity. However, because they often made significant contributions to military peacekeeping operations, the French delegation was concerned that their troops and political leadership might be exposed to politicized prosecution on charges of war crimes.[55]

As the Rome Conference approached its conclusion, the British were the first to draft a proposal along the lines that the French had suggested. They circulated a proposal that would create an optional protocol to the statute by enabling states to exempt themselves from prosecution on charges of crimes against humanity and war crimes for a period of ten years.[56] Under the British proposal, the opt-out protocol would be renewable. The proposal was unable to garner support among the LMG, however pragmatists within the group saw an opportunity to bring France into the fold. Germany offered a counterproposal that would provide a nonrenewable opt-out clause for a period of three years, but was limited only to issues involving war crimes. After intensive negotiation within the Bureau of the Conference, a revised proposal emerged that would later take the form of Article 124 of the Rome Statute, which reads, "Notwithstanding article 12 paragraph 1, a State, on becoming a party to this Statute, may declare that, for a period of seven years after the entry into force of this Statute for the State concerned, it does not accept the jurisdiction of the Court with respect to the category of crimes referred to in article 8 when a crime is alleged to have been committed by its nationals or on its territory."[57]

The proposal was in line with what the French delegation had alluded to in the foreign minister's remarks and ultimately served to expand the LMG design win set so that it overlapped with the French design win set. From the standpoint of the pragmatists among the LMG, Article 124 (as well as Article 16) was the price of the ticket to gain French acceptance of the Rome Statute.[58] Of course, the idealists within the group thought the price they paid was entirely too high.[59] However, on the last day of the Rome Conference, the French joined the LMG in support of the statute.[60]

In short, the fracture of the P5 consensus on ICC design was the product of an exogenous shock stemming from domestic electoral politics in the UK and a combination of design concessions and EU consensus that prompted the French to follow suit. These factors are sequential rather than concurrent because the evidence shows that Britain's defection was instrumental in increasing pressure on France to do the same.[61] In both cases, behavior was shaped more by politics than by principle. In the British case, the broadening of its design win set was more reflective of the internal political dynamics of the Labour Party and the tensions between left and right factions than it was of a changing British identity and the dawn of a more principled foreign policy.[62] Nonetheless, these election-year pronouncements put pressure on the Blair government to back up its campaign promises during the Rome Conference. In addition to domestic political factors, British interests in having a stronger voice within EU governance also pressed for flexibility regarding the design of the ICC. Britain, who held the EU Council presidency in the period leading into the Rome Conference, was succeeded by pro-ICC countries during and after the Rome Conference.[63] In terms of EU politics, Britain (as well as France) had an incentive to change position because changes in leadership within the union could affect a wide array of its interests related to its membership. Once Britain's position changed, it left France as the sole outlier among EU nations. This created pressure to broaden its design win set. When combined with LMG design concessions, the French decided that the compromise provided the strongest net gain given the circumstances. Like Britain, France did not see the Rome Statute as optimal in terms of design. Rather, it was a compromise that retained some Security Council prerogatives (and thus, power) while offering the material and political benefits (i.e., power) of cohesion within the European Union.

The Outlier among the Dissatisfied Countries

The institutional design hypotheses tested in chapter 2 revealed strong support for the notion that dissatisfied states would favor a strong and independent ICC (i.e., removed from the UNSC nest). Among those states who had expressed specific dissatisfaction with the special privileges afforded to the UNSC, the empirical evidence showed unanimous support for such a design.[64] Among those states who expressed a more diffuse dissatisfaction with the two-tiered hierarchy that characterizes contemporary international society, there was also overwhelming consensus.[65] Yet, among this broader group of dissatisfied states, one country did not behave as the theory predicted. Given the general robustness of the findings, the decision by the Guatemalan delegation not to support the Rome Statute should pique our curiosity. Why did Guatemala break ranks with the other dissatisfied powers?

Although global realpolitik cannot account for Guatemala's behavior regarding the design of the ICC, its interests in domestic political survival go a long way in explaining the lone outlier among dissatisfied powers. The Machiavellian politics operating in the case of Guatemala are, in fact, somewhat simpler than those that influenced the behavior of Britain and France among the satisfied powers. Put simply, Guatemala's decision not to support the Rome Statute was a product of two primary factors: (1) individual-level fears of possible prosecution by the court, and (2) the desire of the Frente Republicano Guatemalteco and its political allies to retain power in Guatemala. These two factors are tightly connected.

The issue of individual fears of prosecution centers on the actions of one man, Efraín Ríos Montt, and his political supporters. Ríos Montt was a general in the army during Guatemala's nearly forty-year civil war that pitted government forces against various leftist rebel groups. The civil war, which ended in 1996, resulted in the deaths of over two hundred thousand people.[66] Ríos Montt seized power in a coup d'état on March 23, 1982, and remained in power until August 8, 1983—seventeen months often referred to among Guatemalans as *la violencia*. Upon taking over the country, Ríos Montt initiated a scorched-earth (*tierra arrasada*) policy against some four thousand villages, most of which (some 80%) were Mayan. It is estimated that four hundred to seven hundred villages were completely razed, sending over 1,200,000 people into exile.[67] Two Guatemalan truth commissions placed responsibility for the atrocities committed in Guatemala squarely at the feet of Ríos Montt.[68] Some scholars have suggested that the counterinsurgency policy established during the brief rule of Ríos Montt "was the worst calamity to befall Mayan life and culture in Guatemala since the sixteenth-century Spanish conquest."[69]

The government of Ríos Montt utilized terror and mass casualties as a strategic instrument of power politics: "The Guatemalan violence was designed to disperse and interrupt the guerillas' social base while also killing enough people to ensure that at least some guerillas would be among the slaughtered."[70] How this was carried out in practice was a function of a government calculus of how extensive the guerrilla presence was in a given locale. Villages were coded using a system of colors to reflect the degree of guerilla presence. At one end of the spectrum, villages coded as "red" were seen as largely under complete guerrilla control, while at the other end of the spectrum, "green" villages were seen as largely independent of guerrilla presence. Between them were villages coded as either "pink" or "yellow." For villages coded as red, government forces made little distinction between rebel and civilian and systematically slaughtered everyone in the village, including women and children. In the cases of villages designated as either pink or yellow, the bloodshed was more targeted and selective, and terror was used as an instrument to frighten those who might sympathize with the rebels.[71] A key component of the use of terror in the counterinsurgency campaign was the use of clandestine death squads. As noted by Frank Affillito and Paul Jesilow, "State terror in Guatemala, through the use of death squads as extralegal security and penal forces, was intentionally clandestine. Essentially, the state utilized the death squad forces to hide its responsibility for the political repression. The Guatemalan authorities' use of clandestine forces was designed to provide them deniability. The government, when faced with protest, could always deny involvement and blame the atrocities on other forces such as the guerillas or common criminals."[72] These actions signal government sensitivity to potential political repercussions stemming from the execution of its counterinsurgency campaign. Moreover, it provides evidence of a culture of fear cultivated by the government of Ríos Montt and his supporters. It provides opponents and potential opponents with reason to pause before deciding to challenge its rule.

The fact that Ríos Montt's power was usurped in the 1983 coup d'état does not suggest that his political influence in Guatemala was as short-lived as his presidency. Ríos Montt maintained a high degree of political popularity in Guatemala among those who felt that he represented the embodiment of honesty, law and order, and national integrity.[73] In 1989, he founded the Frente Republicano Guatemalteco, a right-wing political party, and immediately declared himself chairman for life. The newly founded party chose Ríos Montt as its candidate for presidency in 1990; however, the constitutional court ruled that he was not eligible, basing its decision on a provision in Guatemalan law that prohibits those who took part in a coup d'état from assuming the presidency. That did not stop Ríos Montt from exerting domestic political influence. He was instrumental in ensuring that his political allies gained the necessary support to win the presidency in elections in 1990, 1995, and 1999. Ríos Montt would serve as congressman from 1994 to 2004, during which period he also served as president of the Congress. Thus, it is clear that Ríos Montt maintained a high degree of political capital among his supporters, while opposition was likely drawn to caution given his history of violence against those he considered his political enemies and the widespread corruption that continued to plague the government in Guatemala.

Placed in this historical context, the behavior of the Guatemalan delegation at the Rome Conference in 1998 becomes much easier to understand. At the time, however, there were none who would identify the problem as primarily a political one. Instead, opponents of Guatemala joining the ICC focused on a potential legal obstacle. They argued that joining the ICC would be unconstitutional because Guatemalan law dictates that only Guatemalan courts can indict and prosecute Guatemalan citizens. A judgment by the Guatemalan Constitutional Court in 2002, however, found that there were no legal or constitutional impediments to Guatemala joining the ICC. Gert Rosenthal, Guatemala's ambassador to the United Nations, was among the few who would later begin to acknowledge the political obstacles to support for the Rome Statute and Guatemalan participation in the ICC. He suggested that the political obstacle to support for the ICC "had its origins in the fact that the Secretary General of the then ruling party, the Frente Republicano Guatemalteco, was none other than General Efraín Ríos Montt. . . . Although the lawyers of the party understood that the Court would not have jurisdiction over crimes committed before July 2002, they did not want to take any chances."[74] In other words, while Ríos Montt and the party that he headed maintained substantial political clout, there was little chance that Guatemala would support the Rome Statute, regardless of other foreign policy interests that might favor the creation of a strong and independent International Criminal Court.

Once the domestic political situation changed in Guatemala, so too did its position on the ICC. The governments of Oscar Berger (2004–8) and Alvaro Colom (2008–12) both supported Guatemala's accession to the Rome Statute, but faced strong opposition from the Frente Republicano Guatemalteco (FRG). It was clear that Guatemala's accession to the ICC depended on the declining power of Ríos Montt and the political party he created. In the 2007 election, the FRG and its presidential candidate, Luis Rabbe, were handily defeated. Rabbe came in fifth place, garnering only 7.3% of the vote, and the FRG received only 9% of the vote in congressional elections. The declining popularity and influence of the FRG continued in 2011, when the party received just 2.7% of the vote in congressional elections. Otto Perez Molina of the Pardido Patriota (Patriotic Party) won the election and in his inaugural address declared that his government would seek to join the ICC. Guatemala deposited its instrument of accession to the Rome Statute on April 2, 2012.

Ultimately, Guatemala's accession to ICC is consistent with the expectations of the dissatisfied-powers hypothesis forwarded in chapter 2, though the timing of its behavior was anomalous to others included in the group of dissatisfied powers. A closer look inside the domestic politics of Guatemala around the time of the Rome Conference sheds light on the political obstacles that impeded the country's support for a strong and independent court. The case of Guatemala remains consistent with a narrative driven by the notion of interests defined in terms of power. In this case, however, the FRG's interest in protecting its leader from potential prosecution and maintaining its domestic political power trumped broader foreign policy concerns.

This chapter attempts to account for the behavior of Britain, France, and Guatemala as outliers in a structural theory of institutional design preferences for the ICC. The structural theory could not account for why Britain and France broke ranks with their fellow P5 members to support a Rome Statute design that wrested control of the ICC from the UNSC. Moreover, the structural theory predicted that dissatisfied powers would seek to use the institutional design of the court as a way to equalize global power imbalances and revoke the privileged position afforded to the P5. Although this explanation holds for nearly all countries identified among the group of dissatisfied powers, Guatemala's failure to support the Rome Statute stood out as a conspicuous outlier.

To account for these outliers, this chapter moves away from the structural level of analysis and examines the politics taking place within states. My aim here is not to develop and test a specific theory of domestic politics. Instead, to complement the outward-oriented theory developed in chapter 2, I draw on a two-level game framework of analysis that focuses on interests defined in terms of power. Doing so draws attention to the interests and behavior of those vying for control of the state—individual politicians and the political parties from which they draw primary support. This framework illustrates that while there may be significant national interests at stake at the international level, domestic-level actors may give priority to their domestic political interests over the country's international interests. Drawing on the logic of two-level games allows us to explore the interplay between interests generated at the international level and those that operate domestically. Helen Milner argues that "cooperation among nations is affected less by fears of other countries' relative gains or cheating than it is by the *domestic distributional consequences* of cooperative endeavors. Cooperative agreements create winners and losers domestically; therefore they generate supporters and opponents. . . . All aspects of cooperation are affected by domestic considerations because cooperation is a continuation of domestic political struggles by other means."[75] While this argument makes a lot of sense when cooperation involves economic interests—either in the form of trade, investment, or monetary policy—it is a bit more difficult to use when applied to cooperation in the domain of human rights and international criminal justice. What, exactly, are the "domestic distributional consequences" of joining the ICC?

Certainly, domestic distributional consequences are easier to recognize and understand in situations where costs and benefits are highly concentrated, as is the case of Guatemala. Although the Guatemalans have expressed dissatisfaction with the international balance of power and their relative position within international society, using the institutional design of the ICC to constrain the power of the relative power of the P5 offers them very diffuse benefits. In contrast, the potential costs for Ríos Montt and the FRG were highly concentrated. Thus, so long as they held political power within Guatemala, these acute domestic political interests trumped the more diffuse international interests. The result was that Guatemala did not sign the Rome Statute as their fellow dissatisfied powers had. Once these domestic political conditions changed, however, Guatemala's behavior regarding the ICC conformed to those of its fellow dissatisfied powers.

It is much more difficult to tease out the domestic distributional consequences in the cases of Britain and France because neither faced a substantial amount of domestic political pressure to join the ICC, much less to accept the design proposed in the Rome Statute. However, both Britain and France reap diffuse benefits of their various institutional memberships. Two of the most significant for these states are membership in the UN Security Council and membership in the European Union. Yet, their membership in these two institutions pulled them in opposite directions with regard to the Rome Statute and the ICC. So, how is this tension reconciled, particularly in such cases where it is difficult to determine which relationship offers the most net benefits? In the case of Britain and France, the evidence suggests that domestic politics in Britain set in motion events that would ultimately swing the balance in favor of each breaking ranks with the P5 consensus and backing the Rome Statute.

Power and principle intersected in British politics in often subtle ways. As shown in this chapter, New Labour made a commitment to the ICC, but not necessarily as a result of organized domestic political mobilization. Rather, it was a relatively low-risk means for New Labour to differentiate itself from both the Conservatives and from prior Labour platforms. In other words, it used principle strategically, yet was not necessarily reflective of the political power of principled norms. Instead, the political effect of utilizing principled rhetoric manifested itself primarily in a desire by the new Blair government to minimize a potential weakening of public trust by reneging on a concrete election promise so early in its tenure. Thus, the articulation of a new "ethical foreign policy" and a firm commitment to the creation of the ICC are linked to important principles that form the cornerstone of international humanitarian law. Yet, the British case shows that the driving force behind its choice to break from the P5 consensus during the Rome Conference was as much a product of realpolitik as it was of idealpolitik. Thus, combined with strategic design concessions offered by the more pragmatic members of the LMG, the British win set was sufficiently altered to bring the UK on board with the Rome Statute. Subsequently, Britain's defection increased the potential audience cost for the French and ultimately pressed them to follow suit.

Chapter 4

Power, Principle, and Pragmatism in Prosecutorial Strategy

Geopolitical implications of the location of a situation . . . are not relevant criteria for the selection of situations under the Statute.

—ICC Office of the Prosecutor

It was an unprecedented event in the relatively short history of the International Criminal Court (ICC). On September 5, 2013, members of the Kenyan parliament approved a motion to withdraw from membership in the ICC. At issue were ICC charges of crimes against humanity against President Uhuru Kenyatta and Deputy President William Ruto. The charges stemmed from mass violence in the 2007 election that brought the two men into power. During the widespread violence over one thousand people were killed and more than a half million people were forced from their homes. Both Kenyatta and Ruto have repeatedly demanded that the charges against them be dropped and have characterized the ICC action as a politically motivated assault on Kenyan sovereignty by foreign interests.

Though the Kenyan move was uniquely provocative, the sentiments expressed during the meeting reflected a broader and growing skepticism of the ICC evident across Africa. Critics point out that among the nineteen situations currently under ICC review, formal investigations and subsequent legal proceedings have been established in only eight—all in African countries.

The results of the court's reviews have generated considerable skepticism in the region. For example, Rwandan president Paul Kagame suggested that the ICC "was made for Africans and poor countries." Similarly, Jean Ping, president of the African Union (AU) Commission, declared that "the ICC seems to exist solely for judging Africans."[1]

This emerging narrative of an institutional bias against African nations has found a receptive ear, both in African civil society as well as in wider academic and policy circles.[2] Choices made by the ICC's Office of the Prosecutor (OTP) fuel the fire of this rhetoric, as observers point out apparent inconsistencies in the application of justice at the ICC. Why did the OTP utilize its *proprio motu* power authorized under Article 15 of the Rome Statute to seek permission to open a formal investigation into the election violence in Kenya in 2007, yet decline to move forward with investigations into situations characterized by a significantly larger number of civilian casualties, including Afghanistan and Iraq? One critic remarked, "When the Prosecutor quickly decides to open an investigation—as in the Kenya situation—without making a decision about long-term preliminary examinations—in places like Colombia and Afghanistan—it can taint perceptions of the Prosecutor's impartiality and give rise to the impression that the Prosecutor has been influenced by non-legal factors."[3] These case-specific criticisms beg the broader question regarding the determinants of situation selection. In other words, why does the court pursue some cases but not others? Moreover, why does it seem to move more aggressively in some cases and more cautiously on others?

Presumably, the OTP makes prosecutorial choices solely in accordance with accepted norms of jurisprudence. Not surprisingly, the OTP consistently forwards this position in all court statements and documents. However, as pointed out earlier, a strictly legal perspective has difficulty in accounting for some of the inconsistencies evident on the court's docket. In response, some have argued that prosecutorial strategy is the product of politics—of institutional capture by external influence or bias.[4] Such arguments appear quite extreme and face a formidable burden to prove their claims. In addition to providing concrete evidence of external efforts to influence the decisions of the OTP, scholars would need to provide evidence that its decisions were predicated in response to coercion or bias. The OTP is unlikely to concede any such admission and has vigorously denied such accusations. The court's first chief prosecutor, Luis Moreno Ocampo, maintained that "the Statute provides that the Office of the Prosecutor shall act independently on instructions from any external source. Independence goes beyond not seeking or acting on instructions; it means that the Office decisions shall not be altered by the presumed or known wishes of any party or by the cooperation seeking process."[5] Moreno Ocampo's successor, Fatou Bensouda, has also emphatically defended the autonomy of the OTP: "We are a new tool, a judicial tool, not a tool in the hands of politicians who think they can decide when to plug or unplug us."[6] This chapter forwards a theoretical explanation of prosecutorial strategy at the ICC that explores the intersection of these two extremes—one based solely on legal idealism, the other based primarily on political influence. The chapter develops a theory of prosecutorial strategy that explains why egoistic institutional interests may internalize the preferences of external actors. In particular, the theoretical framework provides a rationale for why the strategic interests of three of the most powerful nonmember states may be internalized by the OTP. These states who are not parties to the Rome Statute include the United States, Russia, and China. Using this theoretical framework, the chapter argues that prosecutorial strategy emerges from the intersection of principle, power, and pragmatism. Although international legal principles press the OTP to place greater emphasis on situations deemed to be the most grave, institutional pragmatism prompts the court to move much more cautiously in cases involving the strategic interests of these three nonmember states.

Developing a Theory of Prosecutorial Strategy

Given that the ICC is such a new institution on the international landscape, it is not surprising that little theoretical research has been done to explain the behavior of the court.[7] It is only now that enough time has passed that we have a large enough sample to begin to identify possible patterns of ICC behavior. Because there is not a developed theoretical literature focused on the behavior of the ICC, it may be useful to seek inspiration and guidance from research aimed at explaining the behavior of other international courts (ICs) with longer track records, such as the International Court of Justice (ICJ), the European Court of Justice (ECJ), and the European Court of Human Rights (ECHR).

A number of scholars have turned to principal-agent (PA) theory to address questions regarding the behavior of international courts and other international institutions and organizations.[8] PA theorists examine the relationship between principals and agents and the mechanisms through which principals attempt to get agents to pursue their preferred course of action. Unfortunately, the models do not provide a clear picture of whether international courts are autonomous. Some posit that being a principal provides specific tools of leverage that can shape outcomes; that is, control over the terms of the delegation contract that confers a hierarchical control of the principal over the agent.[9] For example, applying this framework to the study of international courts, Geoffrey Garrett and Barry Weingast suggest that the ECJ has little autonomy and generally selects outcomes that the court's most powerful principals prefer.[10] Additional studies also provide support for the notion that IC behavior is influenced by politics. Geoffrey Garrett, R. Daniel Kelemen, and Heiner Schulz suggest that, although legal precedent is taken into account in court rulings at the ECJ, judges do take into account the likely reactions of member state governments.[11] This would seem to suggest that political factors may have a significant influence on outcomes and challenge those who argue that the ECJ is largely independent of such considerations. Similarly, in their study of the ICJ, Eric Posner and Miguel F. P. de Figueiredo found that judges tend to favor the states that appoint them and those whose wealth level is commensurate with their home country.[12] Moreover, Clifford J. Carrubba, Matthew Gabel, and Charles Hankla argue that preferences of member–state governments "have a systematic and substantively important impact on ECJ decisions" through the use of threats of noncompliance and override.[13]

Other scholars counter that international courts are more independent than PA models would generally anticipate. For example, in his analysis of rulings at the ECHR, Erik Voeten found that judges displayed a high degree of independence from political influence.[14] A similar argument is made by Karen Alter, whose work on the European Court of Justice supports the notion that rulings have become increasingly independent of the interests of member governments, suggesting again that international courts have the capacity to remain independent of political pressure.[15] Subsequent research by Mark Pollack and Jonas Tallberg offers similar findings of judicial autonomy.[16] More recently, Alec Stone Sweet and Matthew Brunell argue that threats of override against ECJ decisions are not credible, and member states were largely unsuccessful in the small number of cases where they sought to curb the court and constrain future developments.[17]

Though sharp disagreement remains among scholars regarding the issue of the autonomy of international courts, the PA framework is useful in that it prompts us to think carefully about the relationship between the ICC and the states that established it. Of particular utility is the consideration of the egoistic interests of the parties who make up the ICC and the delegation contract (Rome Statute) that defines the terms of the arrangement. However, though these factors are not sufficient to capture the process leading toward the creation of a prosecutorial strategy, they do serve as a good starting point in the process of additional theory building.

This chapter begins by considering the interests of the states that created the ICC—the states parties to the Rome Statute. Though states may have had different reasons for wanting to create and then join the court, the largest was represented by the Like-Minded Group (LMG), a coalition of some sixty countries whose primary stated interests centered on notions of the court as an instrument of principled justice.[18] We can consider the LMG as representative of the principal in this case because the group's interests were for the most part reflected in the final design of the Rome Statute and its membership constituted most of those whose prompt ratification brought the Statute into force on July 1, 2002.[19] Among the most prominent of these principles of justice was the notion of equality under the law. From the standpoint of the principals that created the court, the mandate of the ICC was clear—to pursue justice independent of considerations of the political power and interests of the actors involved. This mandate is reflected in the process of design during the Rome Conference, where the idealist LMG sought to secure the institutional independence of the court by freeing it from UN Security Council (UNSC) control. Thus, the OTP is charged with facilitating this pursuit of justice under this premise. For the principals, among the most significant achievements possible would be for the court to finally hold the leadership of a powerful country accountable for their actions.

At first glance, the interests of the principals would seem to be perfectly congruent with the institutional interests of the court itself and could explain the extremely high degree of delegation afforded to the ICC. As with other international courts, high levels of delegation are intended to promote judicial independence and insulate the courts from political influence.[20] Moreover, this delegation was accompanied by an unusually high level of discretion afforded to the OTP. As pointed out by Moreno Ocampo, "States established two key provisions in order to enhance the impartiality and independence of the new Court: they made it a permanent body, and they decided that the selection of situations would be a judicial decision."[21] Presumably, this means that decisions regarding the selection of situations would be soundly rooted in definitive legal thresholds to be met, including jurisdictional limitations as articulated in the statute and whether the principle of complementarity applies in a given instance. Yet, the ICC statute provides tremendous discretion to the OTP in the selection of cases, a point not lost on the court's first chief prosecutor: "Few commentators on the Statute have noted that the most distinctive feature of the Court, as compared to the other international tribunals, is the power given to the Court to independently select the situations to investigate."[22] Presumably, such discretion would simply provide the court the independence it needs to remain insulated from political factors that might influence these crucial decisions. Applied to the question of prosecutorial strategy, this autonomy manifest in the Rome Statute would lead us to predict that the OTP would pursue a strategy based solely on issues of jurisprudence and international legal principles.

Ironically, the discretion afforded to the OTP that was intended to increase the independence and legitimacy of the court may also open the door to political considerations and strategic behavior on the part of the prosecutor.[23] It consolidates the power of the prosecutor to define both the institutional interests of the court and plot the course to achieve these objectives. But would these interests remain congruent with the principled goals laid out in the Rome Statute by its member states? Over the long-term—absolutely. The ICC's most ardent and principled supporters have long envisioned a court that would serve two functions: (1) to provide justice for victims of war crimes, crimes against humanity, and genocide necessary to facilitate postconflict peace and reconciliation; and (2) to serve as a deterrent against the commission of future atrocities by holding those most responsible to account for their crimes. If successful on both counts, the ICC stands to make a significant and lasting impact on global peace. In the short term, however, stand formidable obstacles. Two elements figure prominently for the OTP: (1) the ICC is a new institution that must overcome considerable inertia on the road to becoming a well-functioning and powerful force in international society, and (2) the ICC is a weak institution that depends on cooperation of states. Achieving success in the long term depends on successfully navigating these challenges. As outlined in the following, these challenges create an institutional dependence on the UN Security Council that influences the manner in which the OTP pursues its mission to promote international justice.

To gain support and build legitimacy, new (and thus, relatively weak) institutions face considerable pressure to produce positive results quickly and achieve some measurable evidence of progress in the short run. For the ICC, this meant that becoming a functioning court involved more than gaining the requisite number of states to ratify the Rome Statute—it meant having defendants to prosecute. Thus, the choices regarding initial investigations and prosecutions would likely sacrifice some degree of principle in the name of pragmatism. This pressure toward pragmatism was evident in the ad hoc criminal tribunals that preceded the ICC, both of which depended on securing the cooperation of the states involved.[24] Even though the International Criminal Tribunal for the Former Yugoslavia (ICTY) was based on a principle of decollectivization of guilt that pressed for prosecution of those most accountable for atrocities (i.e., leadership), it began by prosecuting the case of Dusko Tadic, a low-level official at the Omarska prison camp.[25] This choice was restricted because hostilities were still ongoing at the time the court began operation and apprehending political or military leadership was simply not feasible. The ICC faced similar choices at the time it became operational. Given that prosecution is limited by the court's *jurisdiction ratione temporis*, the OTP had to face the fact that defendants would likely come from ongoing situations where stability and order have not yet been achieved.[26] In such situations, the OTP will likely only be able to try rebels apprehended by government forces (most likely, not the top leadership), or would need states to provide the military intervention necessary to stabilize the situation, apprehend political and military leadership, and turn these defendants over to The Hague for trial. For the latter, the court depends on the support of the UN Security Council.

Because the Rome Statute itself does not confer authority on the ICC to take coercive action, the OTP is dependent particularly on the UN Security Council. Under the UN Charter, the Security Council has the authority to legitimize coercive action to stabilize a situation through its Chapter VII powers. One example of the need for coercive action sanctioned by the UNSC to forward war crimes trials was the application of NATO airstrikes in the Bosnian conflict. Operation Deliberate Force played a decisive role in equalizing the balance of power among warring parties, brought the political leadership to the negotiating table, and ultimately paved the way to the stability needed for the ICTY to conduct investigations, apprehend accused war criminals, and forward the process of adjudication. The situation in Libya is another prime example. The ICC was granted jurisdiction over the situation in Libya on February 26, 2011, to investigate crimes committed by Muammar Gaddafi against civilian protesters during the ongoing civil war. It is unlikely that the ICC's arrest warrant for Colonel Gaddafi would bring him into the court's custody absent international military support of the rebel forces. On March 17, 2011, the UN Security Council issued Resolution 1973, which provided the legal basis for international military intervention. The council's action was instrumental to the fall of the Libyan regime and to the apprehension of Gaddafi. Unfortunately for the ICC, Gaddafi was executed by the mob that discovered him before he could be brought into custody to stand trial. The situation in Sudan serves as another example, though in the reverse. Though the OTP issued an arrest warrant for Sudanese president Omar al-Bashir, lack of international military intervention enabled the regime to maintain its hold on power. As a result, al-Bashir remains a free man.

As major world powers, the UNSC's five permanent members (P5) can also help to gain cooperation that the court needs from states involved through the use of political pressure and suasion. For example, the United States used the threat of withholding a $50 million aid package to Serbia if they did not cooperate with the ICTY by arresting Slobodan Milosevic and turning him over to The Hague for prosecution.[27] Similarly, the European Union (EU) linked Serbia's bid for accession to cooperation in securing the arrest of indicted war criminal Ratko Mladic. Following the apprehension and surrender of Mladic, French president Nicholas Sarkozy declared that the arrest represented "one more step towards Serbia's integration one day in the European Union."[28] Although the permanent members of the UNSC are not the only powerful states that can be called on to apply such political pressure, they are among the most important. Moreover, if P5 members seek to actively block ICC action in a given situation, it is highly unlikely that the court could successfully promote its mission. For example, U.S. opposition to the court under the George W. Bush administration produced a number of measures aimed at weakening the ICC. These included threatening to veto UN peacekeeping missions unless the UNSC provided a resolution granting immunity for military personnel from non-ICC member countries, including the United States.[29] It also included a massive diplomatic campaign to secure bilateral nonsurrender agreements from nations around the globe.[30] Although the former chief prosecutor maintains that the court "managed" to operate in the face of this opposition, such obstacles clearly did not make the OTP's job easier nor facilitate the pursuit of justice.[31] In another example, both Russia and China vetoed a UN Security Council resolution to refer the situation in Syria to the ICC, denying the court jurisdiction to act where human rights organizations have documented massive human rights violations and atrocities.[32]

Cooperation from the Security Council is also essential for the court to expand its jurisdictional reach. The Rome Statute limits the court's jurisdiction to the territory and nationals of member states. Yet, jurisdictional limitations do little to quell the calls for justice for situations arising in states that are not party to the statute. Sudan (Darfur) and Libya are two significant examples. To answer the calls for justice, the court required referral by the UNSC under the authority afforded to it under the Rome Statute. The capacity for expanding its reach through UNSC referrals must be considered essential to addressing human rights violations even when they fall outside the ICC's statutory jurisdiction. Though the former chief prosecutor maintains that the OTP has never lobbied the council for referrals, having a council willing to refer situations to the ICC is essential to its global mission to end impunity.[33] Had it not secured a Security Council referral in the case of Sudan, the ICC would have remained a witness to a situation characterized by many as genocide.

In short, it is clear that the ability of the ICC to achieve its mandate for justice is greatly facilitated when it enjoys the support of the Security Council and can be greatly hampered if these states actively oppose it. Indeed, Moreno Ocampo remarked that at the time he took office he considered obtaining the cooperation of the Security Council to be "crucial" to the success of the court.[34] The ICC already has the support of two of the five permanent members of the Security Council—Britain and France. Indeed, their high level of support for the court was on display when they served as key players in securing a Security Council referral for the situation in Sudan.[35] Thus, it is rational for the OTP to pursue an institutional course aimed partially at forging better relations with the three remaining permanent members of the Security Council that are not members of the court: the United States,

Russia, and China (hereafter referred to as the P3).[36] This is not to suggest that the OTP would be optimistic about all three joining the court. However, U.S. opposition to the court has softened under the Obama administration, suggesting that future membership is not beyond the realm of the possible. It is difficult to envision Russian or Chinese membership in the court in the foreseeable future; however, should the United States join the ICC, it would place some pressure on them to follow suit. At this point, it is highly unlikely that the OTP would seriously consider such an outcome. That does not mean that the OTP does not have a strong interest in bettering relations with these states, even if their eventual membership in the court is extremely unlikely. As outlined earlier, the P3's role on the Security Council can either facilitate the court's mission or create formidable obstructions in its path. Indeed, from its standpoint, the OTP does not necessarily need support—simply actions that do not obstruct the ability of the court to investigate and prosecute alleged crimes. In the case of UNSC Resolution 1593, the ICC was able to gain jurisdiction over the situation in Sudan by virtue of the Chinese and American decisions to abstain during the vote rather than to exercise their individual veto power. It stands to reason that, realistically, the OTP would seek to facilitate eventual U.S. membership in the court and to assuage Russian and Chinese opposition to the point that they do not actively obstruct its mission.[37] Put differently, it is in the *egoistic* institutional interests of the ICC to carefully consider the interests and potential reaction of the P3 in charting a course of action for the court. Thus, it is rational to expect that these interests may be internalized in the process of defining the institutional interests of the ICC.

From this perspective, we now have reason to believe that there is a divergence of interests between the principals (states parties) and the court—at least in the short- to medium-time frame as the institution establishes itself, broadens its support base, and cultivates its legitimacy in international society.[38] This theory of internalization suggests that the egoistic interests of the court take into account the preferences of powerful nonmember states whose cooperation it seeks to secure. In this sense, it goes beyond the scope of PA theory that suggests political dynamics are largely endogenous to the principal-agent dyad. This internalization theory does not propose that the prosecutorial strategy of the OTP is driven primarily by strategic interests and deference to the preferences of the P3. Instead, such internalized interests may serve as a significant *intervening variable* in the process of adjudication. Given this view, we would expect prosecutorial strategy to be first and foremost driven by an interest to respond to the situations characterized by the gravest violations of international law. However, we would also expect the court to act much more cautiously when situations involve the strategic interests of the P3. Specifically, this means that the OTP would be less likely to move forward in cases involving high strategic value to any members of the P3. Moreover, we would also expect the process of investigation to move more slowly where P3 interests are vested. These hypotheses are tested using both qualitative and quantitative methods of analysis, and this research develops and draws on an original data set that includes both legal and political variables.

Research Design

Creating an appropriate research design to test these hypotheses is challenging. The first involves deciding on the unit of analysis. The unit of analysis used in this chapter is the "situation"—generally defined in terms of the geographic location where events took place, but also including a temporal context. Although the ICC prosecutes individuals rather than states and charges are specific to particular instances of atrocities committed, the OTP has made it clear that initial decisions to act are done in consideration of situations, not specific events within them. Thus decisions are also not predicated on the actions of individuals who could eventually face prosecution by the court. A second challenge involves deciding which aspect of the process of adjudication to focus on. Adjudicating possible crimes committed in a given situation involves numerous steps. Key among these is the decision to launch a formal investigation after completing a preliminary investigation of a situation. From the standpoint of responding to calls for justice, little political capital is lost by the OTP on the decision to open a preliminary investigation. Information obtained during this process remains confidential, and unless a formal investigation is launched, no arrest warrants will be issued. More importantly, the OTP exercises little discretion with regard to preliminary investigations. As a matter of policy and practice, the OTP will open "a preliminary investigation of all situations that are not manifestly outside the jurisdiction of the court."[39] In contrast, the decision to open a formal investigation involves much more discretion on the part of the OTP. Moreover, the decision to launch a formal investigation performs two significant signaling functions: (1) it suggests that sufficient evidence exists to warrant further action by the court, and (2) it establishes a firm commitment by the OTP to move the process of adjudication further. Though doing so does not bind the OTP into seeking arrest warrants, closing down the adjudication process at this point would signal that the OTP misread the initial findings and that the expense incurred through the formal investigation was squandered. In short, it would have a significantly negative effect on the legitimacy of the court. Therefore, the dependent variable used here is the decision by the OTP to establish (or the failure to establish) a formal investigation. The universe of cases comprises all situations where the court has opened a preliminary investigation, the necessary precursor to the establishment of a formal investigation. During the process of a preliminary investigation, the OTP determines whether the court has jurisdiction over a given situation.

Although the choice to focus on the decision to open a formal investigation makes much more sense than focusing on preliminary investigations, it presents formidable challenges in terms of research design. Among the most vexing is the size of the universe of cases—in this case nineteen situations under review by the court. Researchers who seek to explain general patterns of ICC behavior face a "Goldilocks problem"—the universe of cases appears too small to rely solely on multivariate regression analysis, but too large for an intensive qualitative analysis encompassing all cases. Moreover, qualitative analysis likely would rely largely on the statements of key individuals involved in the decision-making process. It is extremely unlikely that anyone in the OTP would acknowledge that political considerations influence their decisions. This chapter attempts to address the Goldilocks problem by carefully employing elements of both quantitative and qualitative methods of analysis. Two key independent variables figure prominently: gravity and P3 strategic interests. Because neither is concrete, substantial qualitative analysis is employed to operationalize each. To address the question of what factors shape the decision to begin a formal investigation (or not), the analysis begins with a qualitative inspection of the relationship between gravity and outcomes regarding formal investigation, as well as the relationship between strategic interests and outcomes. Basic probability analysis is highly suggestive, but does not allow for possible interaction with other potentially significant variables. Thus, this qualitative evidence is supplemented with probit regression analysis. To address the second question—which factors determine the speed in which the court moves from preliminary to formal investigation—a similar mixed-methods approach is used. Survival analysis is supplemented with a qualitative examination of outcomes when different modes of referral are employed. For the quantitative analysis, this chapter utilizes an original data set that includes both constant and time-varying variables with situation-month observations. Observations begin for the month in which a preliminary investigation is established and run until the month that either a formal investigation is begun or June 2013. The following sections describe the legal and political variables employed in the analysis.

Legal Factors

One common theme in the literature suggests that support for international criminal courts is a function of a state's commitment to liberal principles of human rights and democracy. From this perspective, we might expect that democracies would be more inclined to prosecute crimes covered by the Rome Statute within the domestic court system. The level of democracy can thus serve as a proxy for complementarity—the principle that the ICC should not be the primary venue for prosecution, but rather a court of last resort.[40] Thus, one might expect that the OTP would be less likely to move aggressively in more democratic countries. I operationalize "democracy" using the Freedom House Index.[41]

Another likely legal factor involves a judgment on whether events that occurred in a given situation are severe enough to warrant ICC involvement. Indeed, the Rome Statute charges the ICC to prosecute the *most serious* international crimes. Of course, determining a suitable measure for such a variable is challenging. Given that many of the crimes the ICC is charged with adjudicating involve atrocities committed against noncombatants, using civilian deaths as a proxy for conflict intensity is initially appealing. However, this variable is problematic for several reasons. First, many of the contemporary conflicts marked by atrocities and followed by calls for international justice have been intrastate rather than interstate—either civil wars or ethnic conflicts.[42] Are rebels and their supporters to be defined as "military" or "civilian"? Second, estimates of civilian casualties are often biased to support political agendas, or what Taylor Seybolt, Jay Aaronson, and Baruch Fischhoff refer to as "efforts to produce official ignorance."[43] They add, counting civilian casualties "is an area where politics is often involved in the most pernicious way."[44] Researchers are left with a combination of cases that lack data on civilian casualties and cases characterized by substantial differences in estimates. Though not an ideal measure, I instead employ aggregated battle-related deaths as an alternative measure to gauge the severity of a conflict, drawing primarily on the Uppsala Conflict Data Program data set. This measure captures both military and civilian casualties recorded in a given situation.

Some readers, particularly legal scholars, may object to using the scale of violence alone as a measure of the significance of a given situation. The criteria put forward by the OTP suggest that the gravity of a situation goes beyond consideration of scale and includes consideration of more subjective factors such as "nature, manner, and impact of the alleged crimes committed in the situation."[45] Yet, the statute provides little precise guidance regarding how the "gravity threshold" is to be applied. Margaret de Guzman points out that "in light of the serious repercussions of labeling an international crime 'grave,' one might expect the concept of gravity to have reasonably well-defined and accepted content in international law. In fact, the opposite is true. Individuals who craft, apply, and write about international criminal law invariably reference the seriousness of the crimes at issue but rarely specify what they mean."[46] This lack of specificity had led to some glaring inconsistencies. For example, the chief prosecutor argued that he was hesitant to open a formal investigation into possible crimes committed in Iraq because they involved a small number of victims, yet he was willing to open a preliminary investigation into the situation in Korea that involved a similarly low volume of casualties.[47] In rationalizing his decision on Iraq, the chief prosecutor writes, "The alleged crimes committed by those nationals of States Party in Iraq appeared isolated and did not meet the required gravity threshold."[48] Because the statute does not offer a precise means of determining the level of gravity, finding an appropriate measure to be used in this analysis is problematic. Consideration of factors such as the nature, manner, and impact of crimes is inherently subjective. Utilizing the stated assessments of the chief prosecutor is inappropriate because, as a variable, such remarks would suffer from endogeneity.

One solution was offered by Allison Danner, who argues that gravity could be reflected in a hierarchy of crimes. Noting that a "hierarchy of crimes seems to emerge from the case-law of the ICTY," she suggests that genocide is the most grave and points out that the International Criminal Tribunal for Rwanda (ICTR) frequently referred to it as the "crime of crimes."[49] Citing similar references in the case law drawn from the ad hoc tribunals, she further suggests that war crimes can be considered "lesser crimes" (i.e., less grave) than crimes against humanity. Thus, gravity could be measured on a 1–3 scale. The problem with operationalizing gravity in this manner is that it applies to individual acts, not necessarily to situations as a whole. Most of the situations brought to the attention of the court show evidence of crimes across the hierarchy of crimes; thus we are left with little to differentiate level of gravity between situations. In other words, garnering a subjective assessment measure from the OTP suffers from endogeneity, while utilizing a categorical hierarchy loses precision at the level of the situation.

This chapter addresses these limitations by using original survey data drawn from sources with backgrounds and experience commensurate with those of the chief prosecutor. Twenty of the world's most noted international legal scholars/practitioners drawn from five continents were surveyed, selected because of their extensive expertise in the area of international criminal justice. Survey participants were asked to gauge the gravity of situations under investigation by the court on a scale of 1–10 (10 being the most grave), using only the ICC's published criteria as guidance in their determination.[50] The mean score for each situation, as reflected in the surveys received, was used in the analysis.

Political Factors

The high degree of discretion given to the OTP under the statute raises questions regarding whether external political factors influence the judgment and action of the prosecutor. The broader literature on the court prompts us to consider several likely factors.

One possible political factor could involve public pressure. This argument is in line with those who cite the influence of global civil society on the creation of the court in the first place.[51] From this perspective, one might predict that increased levels of public attention on a given situation will increase the probability that the court will establish a formal investigation. This chapter utilizes original data compiled from content analysis of news stories on situations considered by the court that were published in major world publications from

July 2002 through June 2013. Stories on situations under review by the ICC were analyzed to confirm that they involved aspects germane to the court (i.e., war, casualties, deaths, etc.) as opposed to other news from the country (e.g., the economy). The data set included 190,462 news stories published in major world publications, and observations were made on a country-month basis.

Nongovernmental organizations may also serve to create political pressure to act. Numerous scholars have documented the role that NGOs played in the process leading up to the signing of the Rome Statute, and the number of such organizations has grown substantially over time.[52] Many NGOs acknowledge that they actively press for ICC action by providing information to the OTP via communiques. Moreover, the OTP has made clear that it pays close attention to the reports that groups such as Amnesty International and Human Rights Watch generate. In describing the preliminary investigation on the situation in Iraq, the chief prosecutor noted that "we conducted an exhaustive search of all readily-available open source information, including media, governmental, and non-governmental reports. Significant additional material collected from open sources includes, among others, the findings of Amnesty International, Human Rights Watch, Iraq Body Count, and Spanish Brigades against the War in Iraq."[53] To measure the level of pressure human rights NGOs direct toward the OTP, the number of published press releases and reports produced regarding a specific situation were counted. These data are drawn from the archive established by the Coalition for the International Criminal Court (CICC), an NGO that serves to bring together a wide array of organizations that support an active role for the ICC in dealing with human rights issues. For the period 2002–13, I reviewed 2,399 press releases and reports that appear in the CICC archive and recorded the number that applied to each situation where a preliminary investigation was opened by the OTP.

Lastly, the internalization theory posed here generates the final political variable tested in this analysis: the strategic interests of the P3 vested in a given situation. What constitutes "strategic interests" in the sense used here? Defining this term is an inherently subjective enterprise and is challenging to operationalize because no single measure can capture it adequately. For this reason, this chapter employs qualitative analysis of bilateral relationships between individual members of the P3 and countries where primary investigations have been established by the ICC. The chapter attempts to utilize the most parsimonious measure possible in making strategic interests operational. Thus "strategic interests" in this setting is defined in terms of the combination of three primary components: (1) the level of involvement in a situation, (2) the strategic military value, and (3) the significance of economic ties.

Level of involvement reflects the degree to which a member of the P3's actions contributed to the commission of atrocities—either directly or indirectly. An example of direct involvement would be Russia's actions in Georgia in summer 2008. On August 6, 2008, Georgian military forces launched an assault in South Ossetia. The following day, Russian forces responded in kind, opening a week-long military clash before a cease fire was established on August 15. Human Rights Watch noted that "the week of open conflict, and the many subsequent weeks of rampant violence and insecurity in the affected districts, took a terrible toll on civilians, killing hundreds, displacing tens of thousands, and causing extensive damage to civilian property."[54] Although Russia was not a member of the ICC, the court could try Russian defendants because the alleged crimes were committed on the territory of a member state, putting the Russian military and its political leadership at risk. In general, where the level of P3 involvement is high, the possibility of OTP prosecution presents a risk to leadership in those countries should the ICC proceed to a formal investigation. In addition to direct involvement in the commission of prosecutable crimes, indirect linkages may also increase the strategic importance of a given situation.

Indirect actions might be financial or military support for those who perpetrated atrocities in a given situation. One example is U.S. support for Colombia. The contemporary centerpiece of U.S. policy on Colombia is manifest in Plan Colombia, an antinarcotics program supported by U.S. aid to Colombian military and police operations. The latter included government efforts to combat the insurgency of the Fuerzas Armadas Revolucionarias de Colombia (FARC). The levels of aid afforded through Plan Columbia made it the third-largest recipient of U.S. foreign aid and the largest in the Western Hemisphere. In 2006, U.S. assistance to Colombia amounted to an estimated $728 million, approximately 80% of which was military and police assistance.[55] In addition to monetary support, the United States provided military personnel to train local military and police forces. Amnesty International has documented that the Colombian government's struggle with the FARC insurgency and the narcotics industry has been marked by torture, massacres, "disappearances," and killings of noncombatants.[56] Moreover, "widespread collusion between the armed forces and paramilitary groups continues to this day."[57] Critics have argued that "as a consequence of United States anti-narcotics policy and the War on Drugs in general, the U.S. government is both directly and indirectly implicated in the growing human rights crisis in Colombia."[58] Amnesty International adds, "The US has continued a policy of throwing "fuel on the fire" of already widespread human rights violations, collusion with illegal paramilitary groups and near total impunity."[59] Judging by U.S. actions, policymakers are aware of how U.S. support may be indirectly contributing to atrocities in Colombia. In July 2003, the Bush administration froze military aid to Colombia unless it signed a bilateral immunity agreement with the United States.[60] As a supporter of the ICC, Colombia initially refused to do so. However, as U.S. pressure mounted, it relented and signed an accord on September 17, 2003. Sensitivity to potential prosecution of U.S. personnel is certainly exacerbated in the Colombian case because U.S. policies could be directly or indirectly linked to crimes prosecutable by the ICC. Other examples of indirect support include Russian support for Venezuela and Chinese support for North Korea. Although cases involving indirect involvement are a much lower risk in terms of vulnerability to prosecution, information made public during the investigation and possible trials could pose a substantial threat to a P3 member's soft power. Among the three components of strategic interests employed here, level of involvement is likely the most sensitive. For this reason, it is weighted double relative to the other two measures included in the composite strategic-interests variable.

The second component used to gauge the level of strategic interests vested in a given situation involves its military value. Strategic military value considers multiple factors, including alliance relationships and the regional military importance of the relationship. In addition to whether an alliance relationship exists for a given dyad, the qualitative nature of the relationship was carefully considered when determining the overall strategic value. These include the so-called special relationships that countries may have. A prime example of where both elements figure prominently is the U.S. alliance relationship with Israel. Its strategic military importance is related to both its position in the region as well as to the qualitative nature of the relationship. Israel is the primary ally of the United States in the Middle East. As noted by the U.S. State Department, "Commitment to Israel's security has been a cornerstone of U.S. policy in the Middle East since Israel's creation."[61] In support of this key ally, the United States provides over $3 billion in security assistance annually. Since World War II, Israel has received more aid from the United States—primarily military aid—than any other country.[62] The value of the American alliance with Israel is sometimes likened to the special relationship between the United States and Great Britain.[63] Because U.S. presidents played a key role in founding the Jewish state after World War II, they have frequently pointed to the U.S. relationship with Israel as exceptional among its allies. Bill Clinton remarked, "America and Israel share a special bond. Our relations are unique among all nations."[64] This sentiment was echoed by his successor, George W. Bush, who declared, "The alliance between our governments is unbreakable, yet the source of our friendship runs deeper than any treaty."[65] Most recently, President Obama reaffirmed the American position: "A strong and secure Israel is in the national security interest of the United States not simply because we share strategic interests . . . America's commitment to Israel's security flows from a deeper place—and that's the values we share."[66] Another example of a particularly vital strategic alliance is the one between China and North Korea. China has what could be considered a special relationship with North Korea.[67] China has been North Korea's closest ally ever since Chinese troops entered the Korean War in 1950.[68] An alliance relationship was formalized in 1961 with the signing of the Sino-North Korean Treaty of Friendship, Cooperation, and Mutual Assistance that articulated a Chinese commitment to defend North Korea in case of military attack. It has steadfastly provided military and economic support for the autocratic North Korean leadership across several regimes, including Kim-Il Sung, Kim Jong-Il, and Kim Jong-Un. For the Chinese, the Democratic People's Republic of Korea (DPRK) provides a buffer between its borders and democratic South Korea.

The regional importance of a bilateral relationship need not entail a special relationship, but also may elevate the relative significance of the alliance. One example is Russia's alliance with Venezuela. Since 2001, Russia has sought to increase its influence in the Western Hemisphere by strengthening its ties with Venezuela. Venezuela has been one of the largest importers of Russian-made weapons, the two countries have carried out joint military exercises, and Russian military forces have utilized Venezuelan bases. A bilateral commission meets regularly to explore ways to deepen the relationship.[69] In mid-2013, a major Russian oil company and Venezuela's state-owned oil firm announced plans for a joint venture designed to exploit a new field.[70] In all, the Russia government calculates that it has invested more than $20 billion in Venezuela. The significance of the relationship is increased because of Russia's relative lack of political influence in the hemisphere.

Economic ties are the third component considered when assessing the strategic value of a given situation. The significance of economic ties reflects the relative importance of the relationship and considers the country's position among the bilateral trading relationships of P3 countries. The level of exports from the P3 member country is given priority over level of imports, except in cases involving strategic resources, especially oil. In several instances, military and economic interests vested in a given relationship overlap considerably. A prime example includes the People's Republic of China's (PRC's) relationship with Nigeria. China's interest in close relations with Nigeria is a function of its oil resources as well as an important step in the PRC's grand strategy to increase economic and political influence on the continent.[71] In 2006, Chinese firms signed a multibillion dollar deal to revitalize Nigeria's railway.[72] Chinese state-owned oil companies have received major concessions and have invested significantly in the country's oil sector. In 2012, the volume of bilateral trade between China and Nigeria reached $10.5 billion, making Nigeria China's third-largest trading partner.[73]

Table 4.1 lists the strategic interest values for each component as well as the combined value used in the analysis. Along each component, situation-countries are coded on a 1 (low) to 3 (high) scale, with values doubled for the level of involvement component. The total strategic value of a relationship is determined by a sum of these scores, which are then converted back to a 1–3 scale to correspond with low, medium, and high strategic value.[74] Several of the situations as identified by the ICC actually involve other states of strategic interest to one of the P3 members. Because Israel is the object of the complaints stemming from situations identified as "Palestine" and "Comoros," strategic interests are considered involving Israel. Similarly, the situation in Korea involves the potential prosecution of defendants from North Korea (a non-ICC member state). When determining the strategic interests involved, the object of prosecution was used rather than the situation as identified by the ICC for these cases. The relevant state in terms of strategic interest is noted parenthetically.

Table 4.1. Level of P3 strategic interests related to specific situations

Situation	Involvement	Military Value	Economic Value	Combined
Afghanistan	6	3	1	High (10)
Central African Republic (CAR)	2	1	1	Low (4)
Colombia	4	1	2	Medium (7)
Comoros (Israel)	4	3	2	High (9)
Congo (DRC)	4	1	1	Low (4)
Cote d'Ivoire	2	1	1	Low (4)
Georgia	6	3	1	High (10)
Guinea	2	1	1	Low (4)
Honduras	2	1	1	Low (4)
Iraq	6	3	1	High (10)
Kenya	2	1	2	Low (5)
Korea (DPRK)	6	3	3	High (12)
Libya	2	1	2	Low (5)
Mali	2	1	1	Low (4)
Nigeria	2	2	2	Medium (6)
Palestine (Israel)	4	3	2	High (9)
Sudan	2	2	2	Medium (6)
Uganda	2	1	1	Low (4)
Venezuela	4	2	3	High (9)

Gravity and Strategic Interests

The empirical evidence provides strong support that the gravity of a situation and the level of P3 strategic interests vested in a given situation have a strong influence on the choices made by the OTP, both the choice to pursue a formal investigation and the swiftness with which they do so. A simple summary of court actions when considering these two variables provides initial support for the hypotheses offered here. As shown in table 4.2, formal investigations have been established in 75% of the cases deemed to reflect the gravest violations of crimes covered under the Rome Statute. Consistent with the hypotheses, both of the situations where formal investigations have not been established involve cases with high or medium levels of strategic importance to a member of the P3. Though striking, this cursory analysis is a

Table 4.2. Investigation type for situations deemed the most grave

Situation	Gravity	Formal Investigation
Democratic Republic of Congo	8.5	Yes
Sudan	8.5	Yes
Uganda	7.3	Yes
Nigeria	5.8	No
Central African Republic	5.5	Yes
Afghanistan	5.3	No
Cote d'Ivoire	5.3	Yes
Libya	5.3	Yes

rather blunt instrument on which to make substantive judgments regarding causal inference. Thus, additional quantitative tools of analysis were utilized to provide additional support and clarity.

A series of probit regressions were performed to check their effect on whether the court established a formal investigation across cases.[75] Probit regression tests the probability that an observation with certain characteristics (i.e., defined by the covariates included) will fall into either of the two outcome categories. The results of the probit regression can then be transformed to establish their marginal effect on outcomes. Marginal effects show the effect that a one-unit change in the covariate will have on the probability that a formal investigation will not be established for a given situation. Regressions were run with only two covariates at a time because of the small number of observations available for analysis. The probit results provide further evidence that the decision regarding whether to open a formal investigation is strongly influenced by the level of gravity witnessed in a given situation ($p = .015$). Moreover, the evidence suggests that strategic interests also play an important role in outcomes. Strategic interest is statistically significant ($p = .016$), whereas most other variables have little statistical significance on outcomes. The results of the probit regression become more meaningful when converted into their marginal effects, as shown in table 4.3. In the case of gravity, a one-unit change in the level of gravity increases the probability that a formal investigation will be established by roughly 30% ($dy/dx = 0.317$). Conversely, for each unit increase in the strategic value of a given situation, the probability that a formal investigation will be established *decreases* by over 50% ($dy/dx = 0.509$). As reflected in figures 4.1 and 4.2, the more grave the

Table 4.3. Marginal effects after probit (paired covariates)

	Formal Investigation
P3 Strategic Interest	−0.510**
	(0.172)
NGO	−0.00484
	(0.0170)
Gravity	0.317
	(0.266)
Battle Deaths	−0.0000701
	(0.0000473)
Media Coverage	0.000212
	(0.000171)
HR Reputation	0.0782
	(0.0713)

Note: Marginal effects; standard errors in parentheses (d) for discrete change of dummy variable from 0 to 1: * $p < 0.05$, ** $p < 0.01$, *** $p < 0.001$.

situation, the more likely a formal investigation will be established, whereas the more strategic importance P3 countries place on a given situation, the less likely a formal investigation will be established.

The probit analysis provides further support for the qualitative empirics that P3 strategic interests shape institutional choices regarding the selection of situations to investigate. It does not suggest that the court is beholden to or captured by the P3. Rather, it suggests that the court is more likely to establish formal investigations for those situations deemed most grave, but also takes into account the perceived interests of powerful states whose support it would like to gain. This would be consistent with a principled, yet pragmatic prosecutorial strategy. However, a closer look at the data gives reason for caution with regards to the application of the gravity threshold. Figure 4.3 shows patterns drawn from the results of the survey conducted regarding situational gravity. The graph plots the range of gravity levels assigned to a situation across the universe of survey respondents as well as the mean score used in the quantitative analyses. Although the gravity variable was statistically significant in the probit model, figure 4.3 shows the degree of variation in respondents' assessment of the gravity of a given situation. For many of the situations there was a significant degree of disagreement among respondents

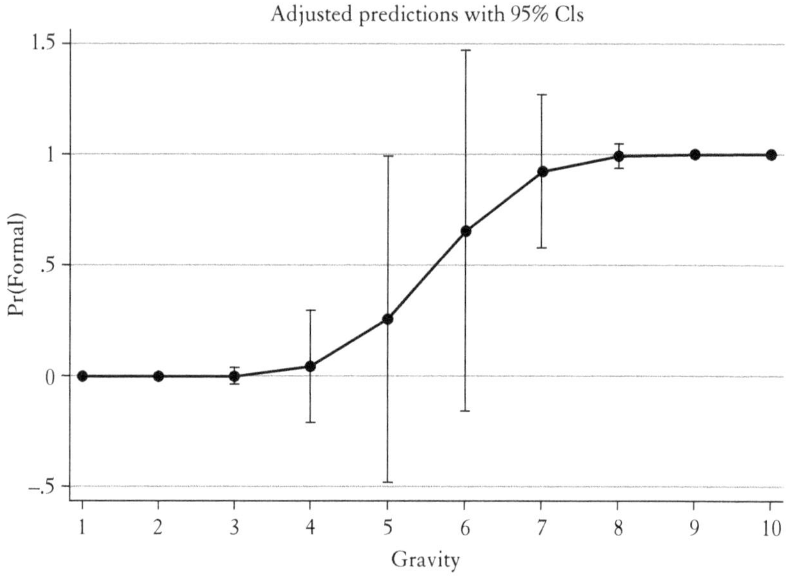

Figure 4.1. Effect of increases in gravity on probability of formal investigation

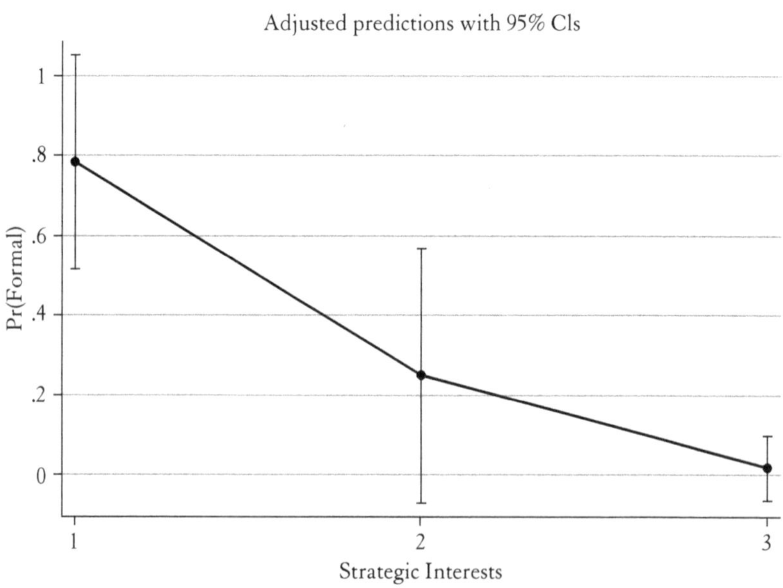

Figure 4.2. Effect of increases in strategic interests on probability of formal investigation

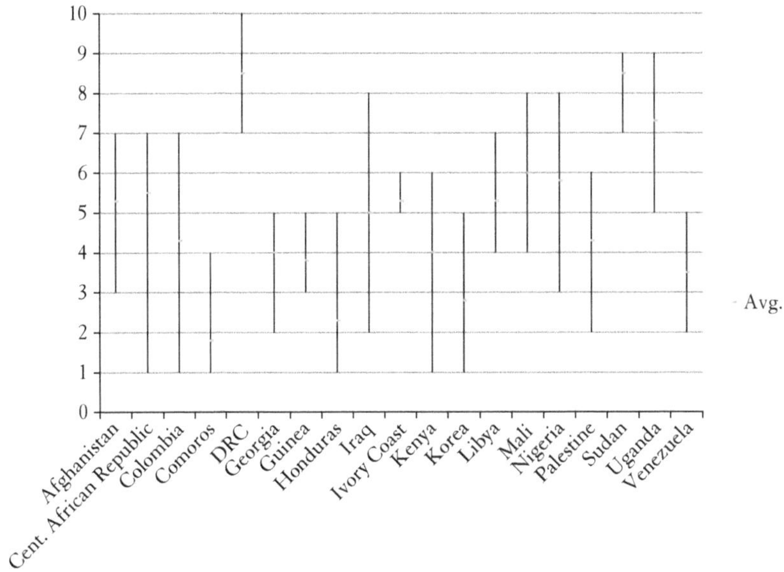

Figure 4.3. Gravity of situations under investigation by the ICC

regarding the level of gravity. In particular, variation was particularly high for the cases of the Central African Republic, Colombia, Iraq, Kenya, and Nigeria, each having a range of at least 5 scale points between the low and high values. However, the mean in many cases clearly deviates from the median, suggesting that the size of the range across situations is a function of outliers in the survey pool. On the one hand, that should give some confidence that the correlation between assessments of gravity and the choices made by the OTP with regard to investigations is indeed robust. However, the presence of such significant outliers, combined with the institutional discretion afforded to the OTP, also suggests that there is the potential for significant deviation regarding the assignment of situational gravity, depending on the perspective of a given individual holding the office of chief prosecutor.

Do these factors also affect the speed of the adjudication process? To answer this question, survival analysis was used to examine likely legal and political variables that may affect outcomes. The analysis begins with a simple test of how strategic interests affect the process of adjudication. Figure 4.4 presents the Kaplan-Meier (K-M) "survival function" for situations involving low, medium, and high levels of strategic interest to one or more of the P3.[76]

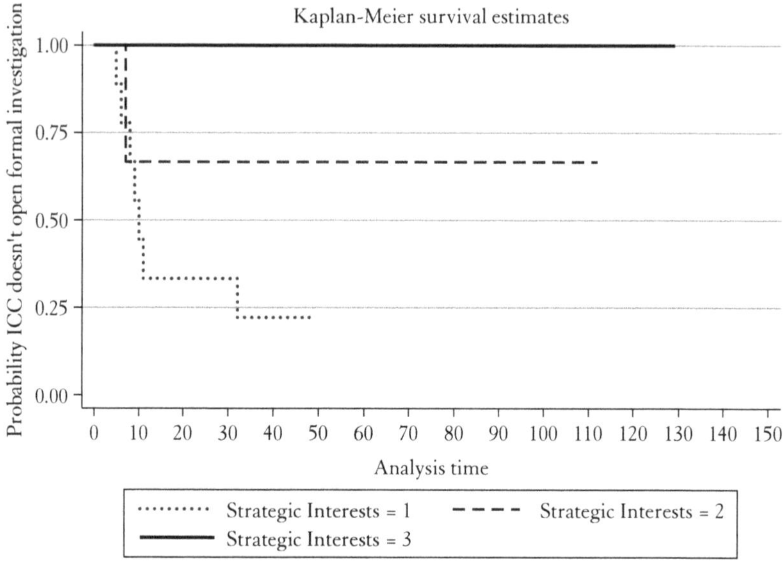

Figure 4.4. Effect of increases in strategic interest on probability that the ICC does not open a formal investigation

Each line represents the probability that an inquiry open for a given number of months "survives" to the next month (i.e., that the ICC does not open a formal investigation at that time). The graph reinforces the qualitative results regarding the decision by the OTP to open a formal investigation: situations that have high (level 3) strategic value to the P3 have a 100% probability that a formal investigation *will not* be established. Of course, this could change because most still have open primary investigations underway. However, even if the OTP eventually decides to open formal investigations for some of these situations, the difference in duration between those with high strategic value and those with lower strategic value is striking. Figure 4.4 illustrates the declining rate of survival as the strategic value of a situation decreases. Put simply, as the strategic value of a situation declines, the probability that the OTP will open an investigation rises sharply, and the time between the preliminary investigation and start of a formal investigation is reduced. To test whether the differences in survival rate reflected in the K-M curve is statistically significant, I ran a nonparametric log-rank test.[77] The results of the log-rank test reveal that the results shown in figure 4.4 are statistically significant ($p = 0.019$).

To gauge the significance of the strategic-interests variable when other covariates are included in the analysis, I utilized Cox proportional hazard regression analysis. The Cox proportional hazard model is a type of event history analysis that in this case tests the extent to which the covariates influence the rate that a formal investigation will not be established. The Cox regression produces a hazard ratio, which is the relative probability of failure due to a one-unit increase in the value of the independent variable. To gauge how sensitive the effect of strategic interest is to the other covariates, I ran a series of bivariate Cox regressions, pairing strategic interest with each of the other covariates.[78] The p-values from these regressions ranged from 0.04 to roughly 0.09, providing a measure of confidence that the effect of strategic interest is not sensitive to model specification. Next, a full model Cox P-H estimate was run that included NGO activity, gravity of the situation, number of battle deaths, amount of media coverage, and human rights reputation. The results listed in table 4.4 show that the only statistically significant variable is strategic interest ($p = .05$). The finding that gravity was not a

Table 4.4. Cox Proportional Hazard Model Results (Full Model)

	Formal Investigation
P3 Strategic Interest	0.0251*
	(0.0471)
NGO	1.034
	(0.0596)
Gravity	1.950
	(0.796)
Battle Deaths	1.000
	(0.000126)
Media Coverage	1.002
	(0.000929)
HR Reputation	1.904
	(0.864)
N	19

Note: Exponentiated coefficients; standard errors in parentheses: * $p < 0.05$, ** $p < 0.01$, *** $p < 0.001$.

statistically significant predictor stands in stark contrast with the results drawn from the probit regressions. This suggests that while gravity may be strongly correlated with the probability that a formal investigation will be established, it may not be highly correlated with the duration of preliminary investigations. However, given the small-*n* available for the full-model analysis, these results should be considered more suggestive than definitive. As such, additional empirical evidence is necessary to supplement these findings.

Another indicator that strategic interest exerts influence on the duration of the process of investigation can be seen when we consider the role of power in the reverse utilizing a qualitative approach. How does the court behave when it receives support from great powers, particularly members of the Security Council? Most of the current situations under review by the ICC were initiated either by member state referrals or by the OTP (*proprio motu*) with authorization by a pretrial chamber. However, two situations, Sudan and Libya, were referred by the UNSC. The first situation referred by the Security Council was in Sudan, which granted jurisdiction to the ICC after passage of Resolution 1593 on March 31, 2005. Passage of the resolution was unanimous, although four Security Council members abstained, including two members of the P3—China and the United States. In this case, a willingness not to block the referral was sufficient support for the ICC to gain jurisdiction over the situation. The OTP opened a formal investigation only nine weeks later on June 6. The second situation was in Libya, which was referred to the ICC by the UNSC through Resolution 1970 on February 26, 2011. Resolution 1970 enjoyed stronger support of the P3, passing unanimously with no abstentions. The OTP opened a formal investigation just five days later on March 3. When comparing the assertiveness of the OTP's response to situations across the different sources of referrals, we see clear patterns of behavior. Figure 4.5 shows the average time between the start of a preliminary investigation and the start of a formal investigation for the three sources of referrals. The average time between preliminary and formal investigations is roughly forty-five weeks for situations referred by states parties to the ICC, whereas those referred by the Security Council average only five weeks.

Although many factors may affect the speed of an investigation, the evidence suggests that the OTP may feel more confident in moving the process forward and making a stronger institutional commitment for situations where the UNSC has offered its support. This is also consistent with the strategic-interests hypothesis, but in the reverse. Where investigations may

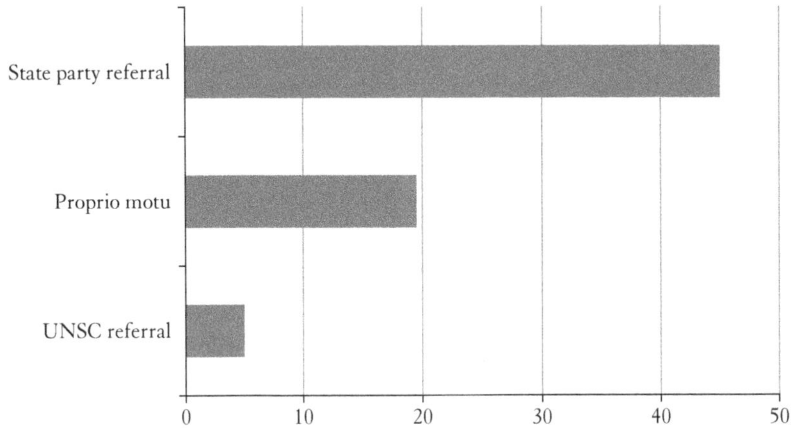

Figure 4.5. Average weeks between preliminary and formal investigation

clash with P3 strategic interests, the OTP has an interest to proceed cautiously. Where the court has the backing of the Security Council, the OTP is more inclined to pursue the case aggressively.

Many are loathe sacrificing principal at the altar of pragmatism, or worse, realpolitik: "In order for the International Criminal Court to build legitimacy over time, it must both act and be seen to act in a neutral way that transcends political pressures."[79] Similarly, Cherif Bassiouni argues, "The legitimacy of the ICC will not be sustained on the basis of occasional referrals based on political expediency but will depend on the consistency of its work."[80] This would certainly include political pressures that might underlie any sort of regional or racial bias. Some critics of the court have argued that its prosecutorial strategy is an extension of great-power bias against weak African countries.[81] Similarly, others have suggested that powerful states have sought to coerce the court to comply with their interests, using direct influence through regular dialogue to pressure the OTP.[82] If the legitimacy of the court is tarnished by questions regarding the OTP's choices regarding which situations it investigates, not only will this potentially hamper its efforts to expand the number of states parties, but risks losing the hard-won support the ICC already has.

Although highly provocative arguments, the "regional bias" and "institutional capture" explanations of ICC behavior are extreme and do not take into account the many non-African situations under preliminary investigation by the OTP or the fact that the current Chief Prosecutor is Gambian. Moreover, they face a formidable burden of proof unlikely to be met by the available evidence. The evidence presented here strongly suggests that great-power interests shape the behavior of the court, but there is no direct evidence that the OTP is beholden to the interests of powerful Western states as some critics have claimed. Rather, a more nuanced explanation of court behavior is gained by examining how the egoistic institutional interests of the OTP are influenced—not determined—by the strategic interests of some important external actors. This is not a case of institutional capture, but rather, reflects the *internalization of external preferences.* It is a reflection of the challenges facing a new, relatively weak institution that depends considerably on receiving cooperation from states, particularly powerful ones. The theoretical framework forwarded here reveals how the interests of powerful nonmember states (and thus, not principles under the more limited PA framework) can be taken into account by the OTP in defining institutional interests and consequently shaping prosecutorial strategy.

The underlying theory and resultant findings are significant to our understanding of the ICC and may also be of interest to those studying other international courts or international institutions more generally. First, they provide a theoretical explanation for the behavior of the ICC and the decisions made by the OTP regarding situation selection in accordance with its prosecutorial strategy. The theory of prosecutorial strategy forwarded here is strongly supported by the available empirical evidence—both quantitative and qualitative. Although there was no attempt to account for initial actions into a situation (i.e., opening a primary investigation), the internalization hypothesis does illuminate a powerful intervening variable in the process of investigation and adjudication by the court. The law may be clear on a principle, but how it is pursued in practice by the court offers considerable latitude to the OTP that can strongly shape the legal process. The evidence presented here illuminates factors that may press the OTP to proceed more cautiously in some cases (those where P3 interests are involved) and more aggressively in others (where referral came from the authority of the UNSC). More broadly, the theoretical framework and the evidence drawn from the ICC reveal how behavior can be affected by institutional dependence on external actors, and how the preferences of these actors may be internalized into the decision calculus—even in legal institutions where procedure is clearly articulated in law. For this reason, these findings may be of interest to those interested in the functioning of international legal institutions more broadly, not just on the ICC.

These findings should also be of interest to those seeking to understand international institutions more broadly. It unpacks the ways that new or weak institutions may be more vulnerable to the influence of great-power realpolitik. This influence need not be the product of direct suasion by these powerful states, but rather as a function of the dependence such institutions have on them and their institutional interests to garner their support. Such insights would seem applicable to institution building across issue areas, including international trade, finance, and environmental protection. Moreover, understanding these processes may facilitate the creation of more successful international institutions charged with addressing crucial global challenges.

Lastly, normative implications can be drawn as well. Idealists critical of the court's apparent consideration of great-power interest—*particularly among those who are not even members of the court*—consider such actions as anathema to the pursuit of justice. Others argue for a more pragmatic course: "The Prosecutor should therefore establish and adhere to a long-term policy which is widely perceived as acceptable, while carefully balancing the need for political support with the need to be perceived as independent and credible."[83] The evidence presented in this chapter suggests that the OTP has done just that and has navigated a very difficult course between principle and pragmatism. The significance of gravity in the series of analyses performed here suggests that the OTP has indeed remained true to the court's mission to prosecute the most serious international crimes. Thus it would seem that the OTP acts in accordance with the wishes of the states parties.[84] On the other hand, the consistently high significance of strategic importance reflects institutional awareness of the very practical dependence the court has on powerful states to successfully prosecute cases and bring the architects of mass atrocities to justice. Moreover, the ability of the court to expand its jurisdictional reach and global influence is dependent on gaining the support of three of its most powerful nonmember states—the United States, Russia, and China. The road to achieving its institutional mandate for international justice requires that the OTP be pragmatic as well as idealistic.

Conclusion

Between Power and Principle

The war in Syria may not represent the end of humanity, but every injustice committed is a chip in the façade of what holds us together. The universal principle of justice may not be rooted in physics but it is no less fundamental to our existence. For without it, before long, human beings will surely cease to exist.

—Stephen Hawking

The civil war in Syria is an epic struggle for power between the government of Bashar al-Assad and an array of nearly one thousand rebel groups, including jihadist groups such as the Islamic State (ISIS) and the al-Nusra Front.[1] On August 21, 2013, chemical weapons were unleashed on the civilian population in Syria, killing thirteen hundred people and turning a dark page in an ongoing civil war that had already claimed the lives of over one hundred thousand.[2] Gruesome images of the victims, four hundred of them children, shocked the world and were accompanied by firsthand accounts of the suffering they endured as they gasped for breath in their final moments of life. As has too often been the case in human history, the powerless again found themselves victims of a violent struggle for political power.

Events like these are why human rights advocates have long pressed for the creation of international criminal courts—to restrain the brutal instruments of realpolitik that are so often unleashed on the innocent. The creation of the International Criminal Court (ICC), the first permanent international court of its kind, has been lauded by many as a landmark achievement, one that not only would provide justice to the victims of atrocities but could potentially serve as a transformative force in the fundamental character of international society.[3] Some have suggested that the prevailing rule of force would be increasingly replaced by the rule of law.[4] Much of the scholarship on international criminal courts, including the ICC, fits this broad narrative emphasizing the growing power of norms of justice and human rights in the creation of international criminal courts. It is a narrative of principles finally emerging triumphant over the frequently ruthless struggle for power.

This book explores the terrain that exists between two opposing takes on international humanitarian law—one that sees justice as transformative, another that sees it as either dangerous or irrelevant. The increasingly dominant view is that international criminal courts are primarily a product of principles, mobilized by key norm entrepreneurs, human rights activists, and NGOs. Although not always framed in terms of principles, this view is generally consistent with a constructivist approach that emphasizes the role of ideals, norms, and social identities in world politics.[5] This view often has been placed in contrast to power-based explanations, and the empirical evidence put forward by constructivists suggests the limits of a realist approach that emphasizes the role of interests defined in terms of power. This is not to say that the existing literature turns a blind eye to the presence of power politics. Indeed, there are scant few extant works that do not acknowledge that interests defined in terms of power have exerted influence on the process of creating international criminal courts at some point. Yet, power politics tend to be peripheral to the primary narrative regarding the growth of human rights norms and the application of evolving principles of justice.[6]

There can be little doubt that evolving human rights norms and principles of justice figure prominently in the creation of international criminal courts. Moreover, it stands to reason that the more political mobilization that is rallied in support of these principles, the greater their potential influence.[7] However, these arguments are hardly counterintuitive. One could mount a similar argument about the formation of the contemporary international trade regime. It is unlikely that we would see the emergence of the World Trade Organization (WTO) or the General Agreement on Tariffs and Trade (GATT) absent the central tenets of Ricardian economics forwarded by influential economic advisers in the post–World War II period. This book does not refute the notion that principles and norms matter. Indeed, it is impossible to imagine the creation of the Nuremberg Principles or the Rome Statute without them. Rather, the empirical evidence offered here suggests that arguments regarding the influence of idealpolitik frequently overstate the role of norms and often fail to recognize how crucial a role realpolitik has played in the evolution of international criminal court. The existing literature far too often imagines idealpolitik and realpolitik as separate and opposed and thus fails to adequately explain how power and principle often overlap in shaping interests and outcomes concerning international criminal courts. This book addresses this critical absence in the literature by focusing on the intersection of power and principle in shaping the origins, design, and operation of international criminal courts.

Principal Findings

This book contributes to our understanding of international criminal courts through the development and application of theory. Theory provides the underlying rationale for the development of falsifiable and empirically testable hypotheses. In this book, I develop and apply both grand theory and middle-range theory to explain the origins, design, and behavior of international criminal courts. I do so in a somewhat eclectic manner. Rather than proposing a monocausal explanation of outcomes or seeking to establish the superiority of one approach, I synthesize elements and insights from several schools of thought. Identifying and explicating the political dynamics involved in international criminal courts requires multiple analytical tools. Instead of drawing solely on one analytical approach, theoretical frameworks used in this book are tailored to the specifics of the facet of institutionalization under investigation.[8] This "theory through synthesis" is consistent with the "eclectic" approach advocated by Rudra Sil and Peter Katzenstein, among others.[9] This approach not only draws from different epistemological perspectives, but may also shift the level of analysis where it is called for.[10] As David Lake notes, "It is precisely this 'mixing and matching' of assumptions, issue areas, units, and interests that makes this sort of theorizing 'eclectic.' "[11]

So what have we learned using these theories and analytical techniques? The following highlights some of the key points raised in the book:

1. Interests defined in terms of power were instrumental in the initial decision to create international tribunals. However, once the decision

> to form them was made, norm entrepreneurs seized the opportunity to institutionalize liberal principles of international humanitarian law within them.

Contrary to the conventional wisdom, the evidence presented in the introduction reminds us that the original impetus for the creation of the International Military Tribunals after World War II was to legitimize Allied actions during the war by establishing that the Axis powers waged a war of aggression. It was not initially driven by concerns regarding human rights, principles of justice, or even the horrors of the Holocaust. The International Military Tribunals not only provided Allied powers the opportunity to legitimize their participation in the war but also their execution of it. This aim to legitimize their use of force during the war did not reflect Allied concerns that they would be vulnerable to prosecution for wartime actions. As instruments of victor's justice, the International Military Tribunals posed no legal threat to Allied leadership. Rather, the Allied interest in adjudicating the crime of aggression was primary rooted in gaining soft power during a period of global transformation where international order was being reconstituted.

2. Growing human rights norms and public outcry may have pressed liberal states to act in the face of atrocities during the early 1990s, but they are not sufficient to explain the UN Security Council's (UNSC's) choice to create international criminal tribunals. Rather, the choice was strongly influenced by interests defined in terms of power for both liberal and illiberal members of the Security Council.

Chapter 1 shows how power and principle shaped the interests of the permanent members of the UN Security Council that created the ad hoc tribunals for the former Yugoslavia and Rwanda. Although opinion polls conducted among the UNSC's liberal democracies showed that the general public had strong concerns regarding atrocities committed during these conflicts, calls for action focused on the question of humanitarian intervention rather than the creation of tribunals. However, the experience in Somalia showed that public support for intervention was fragile. Thus, for the liberal democratic members of the P5 (permanent five members of the UNSC), creating tribunals was a means to respond to public concerns about atrocities in a manner that presented less political risk and lower cost than more assertive policy options (such as military intervention). In other words, interests defined in terms of power shaped the choice to create tribunals. This was also the case for the council's two illiberal permanent members, though in different ways. For these illiberal states, interests defined in terms of power were linked to the liberal states' preferences to create tribunals. At the time the ad hoc tribunals were created, both countries sought closer ties to the West, and supporting liberal states' preferences for tribunals was one way to achieve this objective. Russia's foreign policy at the time was based on a broad strategy of Europeanization and forging better ties with both Europe and the United States. Support for the tribunals offered the Russians the chance to show that post–Soviet Russia supported many of the same principles held by the UNSC's liberal member states. Similarly, China's emphasis on openness and engagement with the international economy also made them reluctant to stand in the way of the tribunals, even though they maintained strong concerns regarding sovereignty. For the Chinese, not opposing the creation of the courts provided an opportunity to begin to rebuild their tattered human rights reputation in the wake of the Tiananmen massacre.

3. The political fault lines regarding the design of the ICC were not simply between supporters and opponents of international humanitarian law. Rather, interests defined in terms of power figured prominently in the design preferences of many states in a battle over the role of the Security Council in the operation of the court.

Chapter 2 shows us that although the original impetus for the creation of the ICC was squarely rooted in principles of international humanitarian law, once the process of negotiations began states sought to shape the design of the court in accordance with other interests. Chapter 2 shows that interests defined in terms of power were among the most significant for a number of states, and these interests created some of the most contentious debates regarding the design of the ICC. For these states, the process of institutional design was part of a broader struggle between those privileged by existing institutional rules and norms and those who sought to use the ICC as a means of equalizing the hierarchical structure of international order—one skewed in favor of the Security Council's five permanent members (P5). These politics were evident at several times during the process of institutional design: initially during the PrepCom meetings, then during the Rome Conference, and lastly during the review conference held in Kampala, Uganda. Where there were significant deviations from expected behavior, chapter 3 shows that these too were strongly shaped by interests rooted in realpolitik. In these instances, realpolitik operating at the global level gave way to interests defined in terms of power at the domestic and regional levels.

4. Though charged with a mission firmly rooted in principles of justice and human rights, egoistic institutional interests press the ICC to pursue a more pragmatic course, one whose principled mission is closely intertwined with the strategic interests of the UN Security Council, particularly its three permanent members who are not party to the Rome Statute.

The book also shows how principle and power intertwine to shape the behavior of the ICC as it seeks to investigate the gravest violations of international humanitarian law. Chapter 4 shows the strong—though indirect—influence that state strategic interests have on the behavior of the ICC. Counterintuitively, this involves the strategic interests of three of the most powerful states who are not party to the Rome Statute—the United States, Russia, and China. However, contrary to the views of some of the court's most vocal critics, the evidence shows that the ICC has not been captured by these powerful countries to do their bidding. Rather, egoistic institutional interests are affected by the court's dependence on powerful states in order to achieve its mandate for justice. As shown in chapter 4, these interests affect both the court's choice to pursue a formal investigation for a given situation and the swiftness of its decision to do so. Future scholarship on the prosecutorial behavior of the ICC can test the proposed theoretical framework against the growing body of empirical data.

The theoretical frameworks developed and applied in this book not only provide us lenses to better understand the form and function of international criminal courts but to varying degrees may be useful to understanding outcomes for other institutions. Grand theories are the most widely generalizable, and this book seeks to contribute to the continued development of grand theory by exploring the overlap between two commonly contrasting schools of thought—realism and constructivism. Examining the frequent overlap between power and principle in the development of international criminal courts reveals that interests in the form of power provided essential windows of opportunity for norm entrepreneurs seeking to advance international humanitarian law. Adopting a more monocausal framework would likely not recognize how interests in the form of power could be integral to the development of interests in the form of principles. Conversely, the approach used here prompts us to reconsider the forms and functions of power so central to realist thought. As shown in chapter 1, Allied leaders sought to use the International Military Tribunals to legitimize their use of force during the war and to increase their soft power in the emerging postwar order. Power is central to the narrative; however, it is not defined solely in terms of brute material force as is common in most contemporary realist scholarship.[12] Rather, interests defined in terms of power over opinion figure prominently, a dimension of power acknowledged by classical realists such as E. H. Carr but more commonly associated with a constructivist view among contemporary scholars.[13] Differing conceptions of power have animated a lively debate among scholars of international relations, yet too often such debates press scholars to choose sides.[14] Instead, the examination of international criminal courts offered here shows the utility of adopting a more nuanced approach that brings together elements of both realist and constructivist (and to some degree, neoliberal institutionalist) perspectives. Although helpful in gaining a sharper understanding of the origins and evolution of international criminal courts, such an approach is certainly not limited to them. Rather, it may be useful in understanding a much broader range of phenomena in international politics.

The middle-range theories developed and utilized in the book are also somewhat generalizable. The theory of institutional design preferences forwarded in chapter 2 is based on an insight not limited to international courts: relative power can either be gained or lost depending on the design of an international institution. Although the design of the ICC clearly had significant implications for the relative power of the UN Security Council and those who sought to remove the prerogatives afforded to its five permanent members, other institutions may have similar effects. One needs to look no further than the Doha round of WTO trade negotiations to see how state preferences were shaped by concerns over relative power as the design of a new trade agreement was being negotiated. Divergent preferences between the global North and global South largely derailed the Doha round talks during the Cancun ministerial meeting in 2003.[15] But the framework forwarded in chapter 2 prompts us to consider more than just how relative power is affected by the design of institutional arrangements. Drawing on (and building on) regime complex theory suggests that such dynamics may be strongly affected by the relationships *between* institutions. Although a growing body of scholarship has focused on how overlapping institutions can affect interests and outcomes, the framework forwarded in chapter 2 illustrates how institutional nesting can have similarly significant effects.

The insights from the internalization theory developed in chapter 4 may also be generalizable and applied beyond the domain of international criminal courts. The notion that international organizations may develop their own egoistic interests independent of the interests of those states that created them was put forward by the architects of principal-agent (PA) theory. The framework used in chapter 4 builds on the central insights by showing how, in some instances, potential influence moves beyond the binary principal-agent relationship to include consideration of third-party actors. Although this insight has relevance in the case of the ICC, it is not specific to the court. Rather, it should not only prompt scholars to consider the formation of egoistic organization interests more broadly but also apply this framework to a broader array of international courts and international organizations.

The Triumph of Principle over Power?

Advocates for the creation of the International Criminal Court have long argued that the court would deter the commission of atrocities and contribute to global peace.[16] Some even went so far as to suggest that the court's creation was a transformative force in the very nature of international politics and world order. Although such rhetoric might easily be dismissed as hyperbole employed in the interests of political salesmanship by the court's most ardent and idealistic supporters, the goals of deterring future atrocities and contributing to peace are expressly stipulated in the preamble of the Rome Statute itself. As the ICC continues in its second decade of operation, we might consider how successful the court has been thus far in constraining the often tragic effects of the pursuit of power in the name of principles of international humanitarian law. Unfortunately, the available evidence is not particularly encouraging.

There is scant evidence to suggest that the ICC's presence acts as a significant deterrent on those whose quest for power knows few, if any, moral boundaries. Alleged perpetrators of crimes covered under the Rome Statute were obviously not deterred in the nineteen situations currently under investigation by the ICC. These include Afghanistan, the Central African Republic (CAR), Colombia, the Democratic Republic of Congo (DRC), Cote d'Ivoire, Georgia, Guinea, Honduras, Iraq, Israel (referral brought by Comoros), Kenya, Korea, Libya, Mali, Nigeria, Sudan, Uganda, and Venezuela. The situation in Libya is a prime example of leaders' general lack of concern regarding ICC prosecution. After using his military in an attempt to crush the growing civilian demonstrations in Libya, Muammar Gaddafi showed little restraint or concern about potential prosecution. In a speech he stated, "We will fight them and we will beat them. . . . If needs be, we will open all the arsenals."[17] At the time, the ICC had been in existence for nearly a decade.

In addition to those situations already under investigation by the court, there are other prominent examples of leaders undeterred by the presence of the ICC. Among the most significant is Syria, where the Assad regime has shown little restraint in its pursuit to maintain its power. Even after President Obama's now-infamous "redline" had been crossed following a chemical weapons attack on civilians in August 2013, there are few signs of any deterrent effect. In addition to a protracted policy to restrict essential aid to civilian populations, the military also resorted to the widespread use of "barrel bombs." These crude weapons are oil drums filled with shrapnel such as nails, which are then dropped from helicopters on the unsuspecting civilians below. In February 2014, U.S. secretary of state John Kerry remarked, "Each and every barrel bomb filled with metal shrapnel and fuel launched against innocent Syrians underscores the barbarity of a regime that has turned its country into a super magnet for terror."[18] Moreover, in June 2014 the Organization for the Prohibition of Chemical Weapons (OPCW) reported that there was evidence to suggest that "toxic chemicals, most likely pulmonary irritating agents such as chlorine, have been used" by the Syrian government in a "systematic manner" long after they agreed to dispose of their chemical weapons cache.[19] Needless to say, it is difficult to find evidence of deterrence in Syria.

Another prominent example of atrocities undeterred is North Korea. On February 17, 2014, an official UN inquiry led by Michael Kirby provided extensive evidence of ongoing atrocities committed by the government of North Korea. Among the evidence forwarded by the Commission of Inquiry on Human Rights in the Democratic People's Republic of North Korea was an overview of the ongoing situation in state-run political prison camps:

> In the political prison camps of the Democratic People's Republic of Korea, the inmate population has been gradually eliminated through deliberate starvation, forced labour, executions, torture, rape and the denial of reproductive rights enforced through punishment, forced abortion and infanticide. The commission estimates that hundreds of thousands of political prisoners have perished in these camps over the past five decades. The unspeakable atrocities that are being committed against inmates of the *kwanliso* political prison camps resemble the horrors of camps that totalitarian States established during the twentieth century.[20]

The report went on to list numerous other violations covered under the Rome Statute, including crimes against humanity. It further concluded that "the gravity, scale and nature of these violations reveal a State that does not have any parallel in the contemporary world."[21] On April 17, 2014, Michael Kirby brought the report to a meeting of the UN Security Council, where he argued for the prosecution of the North Korean leadership. Kirby informed the members present that "in a week of many grave human rights matters occupying the attention of the members of this council, we dare say that the case of human rights in the DPRK (Democratic People's Republic of Korea) exceeds all others in duration, intensity and horror."[22] Pyongyang's representative at the meeting, So Se Pyong, responded to the report by arguing that the United States and "other hostile forces" had fabricated the report in an attempt to "defame the dignified image of the Democratic People's Republic of Korea and eventually eliminate its social system."[23] Pyongyang shows little sign of concern about potential prosecution by the ICC and has shown no signs of change in the wake of the UN report, even though the OTP launched a preliminary investigation.

What is even more damaging to the notion of the deterrent effect of the ICC is evidence of crimes continuing to be committed in situations where the court already has preliminary investigations under way. What behavior do we see among actors who know that the eye of the court is trained on the country? In Nigeria, thousands of innocent people have been slaughtered from 2009 to 2014 by the Islamic militant group Boko Haram. The group seeks to gain power to establish an Islamic state and appears ready to use all means necessary to achieve its goal. This includes the use of child soldiers, kidnapping, selling girls, and mass slayings, including children. In April 2014, Boko Haram kidnapped some three hundred girls from their boarding school and later released a video that declared the girls would be sold as brides. The video generated global shock and outrage, spawning a global Bring Back Our Girls campaign in international civil society. In June 2014, raids in the northeastern state of Borno claimed hundreds of innocent lives. One local leader described the attack on his village: "The death is unimaginable. We have lost between 400 and 500 people in the attacks in which men and male children were not spared. . . . Even nursing mothers had their male infants snatched from their backs and shot dead before their eyes."[24] In addition to these acts, Boko Haram has also begun to utilize children in suicide bombing attacks. According to the United Nations Children's Emergency Fund (UNICEF), 20% of all suicide bombing conducted by Boko Haram have been carried out by children, and the number of children used in such strikes has increased more than tenfold from 2014 to 2015.[25] Those ordering and conducting such attacks do not appear to be deterred by the prospect of international justice.

Iraq is another example where an active preliminary investigation by the court does not appear to serve as an effective deterrent to the commission of atrocities. This involves the actions of members of ISIS, the self-proclaimed Islamic States of Iraq and Syria, led by Abu Bakr al-Baghdadi. In June 2014, ISIS militants attacked numerous villages south of Kirkuk, Iraq, in what witnesses described as massacres aimed at destroying the Shiite Turkmen communities. Witnesses described mass executions and beheadings, and the victims included young girls.[26] We also see continuing violence in Mali, another country where the ICC has already established an investigation. Where actors feel the stakes are high enough, the means to attaining power appear to be of less concern that achieving their primary objective. Not surprisingly, given the available empirical evidence, a number of scholars have cast considerable doubts on the deterrent capacity of the ICC.[27]

Not only are political despots apparently undeterred from using all means they consider necessary to achieve their political objectives but also little evidence suggests that the creation of the ICC has made the world more peaceful. As shown in the most recent data released by the Uppsala Conflict Data

Program, yearly fatalities in organized violence have not been trending downward since the ICC became operational in 2002.[28] In fact, they have risen sharply since 2012. These take into account trends in state-based conflict, nonstate conflict, and one-sided violence. Of course, few (if any) had realistic expectations that the ICC would make violent conflict a thing of the past. Moreover, even though the ICC is nearly halfway through its second decade of existence, it remains an institution that is largely in its infancy. One could argue that it is difficult to establish a deterrent effect until the court has established a proven track record of holding the guilty accountable for their crimes. In addition, with few trials completed as of this writing, it would be reasonable to assume that the court's impact on postconflict reconciliation would be negligible. From the perspective of postconflict reconciliation, the ICC's greatest potential contribution to peace may be its ability to keep conflict-prone societies from recidivism. Gauging the court's success along such lines will clearly require a much longer time horizon. Rather than representing the culmination of a decades-long justice cascade, the ICC is likely better conceived as an institution in its formative stages. Doing so gives us a more measured and realistic perspective regarding its progress and impact.

Striking the Balance between Power and Principle

Even this informal and anecdotal consideration of the ICC makes it clear that we are a long way from the time when principle has the upper hand over power. Although idealists commonly see power as the root of the problems that can often generate profound human suffering, power must play an instrumental role in addressing them. The application of power is not only necessary to protect the innocent and provide a deterrent to those who may do them harm but, as shown in this book, can frequently play a crucial in the process building, strengthening, and diffusing principled norms. Indeed, chapter 1 documented how important the International Military Tribunals were to the development of contemporary international law, even though the rationale behind their creation reflected interests defined in terms of power among the victorious Allied powers. In addition, it is the most powerful states in the world that are in a position to have the strongest impact on peace and security. This notion is foundational to the design of the United Nations and the role of the Security Council. The relationship between power and principle is crucially important to peace, security, and the protection of the innocent. However, the most effective means of combining these forces in the interests of reducing human suffering is not clear. This raises important normative questions for policymakers in the world's most powerful states. To what degree should idealism (principle) or realism (power) shape how powerful states respond to violent conflict and the atrocities commonly committed during them? Moreover, what role should the ICC play in this response?

Realists do not consider justice to be the primary objective when addressing conflict and the suffering it inflicts. Rather, most would likely argue that stopping the violence and reestablishing stability should be the primary objective. This can be achieved either by altering the balance of power among the combatants or by using their power to bring the warring parties to the negotiating table to broker a political settlement. Direct military intervention would clearly have the greatest impact on the balance of power in a conflict situation, but such action is unlikely to be taken in situations where few strategic interests are at stake for the intervening power. Direct military intervention incurs substantial material and political costs, yet in cases with few strategic interests involved, have little to offer from the standpoint of interests defined in terms of power. In these cases, the more common response by the world's powerful countries is to provide material or advisory support for one side in the conflict, an approach sometimes referred to as "building partner capacity." Yet, as the American experiences in Iraq and Afghanistan have shown, such programs too often fail.[29] Moreover, depending on the existing alliance relationships involved in a given situation, providing support to one side may cause powerful states allied with the other side to enter the fray, potentially escalating both the scale and scope of the conflict. Most states would be hesitant to become ensnared in a civil war or ethnic conflict if doing so risks a more substantial military engagement with another powerful state. Given high risks and limited rewards, a realist approach would prefer to either (1) remain disengaged from the conflict until one side is able to secure victory, or (2) promote a political solution to the conflict. Of course, states often may seek to alter the local balance of power in a situation and then quickly push to broker a political settlement to take advantage of short-term gains while minimizing long-term commitments. Regardless of the specific approach taken, the bottom line is that achieving stability takes priority over achieving justice. Realists would not generally welcome any participation by the ICC into the situation until a political settlement has been reached.

Human rights advocates are all too familiar with the realist logic. They can point to the obvious shortcomings of the realist approach. Perhaps most importantly, many of the atrocities evident in international society take place in countries with limited strategic value to the world's great powers. In practice this means that it is unlikely that powerful states will be motivated to become involved at all in stemming the violence. Moreover, the realist approach maintains a system in which the powerful remain largely immune to constraints on their use of power. This not only includes their use of power directly but also in their capacity to provide material support to oppressive regimes to which they are allied. To paraphrase Thucydides, in such a system the powerful do what they can while the weak suffer what they must.[30] For idealists, this is the reality that not only produces the atrocities they are trying to address but also often shields those most culpable. Indeed, the quest for political power often leads to profound human suffering. As Rudi Rummel put it, "power kills."[31]

For these reasons (and others), many idealists place a high priority on principles of human rights and justice in guiding foreign policy regarding violent conflict. For the more legalistic among them, this means framing a given situation through the eyes of international humanitarian law and includes promoting an active role for the ICC in addressing situations where violence is marked by atrocities and profound human suffering. This includes identifying perpetrators of atrocities as war criminals and documenting evidences of crimes to be used in prosecution. Presumably, this perspective includes a preference for regime change because idealists would certainly not consider a government led by a war criminal to possess any legitimacy. Moreover, idealists are not likely to be comfortable with waiting on the sidelines until a military or political solution is reached. Where mass crimes are being committed, the law must take action through the ICC. This position was evident in the case of Darfur. Though the violence in Sudan was ongoing, human rights NGOs pressed the ICC prosecutor to take action. He did so by obtaining a referral from the UN Security Council and issuing arrest warrants, first for Sudan's interior minister, Ahmed Haroun, and then for its standing president, Omar al-Bashir. At the press conference held to announce the OTP's request for an arrest warrant for Bashir, the chief prosecutor explained his motive: "These people are waiting for our protection."[32]

Legal idealists argue that such actions can deter continued violations in the short run because perpetrators will know that the eyes of the ICC are on them and that they will have to answer for their actions in a court of law. Proponents believe that, as the body of successful prosecutions mounts over time, the actions of the court will contribute to the strengthening and global diffusion of norms that, in turn, will contribute to deterrence more broadly. Moreover, this ability to facilitate compliance with international humanitarian law is affected by the degree of legitimacy enjoyed by the courts that adjudicate them.[33] Again, the relationship between power and principle looms large. Many legal experts have argued that the principle of equality under the law is the cornerstone of its legitimacy and, subsequently, its compliance pull.[34] Among them, Abram Chayes and Anne-Marie Slaughter suggest that equality under the law is the "one essential factor" of ICC legitimacy and that "exemption of any nation—especially the richest and most powerful—from important legal requirements strikes at the foundation notion of equal treatment under the law."[35]

Though successful enforcement of these norms of justice is necessary for them to gain strength, in the long run idealists suggest deterrence will be not be achieved primarily through threat of prosecution, but rather through the internalization of these norms.[36] Critics may point out that until this norm "tipping point" is realized, ICC involvement in a situation will likely complicate political efforts to establish peace or even a cessation of hostilities.[37] The threat of ICC prosecution has shown little effect on curbing the behavior of leaders cast in the court's spotlight and, in fact, seems more likely to cause them to become even more resolute. In the case of Sudan, for example, President Omar al-Bashir was defiant in the face of the ICC warrant for his arrest, and the African Union's Peace and Security Council argued that the ICC action was undermining the peace process. When addressing the issue of the timing of the ICC arrest warrant against Ahmed Haroun, the chief prosecutor asked the UN Security Council, "When is a better time to arrest Haroun?"[38]

Of course, even the most idealistic supporters of the ICC and human rights more generally do not believe that the court can end atrocities and facilitate peace on its own. Neither a purely realist-based approach nor a purely legal idealist-based approach would be the most effective approach to dealing with the problems of conflict atrocities. The challenge facing policymakers is finding the right mix between power and principle. Proponents of the doctrine known as the Responsibility to Protect (R2P) suggest that until norms of international humanitarian law reach the tipping point in which they become broadly internalized throughout international society, state power must be brought to bear in defense of civilian populations caught in the crossfire of conflict. These principles gained widespread acceptance at the 2005 World Summit, where all members of the UN General Assembly made a commitment to the Responsibility to Protect doctrine as detailed in the World Summit Outcome document.[39] In addition to committing to protect their own citizens, states accepted the premise that the international community has an obligation to use all appropriate means to protect the innocent from genocide, ethnic cleansing, war crimes, and crimes against humanity. By exacting a commitment to support humanitarian principles, R2P proponents hoped to compel states to utilize their power in support of the doctrine. Although the document stipulated a preference for nonmilitary means of action, including mediation and economic sanctions, the use of force was also sanctioned if peaceful means were inadequate. However, force must be sanctioned by the Security Council under Chapter VII of the UN Charter.

Applying this doctrine and finding the right mix between power and principle is fraught with challenges. Taking a more passive approach, such as economic sanctions, places pressure on actors to comply, yet rarely produces an immediate effect. Doing so risks that mass casualties and grave atrocities will continue to be committed for some time, exacting a profound human toll. As Moreno Ocampo observed, genocidaires require only two things to achieve their goal: global indifference and time.[40] Military intervention provides the most direct and immediate means of protecting the innocent. However, even if policymakers are willing to apply military power to cases involving humanitarian interests, other factors raise important questions about utilizing the military option. For powerful states charged with the task of intervention, military engagement carries significant domestic political risks. In addition to likely concerns about bearing the economic burden of military action, mounting casualties invariably result in declining public support. Although liberal democratic states may be more vulnerable to such domestic political costs, illiberal states are not immune to them.[41] Providing arms but not soldiers may reduce these risks, but doing so raises other potential problems. For example, in the fall of 2015, the U.S. Central Command acknowledged that a $500 million program to train and equip

Syrian rebel forces resulted in a significant amount of these resources passing through the rebels' hands and into the hands of al-Qaeda.[42] Moreover, it suspected that a large number of the fighters trained by U.S. military advisers had changed sides and were now fighting for the Islamic State. Only four or five fighters of a force intended to number some three thousand to five thousand soldiers remained in active battle against ISIS.[43] There is also the potential that consistently backing rebel groups in the name of defending the civilian population risks moral hazard. Some scholars have raised the question of whether rebel groups may provoke genocidal retaliation against their own group in order to secure outside military intervention that may tip the balance of power in their political struggle.[44] Needless to say, the choice to intervene and how to do so is both weighty and fraught with difficulties.

Lessons from the Syrian Civil War

The situation in Syria provides an excellent example of the difficulty in finding the right balance between principle and power, as well as the potential pitfalls along the way. The roots of the conflict began in March 2011 after Syrian security forces opened fire on pro-democracy protesters in the city of Deraa. The incident triggered mounting protests across the country, and by July, hundreds of thousands of Syrians were taking part. The situation became steadily more violent as antigovernment groups organized and took arms in order to expel security forces from their local areas. Within two years, the UN estimated that some ninety thousand Syrians had perished in the conflict.

American president Barack Obama was under pressure to bring U.S. power to bear onto the mounting crisis in Syria by idealists among his advisory staff. Samantha Power, a member of Obama's National Security Council staff and a strong proponent of the Responsibility to Protect doctrine, pushed the president to provide arms to the Syrian rebels in their fight against the Assad regime. She was joined by Secretary of State Hillary Clinton in calling for a robust American response to the violence in Syria. Generally speaking, an idealistic approach would involve providing material support for the Syrian rebels to topple the autocratic Assad regime, supporting the arrest and trial of Assad for violations of international humanitarian law, and promoting a Syrian transition to democracy. At the same time, however, former defense secretary Robert Gates frequently cautioned against overextending U.S. power in the Middle East. Reportedly, Gates quipped on more than one occasion during meetings, "Shouldn't we finish up the two wars we have before we look for another?"[45] The realist preference would be to avoid overextension and becoming embroiled in yet another war in the Middle East. Instead of siding strongly toward one approach or the other, Obama preferred to chart what he considered to be a more pragmatic course that navigates the terrain between power and principle:

> I am very much the internationalist. And I am also an idealist insofar as I believe that we should be promoting values, like democracy and human rights and norms and values, because not only do they serve our interests the more people adopt values that we share—in the same way that, economically, if people adopt rule of law and property rights and so forth, that is to our advantage—but because it makes the world a better place.... Having said that, I also believe that the world is a tough, complicated, messy, mean place, and full of hardship and tragedy. And in order to advance both our security interests and those ideals and values that we care about, we've got to be hard-headed at the same time as we're bighearted, and pick and choose our spots, and recognize that there are going to be times where the best that we can do is to shine a spotlight on something that's terrible, but not believe that we can automatically solve it. There are going to be times where our security interests conflict with our concerns about human rights. There are going to be times where we can do something about innocent people being killed, but there are going to be times where we can't.[46]

Although taking a more pragmatic course between power and principle makes sense, charting this path effectively is extremely challenging. In the case of Syria, U.S. policy took a very public stance rooted in principled idealism, yet was not fully committed to bringing U.S. power to bear on achieving these aims. Moreover, several missteps were taken in managing the elements of realpolitik essential to securing peace and stability and, subsequently, minimizing human suffering.

The Obama administration and its European allies defined the situation in Syria as a conflict emanating from a pro-democracy movement similar to others that characterized the "Arab Spring." Thus the stated aims of policy to address the situation emphasized supporting regime change in Syria rather than stability through a brokered peace agreement that would allow

Assad to remain in power. Initially wary of making a definitive commitment to regime change given the recent experience in Libya, governments on both sides of the Atlantic publicly stated in August 2011 what some policy analysts now refer to as "the magic words": Assad must go. On August 18, Secretary of State Hillary Clinton stated, "The transition to democracy in Syria has begun and it's time for Assad to get out of the way."[47] President Obama echoed this sentiment: "For the sake of the Syrian people, the time has come for President Assad to step aside."[48] These policy pronouncements were coordinated along with those of France, Germany, and the UK who issued similar calls for Assad's ouster. Many inside the Obama administration believed that Assad's hold on power was precarious and that he would soon fall without foreign intervention. As Dennis Ross, former Middle East adviser to Obama, put it, "He thought Assad would go the way Mubarak went."[49] Not surprisingly, American efforts to bring about regime change did not apply much power. Instead, policy took the form of targeted economic sanctions.

Unfortunately for Obama and America's European allies, Assad would not, to quote Dylan Thomas, "go gentle into that good night."[50] At this point, these governments were now bound by their public statements, yet were reluctant to bring significant additional power—particularly military power—to bear on the situation. Obama would later justify American reluctance to use its military power to achieve regime change: "The notion that we could have—in a clean way that didn't commit U.S. military forces—changed the equation on the ground there was never true."[51] This disjuncture between interests defined in terms of principle and interests defined in terms of power not only locked the United States and its EU partners to their preferred outcome but also complicated any efforts to negotiate a political solution. In short, by taking the position that Assad has to go, the United States and its allies made him less inclined to enter into negotiations. Bruce Jones, vice president of the foreign policy program at the Brookings Institution pointed out, "If you call for Assad to go, you dramatically drive up the obstacles to a political settlement. If you're not insisting on him leaving, there are more options. If you say Assad must go as the outcome of a settlement, he has the existential need to stop that settlement."[52] Moreover, by not backing up the principled rhetoric, the U.S.-EU policy likely emboldened Assad not to consider negotiations necessary for his political survival. Jones added, the call for Assad's exit "was a classic case of talking loudly and carrying a small stick."[53]

As the Syrian conflict grew in scale, scope, and gravity, the emphasis on interests defined in terms of principle was not only maintained, but expanded. In addition to the issue of regime change and the promotion of democracy in Syria, American and European rhetoric increasingly focused on defense of human rights and promotion of international humanitarian law in Syria. This raised the question of whether the ICC would have a role to play in this process. On the same day that American and EU leaders called for Assad to step down (August 18, 2011), the Office of the United Nations High Commissioner for Human Rights (OHCHR) released a report that defined the Syrian government's attacks on civilians as crimes against humanity.[54] Moreover, the report urged the UN Security Council to refer the situation to the ICC for investigation.[55] Although the Obama administration did not immediately frame interests in terms of justice, there was a growing linkage created between U.S. interests in Syria and the possible violations of international humanitarian law occurring there. In February 2012, Secretary of State Hillary Clinton declared in a Senate hearing that president Assad "fits the definition of a war criminal."[56] In the summer of 2012, president Obama suggested that continued violations of international humanitarian law would prompt a strong—presumably military—response from the United States. Specifically, Obama stated that the use of chemical or biological weapons by the Assad regime would cross a "redline" and Assad would be held accountable: "We have communicated in no uncertain terms with every player in the region that that's a redline for us and that there would be enormous consequences if we start seeing movement on the chemical weapons front or the use of chemical weapons."[57] Most interpreted Obama's ultimatum as a signal of American resolve to use military power should the "redline" be crossed. However, one year later it appeared that the line had been crossed when reports that rockets carrying sarin were fired at the Ghouta suburbs of Damascus. Western powers believed that only the Syrian government could have carried out the attack. Yet, no military reprisal was forthcoming from the United States in the aftermath of the attack. Instead, a U.S.-Russian proposal to force the Syrian government to relinquish and destroy its chemical weapons stockpile was passed through the UN Security Council.[58] Under the agreement, Syria had until mid-2014 to destroy its chemical weapons stockpile. Airstrikes were eventually initiated by a U.S.-led coalition in September 2014, but Syrian government forces were not the targets. Rather, the airstrikes were used against ISIS targets, one of the groups seeking to overthrow the Assad government.

So what effect did the articulation of interests defined in terms human rights and justice have? It certainly had little deterrent effect: reports of atrocities continued to mount following Hillary Clinton's 2012 statement that Assad "fit the description of a war criminal" and President Obama drew his redline regarding the use of chemical weapons. Moreover, even after the August 2013 attack, numerous reports surfaced that chlorine gas was being used in combat. There were, however, political effects stemming from the legal rhetoric. Just as declaring "Assad must go" most certainly decreased president Assad's motivation to engage in negotiations to find a political resolution to the civil war, declaring him to be a war criminal likely contributed to a reluctance to negotiate a political settlement that would remove him from power. At this point, the war not only involved political survival for the Assad regime, but potential prosecution for Bashar al-Assad himself. In fact, Secretary of State Hillary Clinton acknowledged as much in her February 2012 Senate testimony. During her testimony, Clinton noted that labeling Assad a war criminal would likely make it more difficult to get Assad to step down and thus would reduce the chances of finding a political resolution to ending the violence in Syria.[59] On the other side of a potential bargaining table, labeling President Assad a war criminal no doubt made it more difficult for American and European leaders to soften their insistence that "Assad must go." How could liberal democratic states accept a peace agreement that would allow a war criminal to remain in power?

This insistence that any negotiated settlement must be premised on Assad's removal from power complicated efforts to find a political solution. With no flexibility on this point, the United States was unable to take the lead in promoting a negotiated settlement. Instead, Russia was one of the early proponents of a political solution, hoping that a political compromise might succeed in forwarding two realist-grounded interests: restoring stability in Syria and supporting the continuation of the existing Syrian government with which it was allied. In January 2012, the Russian foreign ministry offered to host "informal talks" between the Syrian government and opposition groups. The next month, the Russian ambassador to the United Nations, Vitaly Churkin, offered a three-point plan that reportedly included a willingness to "find an elegant way for Assad to step aside."[60] Presumably, an "elegant way" meant that Assad's exit would not be immediate and that the existing government would not be subject to regime change after Assad's eventual departure. However, as one European diplomat remarked, "At the time, the West was fixated on Assad leaving."[61]

The inability of the world's major powers to find common political ground on Syria resulted in a number of failed attempts at reaching a political solution to the violence. The failure to secure peace between 2012 and 2016 has produced heartbreaking effects: nearly one-half million Syrians have been killed as a direct result of the war, and the conflict has created nearly 5 million refugees and more than 6.6 million internally displaced people (IDPs).[62] The large flow of refugees seeking protection has created subsequent crises in the EU and the Mediterranean region. In the face of these striking numbers, on December 18, 2015, Secretary of State John Kerry announced a profound shift in U.S. policy: the United States was abandoning its demand that Assad step down as a precondition for a peace agreement. Kerry explained, "We began to really come to the reality that this demand was in fact prolonging the war, creating greater agony and suffering, and not getting us anywhere in a stalemate."[63] It is not clear as of this writing whether the change in the U.S. position will facilitate a return to peace and stability in Syria. However, having the United States and Russia on the same page will no doubt be integral to the peace process.

So what lessons does the Syrian civil war have when considering the relationship between power and principle and the role of international justice? Most obviously, Syria makes clear how difficult finding the right mix between power and principle can be. Moreover, there is no one clearly superior option. However, the difficulties the United States and its European allies have encountered in crafting an effective response does provide important lessons for the future. Probably most important lesson is to make sure that action matches rhetoric. In the U.S. case, strong public pronouncements of "redlines" and that "Assad must go" was not followed with equally strong state action. Policy not only resulted in a loss of American credibility but also likely emboldened Assad and his Russian and Iranian allies and made them less willing to make significant concessions toward a negotiated peace settlement. The experience with the Syrian situation has given reason for pause among those who strongly pressed for strong idealistic public pronouncements in the war's early stages. Among them, Anne-Marie Slaughter, Hillary Clinton's director of policy and planning at the State Department, remarked, "In some ways, those of us who want to see more action will often take whatever we can get. So if we're not willing to do more, at least we can make a statement to let people know you're with them. Now many of us think if that's all you can do, maybe you're better off not speaking. If we're going to get people's hopes up when we're not willing to do more, we need to be honest about that and maybe it's better to remain silent."[64]

Idealists may argue that the central lesson is that liberal states simply need to be true to their principles. However, policymakers face real and potentially significant domestic political costs. Until those potential political costs can be reduced, it would be naïve to presume that policymakers would not take them seriously into account. Thus, policymakers find themselves seeking to find that balance between interests defined in terms of principle and interests defined in terms of power. As President Obama put it, "If it is possible to do good at a bearable cost, to save lives, we will do it."[65] The key determinant, of course, is what costs are considered "bearable." Ultimately, it is paramount that policymakers define these parameters at the outset and design policy and resultant public statements so that they are consistent with this calculus.

Another key lesson from the Syrian situation is that great-power cooperation, particularly among the permanent members of the UN Security Council, is essential. Achieving the cooperation necessary requires a deft hand in navigating the realpolitik involved in great power relations. Although the failure to more actively seek a political settlement early in the conflict may be attributed to the United States' miscalculation of Assad's ability to remain in power, it was certainly a missed opportunity with profound implications. Russia's early gestures at seeking a political compromise were largely seen as a thinly veiled attempt to keep their ally Assad in power. Moreover, the idea of granting Russian president Vladimir Putin a leading role as peacemaker was never warmly received in Washington or Europe. This sentiment certainly grew with Western concerns over Russia's actions in Crimea and Eastern Ukraine, as well as accusations regarding Russsia's role in the downing of Malaysian Flight 17.[66] Before U.S. credibility regarding potential intervention in Syria was weakened by its failure to back up its idealistic rhetoric, the Russians appeared keenly interested in finding a political solution. Granting the Russians a leading role in securing a negotiated peace held considerable promise because it offered strong incentives to the Russians to make sure that the process was successful. Putin has made it clear that he wants Russia to be considered a major player in international politics in the wake of its "humiliation" at the end of the Cold War.[67] Facilitating a negotiated peace would not only have given Putin what he wanted, but would have made Russia a stakeholder in the outcome. Failure of the Syrian government to negotiate in good faith and comply with commitments made under a peace settlement would reflect badly on Putin and the Russians. It would seem that the early stages of the Syrian conflict represented a unique opportunity to lock Russian interests into achieving and enforcing the peace. Unfortunately, once it became more confident that Western powers were reluctant to become militarily engaged in Syria, it appears that the Russians recalculated their interests and their policies. Although they remain publicly supportive of finding a political solution, they have steadily extended additional military support to the Assad government.

Efforts to refer the Syrian situation to the ICC through the UN Security Council certainly did not facilitate Russian cooperation in stopping the conflict. In fact, it is more likely that the gesture further antagonized the Russians who had early on insisted that the ICC had no role to play in Syria until peace was achieved. The effort to secure a Security Council referral took place in May 2014 when a proposal was forwarded by France with the support of sixty-five countries. Russia had clearly signaled its intent to veto any such proposal well in advance of the vote. Vitaly Churkin, Russia's ambassador to the UN, suggested that calling for a vote on the proposal was simply a "publicity stunt" and that referring the Syrian situation to the ICC would hamper any efforts to secure a negotiated peace agreement.[68] Even though they knew the proposal would not pass because of Russia's (and China's) veto, supporters insisted that bringing it up for a vote still had symbolic and moral value.[69] After the vote, the Americans and Europeans were quick to publicly express their outrage. British Foreign Secretary William Hague described the veto as "indefensible," while France's representative to the Council suggested that the action was "an insult to humanity."[70] U.S. ambassador to the UN, Samantha Power, added, "The Syrian people will not see justice today. They will see crime, but not punishment. The vetoes today have prevented the victims of atrocities from testifying at The Hague."[71]

Although the moral value of bringing the proposal up for a vote is debatable, the political results are more clear cut. Putting the proposal up for a vote after Russia had signaled its opposition clearly antagonized the Russians, as did the public comments that followed the vote. The Russians viewed the attempt to gain a Security Council referral as detrimental to the unity among the council's permanent members that was seen as a necessary condition to achieve a negotiated settlement in Syria. Ambassador Churkin remarked,

> It is more difficult to figure out the motives of France which initiated this draft and put it to vote, being fully aware in advance of the fate it will meet. One can hear many complaints about the lack of unity on Syria within the Security Council, among P5. Indeed, when that unity is present we manage to achieve concrete positive results. Among them is undoubtedly the Security Council Resolution 2118 on the destruction of the Syrian chemical stockpile—that program is about to be successfully completed. Another important benchmark was the Security Council Resolution 2139 on humanitarian issues. P5 unity is important. After all, it is for a reason that France has been pushing for P5's engagement in the political settlement of the crisis, having failed however to advance any positive substantive ideas. Then why deal such a blow to P5 unity at this stage?[72]

Although idealists may see moral value in speaking justice to power, doing so did little to alleviate the human suffering taking place in Syria. Nor did it facilitate Russian cooperation whose foreign policy is generally based on a realist perspective. Moreover, as was the case with the creation of the ad hoc tribunals, it provided a means through which liberal democratic countries could appear to be making an assertive attempt at dealing with the crisis without incurring the material costs or political risks associated with a more assertive intervention. Syria offers important lessons regarding the need for great-power cooperation, particularly among the five permanent members of the UN Security Council, the role of realpolitik in achieving cooperation, and the need to effectively bring together both power and principle to address human suffering.

In some ways, the principled rhetoric of the ICC's most ardent supporters echoes the idealism of the interwar period of which E. H. Carr was so critical in his seminal book, *The Twenty Years' Crisis*.[73] Carr was critical of the growing assumption during that time that human beings could agree on abstract normative principles to guide the behavior of states and that, once these were ensconced in international law, they would influence nations to act with greater justice.[74] In contrast to the idealists, Carr argued that ideals could only be effectively pursued if policymakers were sensitive to the distribution of power and to national interests defined in terms of power. More recently, Robert Keohane forwarded a similar stance with regard to institutional design. Among his "ten maxims," Keohane argues that "institutional designers should make differential concessions to states, deferring more to those states whose participation is essential to make agreements effective."[75] He adds that "we need some system in which the powerful states will find it in their interest to participate. . . . Institutions should reflect power relations, and they can only operate within the bounded scope of power relations."[76]

What exactly does this involve in the context of the ICC? Most importantly, it requires that idealism give way to higher degrees of pragmatism than has been reflected by many of the court's most ardent supporters. Because international criminal law requires material power to back it up, it is necessary to fit the principles and practice of the law within the hierarchical framework of the existing international order. Just as all states are not equal in the existing international political order, the international legal order pertaining to the atrocities regime should not be too stringent in its adherence to the principle of equality under the law. This is a necessary quid pro quo exchanged for the special responsibilities bestowed on those called on to provide the power necessary to enforce international law.[77] David Scheffer made essentially the same argument during the Rome Conference, noting that "the requirements of those few countries that are still in a position to actually do something by way of accomplishing various human objectives simply have got to be accommodated. And you can't approach this on the model of equality of all states."[78] Without the support of powerful states, particularly those more inclined to take a more central role in applying power in defense of human rights (such as the United States), high-minded principles of justice may be successful only in producing justice for justice's sake. Some have suggested that the failure to take this view into account during the critical design process may have produced a self-defeating court. For example, Jack Goldsmith writes, "An ICC without U.S. support—and indeed, with probable U.S. opposition—will not only fail to live up to its expectations. It may well do actual harm by discouraging the United States from engaging in various human rights–protecting activities. And this, in turn, may increase rather than decrease the impunity of those who violate human rights."[79]

The more idealistic among scholars and practitioners of international law are likely to take exception to calls for sacrificing legal principle in the name of political pragmatism. This was certainly true of the more idealistic members of the Like-Minded Group and members of human rights NGOs participating in the Rome Conference deliberations in 1998. This group already lamented the "unfortunate" design concessions made in the Rome Statute and felt that too much had already been sacrificed at the altar of power politics.[80] In contrast to the idealists, pragmatists give priority to the ultimate goals of institutions and seek to find the most effective ways of achieving their desired end results. In the case of international criminal law, pragmatists do not seek to achieve "perfect justice," but rather a regime that best reduces the probability of future violations that would produce human suffering. Interestingly, as shown in chapter 4, the chief prosecutors of the ICC seem to be more pragmatic about the pursuit of justice than the idealistic international lawyers and activists who were instrumental in the court's initial design. In practice, the court has shown itself to be sensitive to the interests of powerful states, though stopping well short of being completely beholden to them. In time, this de facto sensitivity to power relationships and political realities may whittle away at U.S. fears of an overzealous court that form the basis of American resistance to joining the ICC. Should the U.S. eventually join the ICC, this, in turn, may promote more cooperation for the court by Russia and China.

So does that mean normative principles are irrelevant? Absolutely not. Considering the relationship between power and principle in the context of international criminal courts calls to question the role of law in international society. Idealists see norms as transformative. In contrast to the idealistic perspective, a pragmatic view of norms regarding individual criminal accountability for violations of international humanitarian law might suggest that their role is not to redefine international order through prosecution and punishment. Rather, they are a vehicle to articulate and practice values. Through the process of adjudication, law and courts refresh these norms for international society and help to further the normative consciousness of its members. Principles ensconced in international courts may become an important element that defines a common identity among the states in the international system. In other words, abiding by these principles not only shapes how actors in the international system self-identify but also create an element of a common social identity among all members of international society that have internalized these norms.

This is a book about the relationship between power and principle—a relationship that creates one of the most crucial dynamics in international politics. E. H. Carr was among those who recognized the significance of this relationship. Carr described the antithesis of utopia (i.e., principle) and reality (i.e., power) as being fundamental to international politics: "Most fundamental of all, the antithesis of utopia and reality is rooted in a different conception of the relationship between politics and ethics. The antithesis between the world of value and the world of nature, already implicit in the dichotomy of purpose and fact, is deeply embedded in the human consciousness and in political thought."[81] Although this dichotomy influences international politics in myriad ways, it is perhaps most profoundly felt in the politics surrounding international criminal courts. As shown in this book, the creation of the ICC does not signal the ultimate triumph of principle over power, nor is it the harbinger of a fundamental reordering of international society. Power politics have influenced all aspects of regime formation and continue to have a substantial impact on the continuing operation of the court. This does not, however, suggest that the continuing presence and influence of power necessarily come at a cost to the promotion of human rights and the alleviation of human suffering. Although principle and power are often presented as opposing forces in international politics, nations need not choose one over the other in responding to the world's most pressing global challenges. Instead, effective governance involves managing the complex politics that operates *between* power and principle.[82]

Notes

Prologue

1. Downes 2008, 1.
2. Rummel 1994, 9.
3. Ibid.

Introduction

Epigraph. Annan 1997, 365.

1. Hans Corell, quoted in UN News Centre, "Ratification Ceremony at UN Paves Way for International Criminal Court," April 11, 2002, http://www.un.org/apps/news/story.asp?NewsID=3360&Cr=icc&Cr1#.VPcXfS4V7ng (accessed March 4, 2015).
2. Bosco 2014, 2.
3. Schiff 2008, 259.
4. Bass 2000.
5. Sikkink 2011, 5.
6. Schiff 2008, 41.
7. S.C. Res. 827, UN SCOR, UN Doc. S/RES/827 (1993).

8. Morris and Scharf 1995, 391.

9. Prosecutor v. Tadic, IT-94-1-AR72, P77 (1995).

10. Williams 2001.

11. Bass 2003, 82.

12. Schabas 2011.

13. C. A. Smith 2012; Bosco 2014.

14. In July 2012, Lubanga was found guilty of war crimes stemming from his use of child soldiers and sentenced to fourteen years in prison. See BBC News Africa, "DR Congo Warlord Thomas Lubanga Sentenced to 14 Years," July 10, 2012, http://www.bbc.com/news/world-africa-18779726 (accessed March 4, 2015).

15. ICC-02/05-01/09 (March 4, 2009).

16. The arrest warrant on the charge of genocide came separately in July of 2010.

17. See Luis Moreno Ocampo, "Prosecutor's Statement on the Prosecutor's Application for a Warrant of Arrest under Article 58 against Omar Hassan Ahmad al Bashir," July 14, 2008, OTP, ICC, The Hague, http://www.icc-cpi.int/NR/rdonlyres/A2BA9996-67C3-4A5F-9AD2-B20A7FD2D176/277757/ICCOTPST20080714ENG.pdf (accessed February 16, 2015).

18. Current status information is available at the ICC web page, http://www.icc-cpi.int/en_menus/icc/Pages/default.aspx (accessed March 4, 2015).

19. Slaughter 2004.

20. BBC News, "Jordan Pilot Hostage Moaz al-Kasabeh 'Burned Alive,'" February 3, 2015, http://www.bbc.com/news/world-middle-east-31121160 (accessed February 17, 2015).

21. CNN, "ISIS Video Appears to Show Beheadings of Egyptian Coptic Christians in Libya," February 16, 2015, http://www.cnn.com/2015/02/15/middleeast/isis-video-beheadings-christians (accessed February 17, 2015).

22. Scheffer 2012, 503; Bassiouni 2005.

23. Mearsheimer and Walt 2013, 432.

24. See Sil and Katzenstein 2010.

25. Bueno de Mesquita 1996.

26. Cf. Pace and Thieroff 1999; Glasius 2006; Kelley 2007; Schiff 2008; Struett 2008; Simmons and Danner 2010; Sikkink 2011.

27. Two notable exceptions are C. A. Smith 2012 and Bosco 2014. See also Goodliffe and Hawkins 2009 and Goodliffe et al. 2012.

28. E.g., cf. Arieff et al. 2011; Luckscheiter and Maas-Albert 2012; Hoile 2014.

29. Cf. Hafner-Burton 2009.

30. Stone 2011.

31. Sil and Katzenstein 2010.

32. Koremenos, Lipson, and Snidal 2001.

33. On precision and legalization, see Goldstein et al. 2001.

34. Walt 2002.

35. Grotius [1625] 1962.

36. The former draws on Ikenberry (2001) and Stone (2011). The latter draws on Aggarwal (1998; 2006), Young (1999); Raustiala and Victor (2004); and Alter and Meunier (2006; 2009).

37. Putnam 1988.
38. Busby 2010, 246.
39. Guatemala deposited its instruments of accession to the ICC on April 2, 2012.
40. Office of the Prosecutor 2010, 7.
41. Fatou Bensouda, quoted in D. Smith 2012.
42. E.g., cf. Arieff et al. 2011; Luckscheiter and Maas-Albert 2012; Hoile 2014.
43. On "institutional capture" regarding the ICC, see Bosco 2014.
44. Author interview with Luis Moreno Ocampo, February 6, 2015.
45. Bosco 2009.

1. Power and Principle from Nuremberg to The Hague

Epigraph. Robert H. Jackson, Opening Statement before the International Military Tribunal, November 21, 1945, http://www.roberthjackson.org/the-man/speeches-articles/speeches/speeches-by-robert-h-jackson/opening-statement-before-the-international-military-tribunal (accessed February 25, 2014).

1. Conot 1983. The London Charter is also known as the Nuremberg Charter.
2. Heller 2011.
3. Bass 2000, 203.
4. Ehrenfreund 2007.
5. Quoted in Taylor 2008, 387.
6. Schabas 2006.
7. Beres 1988, 124.
8. Bass 2000, 28.
9. Finnemore and Sikkink 1998. Much of this body of research either draws specifically on this framework or mirrors its major characteristics.
10. Schiff 2008, 15.
11. Sikkink 2011. See also Broomhall 2003; Pace and Thieroff 1999; Glasius 2006; Struett 2008; Fehl 2004; Schiff 2008.
12. Sikkink 2011, introduction.
13. Buergenthal 1997.
14. Glasius 2006, xiii.
15. E.g., cf. Schiff 2008, 27; Schabas 2011; Simmons and Danner 2010, 228.
16. Cf. Bass 2000; Rudolph 2001.
17. This is consistent with the realist tradition in international relations theory. See Walt 1997 and Booth 2011.
18. Cf. Carr 1939; Morgenthau 1985 [1948]; Waltz 1979; Mearsheimer 2001.
19. Keohane 1986, 4–8.
20. However, no specific crime of genocide was articulated under the Nuremberg Charter. Crimes related to the Holocaust were adjudicated under the category of "crimes against humanity."
21. Bass 2000, 148.
22. Hermann Goering, quoted in Moghalu 2006, 30.
23. Curtis LeMay, quoted in Rhodes 1995, 48.

24. Ikenberry 2001.

25. Ginsburgs 1996.

26. Moscow Declaration on Atrocities, November 1, 1943. http://www.cvce.eu/content/publication/2004/2/12/699fc03f-19a1-47f0-aec0-73220489efcd/publishable_en.pdf (accessed February 20, 2015).

27. Bass 2000, 195.

28. Ibid., 160.

29. British Foreign Office papers 371/39202/13673; 371/39202/16398, cited in Bass 2000, 183.

30. Smith 1982, 92.

31. Harry Truman, quoted in Bass 2000, 174.

32. British Foreign Office paper 371/50988/U7378, September 10, 1945, cited in Bass 2000, 174.

33. Trainin 1944, 47–48.

34. Hirsch 2008, 710.

35. D. Maxwell Fife, quoted in Hirsch 2008, 708.

36. Grotius [1625] 1962; Christopher 1994.

37. Walzer 1977, 21.

38. See Grotius [1925] 1962, 641–62.

39. Clausewitz 2008; Walzer 1977, 23.

40. Ikenberry 2001.

41. Hirsch 2008, 722.

42. Ibid., 722.

43. Zorya and Lebedeva 1989, 121.

44. Marrus 1997, 133.

45. Truman to Thomas Murray, January 19, 1953. Harry S. Truman Papers (www.trumanlibrary.org).

46. Truman to Samuel Cavert, August 11, 1945. See also Truman to Richard Russell, August 9, 1945, where he writes, "I certainly regret the necessity of wiping out whole populations . . . and, for your information, I am not going to do it unless it is absolutely necessary. . . . My object is to save as many American lives as possible." Harry S. Truman Papers (www.trumanlibrary.org).

47. On soft power, see Nye 2004.

48. Carr 1939, 132.

49. Robert Jackson, quoted in Bass 2000, 199.

50. Hirsch 2008, 714.

51. Ibid., 713.

52. Bass 2000.

53. Bostdorff 2008.

54. Harry S. Truman, "Address before the Attorney General's Conference on Law Enforcement Problems," February 15, 1950, The American Presidency Project, compiled by John Woolley and Gerhard Peters, http://www.presidency.ucsb.edu/ws/?pid=13707 (accessed February 11, 2013).

55. Robert Jackson, quoted in Conot 1983, 14 (emphasis added).

56. London Charter for the International Military Tribunal, The Avalon Project, Yale School of Law, http://avalon.law.yale.edu/imt/imtconst.asp (accessed February 11, 2013).

57. C.A. Smith 2012, 80.

58. *Time,* May 20, 1946, 24.

59. Hirsch 2008, 730.

60. Tokyo Charter, reprinted in Minear 1971, 185–92.

61. C.A. Smith 2012, 96. See also Horowitz 1950, 480.

62. Douglas MacArthur, Proclamation by the Supreme Commander for the Allied Powers, January 19, 1946, reprinted in Minear 1971, 183.

63. Röling and Cassese 1993, 5.

64. Joseph Keenan, quoted in Baldwin 1946, 36.

65. Piccigallo 1979.

66. Keenan, quoted in Minear 1971, 50.

67. Robert Cryer and Neil Boister, *Documents on the Tokyo International Military Tribunal: Charter, Indictments, and Judgements*, vol. 1. (Oxford: Oxford University Press, 2008), xxxviii.

68. Statement of Justice Jaranilla of the Philippines in the Concurring Opinion, quoted in Minear 1971, 100.

69. G. Acquaviva, N. Combs, M. Heikkila, S. Linton, Y. McDermott, and S. Vasiliev, "Trial Process," in *International Criminal Procedure: Principles and Rules*, ed. Göran Sluiter, Hakan Friman, Suzannah Linton, Salvatore Zappala, and Sergey Vasiliev, 489–938 (Oxford: Oxford University Press, 2013). For critiques of the fairness of the trial's proceedings, cf. Minear 1971; Röling and Cassese 1993; C.A. Smith 2012.

70. Tokyo Charter, reprinted in Minear 1971, 183–92.

71. See Röling and Cassese 1993; C.A. Smith 2012; Minear 1971.

72. MacArthur, quoted in Piccigallo 1979, 46.

73. MacArthur 1964, 287–88.

74. Piccigallo 1979, 17.

75. Minear 1971, 113.

76. Conot 1983, 198.

77. Taylor 2012.

78. ILC 1950.

79. Taylor 2012.

80. Falk 2009, 93.

81. UN General Assembly, Convention on the Prevention and Punishment of the Crime of Genocide, adopted December 9, 1948, Article II.

82. Ibid., Article I.

83. UN General Assembly, Universal Declaration of Human Rights, adopted December 10, 1948, http://www.un.org/en/documents/udhr/index.shtml (accessed February 25, 2013).

84. Ignatieff 2001, 81.

85. UN Universal Declaration of Human Rights, preamble.

86. Ignatieff 2001, 81.

87. ILC, Principle of International Law Recognized in the Charter of the Nuremberg Tribunal in the Judgment of the Tribunal (New York: United Nations, 1950). http://legal.un.org/ilc/texts/instruments/english/draft%20articles/7_1_1950.pdf (accessed March 6, 2014).

88. Ibid.

89. See Willaim Pfaff, "Cambodia Invasion Reminder of U.S. Political Use of Military," *Chicago Tribune*, April 25, 2000, http://articles.chicagotribune.com/2000-04-25/news/0004250036_1_khmer-rouge-cambodian-communist-vietnamese (accessed March 3, 2014).

90. See, e.g., a report issued by the Tibet Justice Center, http://www.tibetjustice.org/reports/occupied.html (accessed March 3, 2014).

91. "Report of the Special Committee on the Problem of Hungary," UN General Assembly, 11th sess., suppl. 18 (A/3592) (1957), http://mek.oszk.hu/01200/01274/01274.pdf (accessed March 3, 2014).

92. International Commission of Jurists, "The Question of Tibet and the Rule of Law," (Geneva, 1959), http://www.claudearpi.net/maintenance/uploaded_pics/1959TheQuestionofTibetandtheRuleofLaw.pdf (accessed March 3, 2014).

93. Olson and Roberts 1998.

94. See, e.g., Hee-Kyung 2013.

95. However, it has been argued that accountability was exacted through domestic legal institutions rather than international courts. See Sikkink 2011.

96. Harry S. Truman, Address Before a Joint Session of Congress, March 12, 1947, The Avalon Project,http://avalon.law.yale.edu/20th_century/trudoc.asp (accessed March 6, 2014).

97. See, e.g., Schmitz 2006.

98. Robertson 2012, 52.

99. Ibid., 58.

100. Schiff 2008, 29.

101. Robertson 2012, 54.

102. GA Res. 897 (IX) (1954), http://daccess-dds-ny.un.org/doc/RESOLUTION/GEN/NR0/096/32/IMG/NR009632.pdf?OpenElement (accessed March 3, 2014).

103. Bassiouni 2011, 177.

104. Ibid.

105. Schiff 2008, 39.

106. Cf. Bass 2000; Simmons and Danner 2010.

107. Mueller 2009, 301.

108. Gutman 1993.

109. Neier 1998, 135.

110. Clarke 1997.

111. Nye 2004, 11.

112. Cf. Page and Shapiro 1983; Hartley and Russett 1992; Holsti 1996.

113. Logan 1996, 156.

114. Kull and Ramsay 2003, 71.

115. Wybrow 2003, 66.

116. Logan 1996.

117. Weiss 1995.

118. Logan 1996, 156.

119. Silber and Little 1997.

120. Des Forges 1999; Gourevitch 1998; Barnett 2002.

121. Kuperman 2000, 101.

122. Weiss 1995, 171.

123. Valentino 2006, 733.

124. Conway-Lanz 2006.

125. Valentino 2011, 65.

126. This budget was set for the first six months of operation; UN Doc. A/48/765 (1993).

127. Neier 1998, 129.

128. P5 refers to the five permanent members of the UN Security Council—namely, China, France, Russia, the United Kingdom, and the United States.

129. Baranovsky 2000.

130. Tsygankov 2013, 57.

131. Andrei Kozyrev, quoted in Tsygankov 2013, 57.

132. Tsygankov 2013, 74.

133. Gorokhov and Gorovstov 1998, 71. See also "Bill Clinton, Boris Yeltsin, and U.S.-Russian Relations," Milestones 1993–2000, Office of the Historian, U.S. Department of State, https://history.state.gov/milestones/1993-2000/clinton-yeltsin (accessed March 8, 2014).

134. Smith 2008, 3.

135. Yeh 1993, 124.

136. Gross domestic product based on PPP valuation of country GDP (current international dollars). Figures rounded to the nearest billion U.S. dollars.

137. Wu 2001, 295.

138. Jacobson and Oksenberg 1990.

139. See BBC News, "Timeline: Tiananmen Protests," June 2, 2014, http://www.bbc.com/news/world-asia-china-27404764 (accessed February 22, 2015).

140. Ross, Whiting, and Harding 1990.

141. Lanteigne 2009.

142. Roy 1998, 35.

143. Krasner 1999.

144. Wu 2009.

145. Wu 2001, 298.

146. Lampton 1994.

147. Zhao 1996.

148. S.C. Res. 827, UN SCOR, UN Doc. S/RES/827 (1993).

149. Yet, the Security Council retained significant control. Although judges are nominated and elected by the General Assembly, the list of nominees must be approved by the Security Council. Moreover, the chief prosecutor is appointed by the Security Council on the recommendation of the secretary general.

150. The first chief prosecutor chosen was Richard Goldstone, justice of the South African Constitutional Court. Subsequent chief prosecutors included Louise Arbour,

justice of the Court of Appeal in Ontario, Canada, and Carla del Pointe, the attorney general from Switzerland.

151. *Annual Report of the International Tribunal for the Prosecution of Persons Responsible for Serious Violations of International Humanitarian Law Committed in the Territory of the Former Yugoslavia since 1991*, UN Doc. A/49/342 (1994), http://www.icty.org/x/file/About/Reports%20and%20Publications/AnnualReports/annual_report_1994_en.pdf (accessed March 10, 2014).

152. Ibid.

153. Schrag 1995, 191.

154. *Annual Report . . . since 1991*, UN Doc. A/49/342 (1994), 14–15.

155. Peskin 2008.

156. Bakuramutsa 1995, 645.

157. LCHR 1997, 23.

158. Alvarez 1999, 397.

159. Bakuramutsa 1995, 648.

160. Howland and Calathes 1998, 161.

161. UN Doc. A/54/646 (1999).

162. Peskin 2008.

163. Cf. Peskin 2005; Creta 1998; Hayden 1999; Johnson 1998; Jokic 2001.

164. Schabas 2010, 537.

165. Cassese 2009, 22.

166. Harmon and Gaynor 2004, 403.

167. Two recent works seek to address this lacuna: C.A. Smith 2012 (dealing with international tribunals generally) and Bosco 2014 (dealing specifically with the experience of the ICC).

168. Snyder and Vinjamuri 2003–4, 5.

169. Franck 1990.

170. Goldstone 2004, 383.

171. See chapter 4.

2. Nested Interests and the Institutional Design of the International Criminal Court

Epigraph. Bull 1977, 76.

1. The statute passed by a vote of 120 in favor, 7 opposed, and 21 abstentions; Lee 1999, 26.

2. Scheffer 2012, 223.

3. Kofi Annan, quoted in Lee 1999, ix.

4. Schiff 2008, 1.

5. Cf. Pace and Thieroff 1999; Glasius 2006; Struett 2008; Sikkink 2011; Schiff 2008; Fehl 2004; Deitelhoff 2009.

6. Simmons and Danner 2010, 236. They add that support will also come from states with a recent history of civil wars.

7. The former draws on Ikenberry (2001) and Stone (2011). The latter draws on Aggarwal (1998, 2006); Young (1999); Raustiala and Victor (2004); Alter and Meunier (2006, 2009).

8. Rationalist IR scholars commonly explain states' willingness to join and comply with international institutions as a function of the benefits they offer—benefits they cannot realize unilaterally. See Keohane 1982, 1984. For a broad overview, see Hasenclever, Rittberger, and Mayer 1997.

9. Danner and Voeten 2010, 43.

10. Kelley 2007, 577.

11. Deitelhoff 2009, 33–34.

12. Ibid., 34.

13. Schiff 2008, 6.

14. Sikkink 2011, 232.

15. Schabas 2011, 23. See also Weller 2002; Bassiouni 1998.

16. Kelley 2007, 580.

17. Franceschet 2009, 200.

18. On the normative discourse argument, see Deitelhoff (2009); on civil-society actors, see Glasius (2006) and Struett (2008). In many ways, Sikkink (2011) combines facets of both in her argument.

19. See, e.g., the review of Struett (2008) in Peskin (2009).

20. Cf. Neier 1998; Cassese 2004; Minow 1998; Rotberg and Thompson 2000.

21. A "dependence network" is defined as a group of "international partners on whom they depend for a diverse set of goods that range from trade and security to votes and support in international organizations." See Goodliffe et al., 2012, 131. A similar argument was made in an earlier work by Goodliffe and Hawkins (2009).

22. Goodliffe et al. 2012, 132.

23. Goodliffe and Hawkins 2009.

24. Kelley 2007.

25. Sikkink 2011, 232.

26. Schabas 2006, 19.

27. Stone 2011, 2.

28. Koremenos, Lipson, and Snidal 2001.

29. Wendt 2001, 1035.

30. Krasner 1985, 1991; Keohane 2006.

31. Ikenberry 2001.

32. A specific, though informal, spheres-of-influence agreement was reached between Churchill and Stalin during the Yalta Conference. See Larson 1985.

33. Hoopes and Brinkley 1997.

34. France was added to the four during the San Francisco Conference.

35. Hurd 2008, 89; see also Hoopes and Brinkley 1997, 198.

36. Hurd 2008, 85–86.

37. Bosco 2009, 3.

38. Cronin and Hurd 2008; Bosco 2009.

39. Cronin and Hurd 2008, 3.

40. On hierarchy in international relations, see Lake 2009.
41. Raustiala and Victor 2004.
42. Cf. Aggarwal 1998, 2006; Abbott and Snidal 2006; Alter and Meunier 2006, 2009; Young 1999.
43. Oran Young (1999, 167) refers to these arrangements as "the principles and practices that constitute the deep structure of international society as a whole."
44. Ibid.
45. Vinod Aggarwal (2006) refers to this type of arrangement as "parallel" or "horizontal" institutions.
46. Ibid., 1.
47. Alter and Meunier 2006; Davis 2009; Hafner-Burton 2009.
48. On the distinction of Westphalian sovereignty from other forms of sovereignty, see Krasner 1999.
49. C. A. Smith 2012, 188. Smith's statement is consistent with the literature on commitment to human rights institutions more generally. Doyle and Gardner (2003, 3) suggest that "the most transformative aspect of the human rights regime for the international system is found not in its growth in scope, instruments, implementation, and players but in its impact on a fundamental principle of international relations: state sovereignty." See also Simmons 2009, 24.
50. Matas 1994.
51. Krasner 1999.
52. Abbott 1999.
53. Schabas 2004.
54. Schabas 2006, Bass 2000.
55. Sandholtz 2008, 131.
56. Organski and Kugler 1980.
57. Ibid., 19–20.
58. I use the notation G20-DN to distinguish this group from the G20 group of major economies.
59. Brasilia Declaration, http://www.itamaraty.gov.br/temas-mais-informacoes/temas-mais-informacoes/saiba-mais-ibas/documentos-emitidos-pelos-chefes-de-estado-e-de/brasilia-declaration/view (accessed November 12, 2013).
60. Ibid., Art. 4. (n4).
61. Ibid., Art. 13. (n4).
62. On hierarchy in international order, see Lake 2009.
63. Maswood 2007, 43 (emphasis added).
64. Organski and Kugler 1980.
65. Schabas 2006, 7.
66. United Nations 1994.
67. ICC Legal Tools, http://www.legal-tools.org/en/what-are-the-icc-legal-tools (accessed November 12, 2013).
68. Nye 2004.
69. Values range from 1 (free) to 7 (not free).
70. Logged, using the data from Simmons and Danner (2010).
71. Bass 2000.

72. Simmons and Danner 2010.

73. Data from Simmons and Danner (2010).

74. Goldstone and Bass 2000, 58.

75. USUN Press Release No. 182, November 1, 1995, 3, 5, http://www.state.gov/documents/organization/65827.pdf.

76. UK Mission to the UN, Press Release 32/95, April 7, 1995, 6. https://www.legal-tools.org/uploads/tx_ltpdb/doc19239.pdf. This point was reiterated in other official statements. In August, 1997, the British mission to the UN declared, "A permanent international criminal court would enable that work to begin more speedily when it is next required; would remove the need for an ad hoc decision that authorized legal processes with respect to that particular country; and would enable its lawyers to retain expertise and authority in this specialized field." See UK Mission to the UN Press Release, August 4, 1997, 1.

77. Author's interview with Cherif Bassouni, vice chairman of the PrepCom delegations, November 9, 2011.

78. Statement of the representative of the Russian Federation to the Ad Hoc Committee on the Establishment of an International Criminal Court, April 5, 1995. https://www.legal-tools.org/en/browse/record/463fff/.

79. PrepCom 1996, L2776 April 4, http://www.un.org/press/en/1996/19960404.12776.html (emphasis added).

80. Hall 1997, 182.

81. Scheffer 2012, 173.

82. Author interview with Bassouni, November 9, 2011.

83. Scheffer 2012, 176.

84. Statement by Hans-Peter Kaul, August 4, 1997, ICC Legal Tools, http://www.legal-tools.org/en/terms-and-conditions-of-use/forPage/%252Fen%252Fgo-to-database%252F.

85. Lorenzo Ferrarnin, quoted in UN Press Release GA/L/3009, October 28, 1996.

86. PrepCom 1996, UN Doc. L/2775 (April 3).

87. PrepCom 1996, UN Doc. L/2776 (April 4).

88. Simonovic 1999, 445.

89. PrepCom 1996, Proceedings of the Preparatory Committee during the Period March 25–April 12, 1996, UN Doc. A/AC.249/CRP.5 (April 8).

90. PrepCom 1996, UN Doc. L/2777, 1–2 (April 4).

91. PrepCom 1996, UN Doc. L/2777 (April 4).

92. UN Press Release GA/L/3009, October 28, 1996.

93. PrepCom 1996, UN Doc. L/2777 (April 4).

94. Lee 1999, 616. See also UN Doc. A/C.6/53/SR.12 (October 22, 1998).

95. Indeed, Coffee Club members strongly opposed the G4 petitions for acceptance on a reconstituted Security Council.

96. "Open the Club," *Economist*, August 29, 1992, 10.

97. Wedgwood 1999, 98.

98. "India Blasts Special Treatment for Security Council," *Terraviva,* June 17, 1998, http://www.ips.org/icc/tv170604.htm (accessed December 16, 2011).

99. Even though the G4 did not abandon their goals of council reform and permanent membership, debates made clear that any future reform would not likely afford veto privileges to new permanent council members.

100. "India Blasts Special Treatment for Security Council."

101. Steinke 2012, 103–4.

102. Steinke 2012, 106.

103. Guatemala submitted its instrument of accession to the ICC on April 2, 2012.

104. Lee 1999, 600. See also UN Doc. A/C.6/53/SR.12 (October 22, 1998).

105. Lee 1999, 587–88.

106. Statement by Manuel de Jesus Pirez Perez, November 1, 2007, http://www.iccnow.org/documents/Cuba.pdf (accessed December 6, 2011).

107. Liberal democracy is significant at the .01 level (p=.002), whereas NGO activity is significant at the .10 level (p = .085).

108. Hafner-Burton 2008.

109. Clark 2010, 1113.

110. Kress and von Holtzendorff 2010, 1194.

111. Van Schaack 2010–11, 518.

112. Ibid., 518–19.

113. Kress and von Holtzendorff 2010, 1195.

114. Stephen J. Rapp, Statement to the Assembly of States Parties at the Kampala Review Conference, November 19, 2009, 2. http://www.state.gov/j/gcj/us_releases/remarks/2009/133316.htm.

115. Kressand von Holtzendorff 2010, 1204.

116. Ferencz 2010, 907–8.

117. Statement of Lourdes Aranda Bezaury, Kampala Review Conference, May 31, 2010, 3. http://www.gob.mx/sre.

118. Such a deferral would not constitute a complete termination of the case, but rather could be maintained through annual renewal of the Security Council deferral.

119. Van Schaack 2010–11, 559.

120. Young 1999, 163–64.

121. Keohane 2006, 26.

122. Schabas 2004, 720.

123. Wedgwood 1999, 97.

3. Explaining the Outliers

Epigraph. Wickham-Jones 2000, 109.

1. Cuba, India, and Indonesia did not sign the Rome Statute in part because they felt that it did not go far enough in insulating the ICC from the UNSC.

2. Putnam 1988; Evans, Jacobson, and Putnam 1993; Milner 1997.

3. Putnam 1988.

4. Deitelhoff 2009.

5. Wendt 1999.

6. Goodliffe and Hawkins 2009; Goodliffe et al., 2012.

7. Goodliffe et al. 2012, 132.

8. Ibid., 132. See also Keohane 1986.

9. Eurostat GDP estimates are from 1999; European Commission, http://ec.europa.eu/environment/enveco/eco_industry/pdf/annex6.pdf (accessed November 22, 2013).

10. In fact, as pointed out by Eurostat, "Taking goods and services together, the EU and the USA account for the largest bilateral trade relationship in the world." See Eurostat 2007, 15.

11. Reynolds 1986.

12. Goldstein et al. (2001) offer an alternative set of design parameters that include membership, scope, centralization, control, and flexibility. See also Koremenos, Lipson and Snidal 2001.

13. Goodliffe and Hawkins 2009; Goodliffe et al. 2012.

14. Putnam 1988; Evans, Jacobson, and Putnam 1993; Milner 1997.

15. For an overview of the liberal approach, see Moravcsik 1997.

16. Machiavelli [1512] 1998.

17. Blair 2004.

18. Ibid., 3.

19. Williams 2004.

20. Blair 2010, 224.

21. Labour Party 1997, 39.

22. Robin Cook, May 12, 1997, quoted in Dunne and Wheeler 2000, 63.

23. Williams 2002, 55. See also Vickers 2000; Williams 2004.

24. Williams 2004, 921.

25. Ibid., 921.

26. Labour Party 1997, 39.

27. Williams 2005, 157.

28. See, e.g., Schiff 2008.

29. Buller and Harrison 2000, 78.

30. Cohen 1999.

31. Wheeler and Dunne 1998, 861.

32. See Andrew Buncombe, Paul Routledge, and Fran Abrams, "Inquiry Finds Sandline Did Breach Arms Embargo," *The Independent*, May 17, 1998, http://www.independent.co.uk/news/inquiry-finds-sandline-did-breach-arms-embargo-1159472.html (accessed February 26, 2015).

33. See, e.g., BBC News, "Million March against Iraq War," February 16, 2003, http://news.bbc.co.uk/2/hi/uk_news/2765041.stm (accessed February 26, 2015).

34. Labour Party 2001.

35. Williams 2002, 59.

36. Robin Cook, quoted in UK Mission to the United Nations, "British Government Support Establishment of an International Criminal Court," press release, August 4, 1997.

37. UK Mission to the United Nations, press release 32/95, April 7, 1995, 2.

38. Williams 2002, 61.
39. Dodd and MacAskill 2000.
40. Schabas 2004, 16.
41. Blair 2010, 187.
42. Bourne and Cini 2000, 175; Daniels 1998.
43. These included Austria, Belgium, Denmark, Finland, Germany, Greece, Ireland, Italy, Luxembourg, the Netherlands, Portugal, Spain, and Sweden.
44. Weller 2002.
45. Rome Statute, Art. 16.
46. Hall 1998, 131.
47. Dutton 2013, 87.
48. Scheffer 2012, 220.
49. Tony Blair, quoted in *The Telegraph*, March 10, 2016, http://www.telegraph.co.uk/news/politics/tony-blair/7974268/Tony-Blair-on-Labours-1997-victory-and-learning-to-understand-politics.html.
50. Dutton 2013, 87.
51. Schuman Declaration, May 9, 1950, European Union, http://europa.eu/about-eu/basic-information/symbols/europe-day/schuman-declaration/index_en.htm (accessed February 26, 2015).
52. Steinke 2012.
53. Richard Dicker, quoted in *Terra Viva*, June 22, 1998.
54. Hubert Vedrine, quoted in *Terra Viva*, June 22, 1998.
55. CICC 1998b.
56. Zimmermann 2008.
57. Rome Statute, Art. 124.
58. Arsanjani 1999; Tabak 2009.
59. Amnesty International called the concession a "license to kill." Cf. McCormack and Robertson 1999; Cassese 2003; Politi 2001.
60. France took advantage of this provision as well. It was one of only two countries that did so; the other was Colombia.
61. Wippman 2004.
62. Vickers 2000, 34.
63. Payton 2009, 116.
64. This is the group comprising the G4 and Uniting for Consensus (also known as the Coffee Club).
65. This is the group that included the G20 Group of Developing Nations (in addition to the G4 and UfC).
66. CEH 1998. Others have offered more conservative estimates of casualties. See, e.g., Schirmer 1998.
67. Cf. Affilitto and Jesilow 2007, 25; Nairn 1993; Roberts 2002; Albesa 1998, 15.
68. CEH 1998; ODHAG 1999.
69. Garrard-Burnett 2010, 7.
70. Affillito and Jesilow 2007, 25.
71. Ibid., 26.
72. Ibid., 118.

73. Garrard-Burnett 2010, 9.

74. Statement of Gert Rosenthal in Assembly of States Parties to the Rome Statute ICC 2009, 19, May 19, 2009, trans. by Daniella Restrepo.

75. Milner 1997, 9–10.

4. Power, Principle, and Pragmatism in Prosecutorial Strategy

Epigraph. OTP 2010, 7.

1. Jean Ping, quoted in Arieff et al. 2011, 27.
2. Cf. Arieff et al. 2011; Luckscheiter and Maas-Albert 2012.
3. Grandison 2012.
4. On institutional capture, see Bosco 2014. Cf. C.A. Smith 2012.
5. OTP 2010, 6.
6. Fatou Bensouda, quoted in D. Smith 2012.
7. There are numerous works directed at explaining ICC actions; however, they do not develop or test a theory of prosecutorial strategy more generally. Cf. Cryer 2005; Clark 2008; Schabas 2008; Dong 2009; Lepard 2010; de Guzman 2012b; Scheffer 2012; Ambos and Stegmiller 2013.
8. Cf. Alter 2006, 2008; Vaubel 2006; Hawkins et al. 2006; Kim 2011; Pollack 2003; Voeten 2008.
9. Hawkins et al. 2006.
10. Garrett and Weingast 1993.
11. Garrett, Kelemen, and Schulz 1998.
12. Posner and Figueiredo 2005.
13. Carrubba, Gabel, and Hankla 2008, 435. For a critique, see Stone Sweet and Brunell 2012.
14. Voeten 2008.
15. Alter 1998.
16. Cf. Pollack 2003; Tallberg 2002.
17. Stone Sweet and Brunell 2012.
18. Schabas 2004, 15–16.
19. According Article 126, the statute would enter into force when it was ratified by sixty nations (roughly the size of the LMG).
20. Alter 2008, 312.
21. Moreno Ocampo 2009, 14.
22. Ibid., 13.
23. Stahn 2009.
24. Peskin 2008; Rudolph 2001.
25. Bass 2000, 206–7.
26. The ICC's jurisdiction is limited to situations occurring after the court became operational in July 2002.
27. Erlanger 2001.
28. Nicholas Sarkozy, quoted in Castle 2011.
29. UNSC Res. 1422 (2002).

30. These are also referred to as bilateral immunity agreements (BIAs) or Rule 98 agreements. See Kelley 2007.

31. Author interview with Luis Moreno Ocampo, February 6, 2015.

32. BBC News, "Russia and China Veto UN Move to Refer Syria to the ICC," May 22, 2014, http://www.bbc.com/news/world-middle-east-27514256 (accessed January 28, 2015).

33. Author interview with Luis Moreno Ocampo, February 6, 2015.

34. Ibid.

35. Bosco 2014, 138.

36. Jack Goldsmith (2003, 89) emphasizes that this dependence is particularly applicable with respect to the United States. He writes, "An ICC without U.S. support . . . will not only fail to live up to its expectations. It may well do actual harm by discouraging the United States from engaging in various human-rights protecting activities."

37. The Chinese have rarely used their veto unilaterally. Thus, it stands to reason that if other members of the P5 would not veto a UNSC resolution calling for a referral to the ICC, the probability that China would do so alone is not likely.

38. This view is consistent with the notion of egoistic organizational interests put forward by Barnett and Finnemore (1999).

39. Office of the Prosecutor, Policy Paper on Preliminary Investigations, November 2013, p. 2.

40. On complementarity, see AMICC 2005.

41. Values range from 1 (free) to 7 (not free).

42. Cf. Lake and Rothchild 1998; Walter and Snyder 1999; Wimmer 2004.

43. Seybolt, Aaronson, and Fischhoff 2013, 44; see also Greenhill 2013.

44. Seybolt, Aaronson, and Fischhoff 2013, 45.

45. OTP 2010, 2.

46. de Guzman 2012a, 21.

47. de Guzman 2012b, 285.

48. Moreno Ocampo 2009, 15.

49. Danner 2001, 469–70.

50. See SáCouto and Cleary 2008.

51. Cf. Schiff 2008; Struett 2008; Glasius 2006; Deitelhoff 2009; Sikkink 2011.

52. Struett 2008; Sikkink 2011.

53. Luis Moreno Ocampo to The Hague, February 9, 2006), p. 2, https://www.icc-cpi.int/NR/rdonlyres/04D143C8-19FB-466C-AB77-4CDB2FDEBEF7/143682/OTP_letter_to_senders_re_Iraq_9_February_2006.pdf (accessed August 14, 2016).

54. Human Rights Watch 2009.

55. Amnesty International, "US Policy in Colombia,"http://www.amnestyusa.org/our-work/countries/americas/colombia/us-policy-in-colombia (accessed August 8, 2013).

56. Ibid.

57. Amnesty International, "US Policy in Colombia."

58. Barry 2003.

59. Amnesty International, "US Policy in Columbia."

60. "Plan Columbia—The Sequel," *The Economist*, August 21, 2003, http://www.economist.com/node/2009304 (accessed August 8, 2013).

61. U.S. Department of State 2012.

62. Sharp 2013.

63. Little 1993.

64. Bill Clinton, remarks to Israeli ambassador Shoval, September 10, 1998, Jewish Virtual Library, http://www.jewishvirtuallibrary.org/jsource/US-Israel/presquote.html (accessed August 8, 2013).

65. George W. Bush, speech to the Knesset, May 15, 2008, Jewish Virtual Library, http://www.jewishvirtuallibrary.org/jsource/US-Israel/presquote.html (accessed August 8, 2013).

66. Barack Obama, speech at the 2011 American Israel Public Affairs Committee Policy Conference, May 22, 2011, Jewish Virtual Library, http://www.jewishvirtuallibrary.org/jsource/US-Israel/presquote.html (accessed August 8, 2013).

67. Bajoria and Xu 2013.

68. Ibid.

69. ITAR-TASS (Russian news agency), "Russian-Venezuelan Intergovernmental Commission Begins Its 9th Regular Meeting in Caracas," April 3, 2013.

70. ITAR-TASS (Russian news agency), "Russian, Venezuelan Oil Companies Set Up Joint Venture," May 22, 2013.

71. Brautigam 2009; Van de Looy 2006; Taylor 2006.

72. See BBC News, "China to Build Nigerian Railway," October 31, 2006, http://news.bbc.co.uk/2/hi/africa/6101736.stm.

73. Kingsley Opurum, "Nigeria is Third Largest Trade Partner of China—Chinese Envoy," *Leadership*, July 10, 2013, http://leadership.ng/news/100713/nigeria-third-largest-trade-partner-china-chinese-envoy (accessed August 15, 2013).

74. Scores totaling more than 8 were coded as "high" (3), those totaling 6–8 were coded "medium" (2), and those less than 6 were coded "low" (1).

75. Logit regression is another technique that can be employed. In practice, the results tend to be similar for both logit and probit analysis, and preferences for one over the other tend to vary by discipline.

76. The KM estimator is nonparametric and is one of the most widely used methods for estimating survivor functions.

77. This nonparametric log-rank test is a basic test of the equivalence of the survival functions across the scores of a covariate, similar to the chi-square test, and is very well equipped to deal with the right-censoring reflected in the data set.

78. I also ran a test of the proportional hazard assumption to justify the use of the Cox model. None of the covariates violated the P-H assumption. The number of independent covariates included in each regression was kept minimal because of the small number of cases to examine.

79. Struett 2012, 83.

80. Bassiouni 2006, 426.

81. Hoile 2014.

82. Bosco 2014, 20.

83. Stigen 2008, 376–77.
84. Schabas 2008, 731.

Conclusion

Epigraph. Stephen Hawking, "A Step Backward for Civilization," *Washington Post*, February 16, 2014.

1. See BBC News, "Guide to the Syrian Rebels," December 13, 2013, http://www.bbc.com/news/world-middle-east-24403003 (accessed March 26, 2016).
2. Hughes and Newey 2013, 4–5.
3. Cassese 2004.
4. Slaughter 2004; Sikkink 2011.
5. Cf. Onuf 2012; Wendt 1999; Katzenstein 1996.
6. Cf. Fehl 2004; Glasius 2006; Schiff 2008; Struett 2008; Simmons and Danner 2010, Sikkink 2011. Two recent exceptions are C.A Smith (2012) and Bosco (2014).
7. Keck and Sikkink 1998.
8. Lake 2013.
9. Sil and Katzenstein 2010.
10. See, e.g., Milner 1997; Lake and Powell 1999.
11. Lake 2013, 573.
12. See Baldwin 2013 for an overview.
13. Carr [1939] 2001.
14. Barnett and Duval 2005, 44.
15. Baldwin 2006.
16. Ferencz 1980; Meron 1997; Pejic 1998; Jo and Simmons 2014.
17. Muammar Gaddafi, quoted in ABC News, "Tripoli Braces for Battle as Gaddafi Digs In," February 26, 2011, http://www.abc.net.au/news/2011-02-27/tripoli-braces-for-battle-as-gaddafi-digs-in/1958692?section=justin (accessed July 24, 2014).
18. John Kerry, quoted in Schonfeld 2014.
19. Gearan 2014.
20. UN 2014, 12.
21. Ibid., 15.
22. Nichols 2014.
23. Park 2014.
24. CNN World News, "Reports: Boko Haram Village Raids Kill Hundreds in Nigeria," June 5, 2014, http://www.cnn.com/2014/06/05/world/africa/boko-haram-village-raids (accessed June 24, 2014).
25. Sieff 2016.
26. Hauslohner 2014.
27. Cf. Snyder and Vinjamuri 2003–4; Ku and Nzelibe 2006; Fish 2010; Cronin-Furman 2013.
28. Melander 2016, 3–4.
29. Carter 2015.
30. Thucydides [431 BC] 2009.

31. Rummel 1997.

32. Luis Moreno Ocampo, quoted in *The Reckoning: The Battle for the International Criminal Court*, documentary film, directed by Pamela Yates (Brooklyn, NY: Skylight Pictures), 2009.

33. Franck 1990.

34. Henkin 1979.

35. Chayes and Slaughter 2000, 238.

36. See, generally, Finnemore and Sikkink 1998.

37. Snyder and Vinjamuri 2003–4.

38. Moreno Ocampo, quoted in *The Reckoning*.

39. UN General Assembly, "2005 World Summit Outcome," October 24, 2005, http://www.un.org/womenwatch/ods/A-RES-60-1-E.pdf.

40. See Moreno Ocampo's remarks in *The Reckoning*.

41. See, e.g., the CIA's assessment of Soviet public opinion regarding the occupation of Afghanistan (CIA 1988).

42. Carter 2015.

43. Ackerman 2015.

44. See Crawford and Kuperman 2006, vii.

45. Robert Gates, quoted in Goldberg 2016.

46. Barack Obama, quoted in Goldberg 2016.

47. Hillary Clinton, quoted in Mufson 2015.

48. Barack Obama, quoted in Wilson and Warrick 2011.

49. Dennis Ross, quoted in Goldberg 2016.

50. Thomas 1952.

51. Barack Obama, quoted in Goldberg 2016.

52. Qtd. in Mufson 2015.

53. Bruce Jones, quoted in Mufson 2015.

54. Lynch 2011.

55. United Nations 2011.

56. Hillary Clinton, quoted in BBC News, "Clinton: Assad 'Fits Definition' of War Criminal," February 28, 2012. http://www.bbc.com/news/world-middle-east-17199446 (accessed April 27, 2016).

57. Barack Obama, quoted in CNN "Obama Warns Syria Not to Cross 'Red Line,'" August 21, 2012. http://www.cnn.com/2012/08/20/world/meast/syria-unrest (accessed April 27, 2016).

58. S.C. Res. 2118, UN SCOR, UN Doc. S/RES/2118 (September 27, 2013).

59. BBC News "Clinton: Assad 'Fits Definition' of War Criminal," February 28, 2012. http://www.bbc.com/news/world-middle-east-17199446 (accessed April 27, 2016).

60. Borger and Inzaurralde 2015.

61. An anonymous EU official, quoted in Borger and Inzaurralde 2015.

62. See Boghani 2016; IDMC 2016; UNHCR 2016.

63. John Kerry, quoted in Meyer 2015.

64. Anne-Marie Slaughter, quoted in Mufson 2015.

65. Barack Obama, quoted in Goldberg 2016.

66. See Samantha Power's comments at the United Nations, August 30, 2014. https://www.youtube.com/watch?v=xTpR0qEe57E (accessed May 2, 2016).

67. Bugajski 2008, 5–6.

68. Black 2014.

69. Ibid.

70. British and French participants, quoted in Black 2014.

71. Samantha Power, quoted in Black 2014.

72. Vitaly I. Churkin, "Statement at the Security Council Meeting on the Explanation of Vote on the Draft Resolution on the Referral of the Situation in Syria to the ICC," May 22, 2014. Permanent Mission of the Russian Federation to the United Nations, http://russiaun.ru/en/news/sc_syr22 (accessed May 3, 2016).

73. Carr [1939] 2001.

74. Goldsmith and Krasner 2003, 47.

75. Keohane 2008, 7.

76. Ibid.

77. Bukovansky et al. 2012; Clark and Reus-Smit 2013.

78. David Scheffer, quoted in Weschler 2000, 102.

79. Goldsmith 2003, 89.

80. Weller 2002.

81. Carr [1939] 2001, 20.

82. Chayes and Slaughter 2000, 245.

References

Abbott, Kenneth W. 1999. "International Relations Theory, International Law, and the Regime Governing Atrocities in Internal Conflicts." *American Journal of International Law* 93 (2): 361–79.

Abbott, Kenneth, and Duncan Snidal. 2006. "Nesting, Overlap, and Parallelism: Governance Schemes for International Production Standards." Memo for Princeton Nesting Conference (February 24).

Ackerman, Spencer. 2015. "U.S. Has Trained Only 'Four or Five' Syrian Fighters against ISIS." *Guardian*, September 16. http://www.theguardian.com/us-news/2015/sep/16/us-military-syrian-isis-fighters (accessed April 21, 2016).

Afflitto, Frank M., and Paul Jesilow. 2007. *The Quiet Revolutionaries*. Austin: University of Texas Press.

Aggarwal, Vinod K., ed. 1998. *Institutional Designs for a Complex World: Bargaining, Linkages, and Nesting*. Ithaca, NY: Cornell University Press.

——. 2006. "Reconciling Institutions: Nested, Horizontal, Overlapping, and Independent Institutions." Memo presented at the Conference on Nested and Overlapping Institutions, February 24, Princeton University.

Albesa, Xavi. 1998. *Amarga Máscara*. Guatemala: Editorial Imprenta El Centro.

Alperovitz, Gar. 1995. *The Decision to Use the Atomic Bomb*. New York: Knopf.

Alter, Karen. 1998. "'Who Are the Masters of the Treaty?' European Governments and the European Court of Justice." *International Organization* 52 (1): 121–48.

———. 2006. "Delegation to International Courts and the Limits of Re-Contracting Political Power." In *Delegation and Agency in International Organizations*, ed. D. Hawkins, D. Lake, D. Nielson, and M. Tierney, 312–38. Cambridge: Cambridge University Press.

———. 2008. "Agents or Trustees? International Courts in their Political Context." *European Journal of International Relations* 14 (1): 33–63.

Alter, Karen J., and Sophie Meunier. 2006. "Nested and Overlapping Regimes in the Transatlantic Banana Trade Dispute." *Journal of European Public Policy* 13 (3): 362–82.

———, eds. 2009. "The Politics of International Regime Complexity." Special issue. *Perspectives on Politics* 7 (1).

Alvarez, Jose E. 1999. "Crimes of State/Crimes of Hate: Lessons from Rwanda." *Yale Journal of International Law* 24 (2): 365–483.

Ambos, Kai, and Ignaz Stegmiller. 2013. "Prosecuting International Crimes at the International Criminal Court: Is There a Coherent and Comprehensive Prosecution Strategy?" *Crime, Law and Social Change* 59 (4): 415–37.

AMICC. 2005. The Principle of Complementarity. Typescript. (Sept. 26). http://www.amicc.org/docs/Complementarity.pdf (accessed February 9, 2015).

Amnesty International. 1998. *Sierra Leone: 1998—A Year of Atrocities against Civilians.* New York: Amnesty International. http://www.amnesty.org/en/library/asset/AFR51/022/1998/en/e950eb45-d99d-11dd-af2b-b1f6023af0c5/afr510221998en.pdf (accessed February 9, 2012).

Annan, Kofi. 1997. "Advocating for an International Criminal Court." *Fordham International Law Journal* 21 (2): 363–66.

Arieff, Alexis, Rhoda Margesson, Marjorie Ann Browne, and Matthew C. Weed. 2011. *International Criminal Court Cases in Africa: Status and Policy Issues.* Washington, DC: Congressional Research Service, July 22.

Arsanjani, Mahnoush. 1999. "The Rome Statute of the International Criminal Court." *American Journal of International Law* 93.

Askin, Kelly D. 2003. "Omarska Camp, Bosnia—Broken Promises of 'Never Again.'" *Human Rights Magazine*, Winter. http://www.americanbar.org/publications/human_rights_magazine_home/irr_hr_winter03_omarskacampbosnia.html (accessed February 10, 2012).

Assembly of States Parties ICC. 2009. *Seminario Sobre Justicia Penal Internacional: El Papel de la Corte Penal Internacional.* New York: United Nations.

Avant, Deborah, Martha Finnemore, and Susan K. Sell, eds. 2010. *Who Governs the Globe?* Cambridge: Cambridge University Press.

Bajoria, Jayshree, and Beina Xu. 2013. "The China-North Korea Relationship." *Backgrounder*, February 21. http://www.cfr.org/china/china-north-korea-relationship/p11097 (accessed August 22, 2013).

Bakuramutsa, Manzi. 1995. "Panel III: Identifying and Prosecuting War Crimes; Two Case Studies—the Former Yugoslavia and Rwanda." *New York University Law School Journal of Human Rights* 12 (3): 631–88.

Baldwin, David. 2013. "Power and International Relations." In *Handbook of International Relations*, edited by Walter Carlsnaes, Thomas Risse, and Beth Simmons, 273–97. London: Sage.

Baldwin, Hanson W. 1946. "Tokyo War Guilt Trials: All Phases of Japan's Conspiracy in Orient Covered in the Prosecution Letter from Prosecutor." *New York Times*, December 4.

Baldwin, Robert E. 2006. "Failure of the WTO Ministerial Conference at Cancun: Reasons and Remedies." *World Economy* 29: 677–96.

Bandow, Doug. 2013. "South Korea: Close Friend of the U.S., and a Defense Welfare Queen." *Forbes*, May 6. http://www.forbes.com/sites/dougbandow/2013/05/06/south-korea-close-friend-of-the-u-s-and-a-defense-welfare-queen/ (accessed August 9, 2013).

Baranovsky, Vladimir. 2000. "Russia: A Part of Europe or Apart from Europe?" *International Affairs* (76) 3: 443–58.

Barnett, Michael. 2002. *Eyewitness to a Genocide*. Ithaca, NY: Cornell University Press.

Barnett, Michael, and Raymond Duval. 2005. "Power in International Politics." *International Organization* 59 (1): 39–75.

Barnett, Michael, and Martha Finnemore. 1999. "The Politics, Power, and Pathologies of International Organizations." *International Organization* 53 (4): 699–732.

———. 2004. *Rules for the World*. Ithaca, NY: Cornell University Press.

Barry, John. 2003. "From Drug War to Dirty War: Plan Colombia and the U.S. Role in Human Rights Violations in Colombia." http://www.mamacoca.org/FSMT_sept_2003/en/doc/barry_drug_war_to_dirty_war_en.htm (accessed August 24, 2016).

Bass, Gary Jonathan. 2000. *Stay the Hand of Vengeance*. Princeton, NJ: Princeton University Press.

———. 2003. "Milosevic in The Hague." *Foreign Affairs* 82 (3): 82–96.

Bassiouni, M. Cherif. 1998. *The Statute of the International Criminal Court: A Documentary History*. Ardsley: Transnational.

———. 2005. *A Legislative History of the International Criminal Court*. Ardsley, NY: Transnational.

———. 2006. "The ICC—Quo Vadis?" *Journal of International Criminal Justice* 4: 421–27.

———. 2011. *Crimes against Humanity: Historical Evolution and Contemporary Application*. Cambridge: Cambridge University Press.

BBC (British Broadcasting Corporation) News. 1999. "Timor Atrocities Unearthed," September 22. http://news.bbc.co.uk/2/hi/asia-pacific/455030.stm (accessed February 9, 2012).

———. 2001. "Omarska: A Vision of Hell," November 2. http://news.bbc.co.uk/2/hi/europe/1634250.stm (accessed February 10, 2012).

———. 2003. "DR Congo Pygmies Appeal to the UN," May 23. http://news.bbc.co.uk/2/hi/africa/2933524.stm (accessed June 6, 2012).

———. 2012. "Clinton: Assad 'Fits Definition' of War Criminal," February 28. http://www.bbc.com/news/world-middle-east-17199446 (accessed April 27, 2016).

Berdal, Mats R. 1996. "The Security Council, Peacekeeping, and Internal Conflict after the Cold War." *Duke Journal of Comparative and International Law* 7 (10): 71–91.

Beres, Louis René. 1988. "Justice and Realpolitik: International Law and the Prevention of Genocide." *American Journal of Jurisprudence* 33: 123–59.

Bijian, Zheng. 2005. "China's 'Peaceful Rise' to Great-Power Status." *Foreign Affairs* 84 (5): 18–24.

Black, Ian. 2014. "Russia and China Veto Move to Refer Syria to International Criminal Court." *Guardian*, May 22. http://www.theguardian.com/world/2014/may/22/russia-china-veto-un-draft-resolution-refer-syria-international-criminal-court (accessed May 3, 2016).

Blair, Tony. 2004. *New Britain: My Vision of a Young Country*. Boulder, CO: Westview Press.

———. 2010. *A Journey: My Political Life*. Toronto: Vintage-Canada.

Boghani, Priyanka. 2016. "A Staggering Death Toll for Syria's Civil War—470,000." *Frontline*, PBS, February 11. http://www.pbs.org/wgbh/frontline/article/a-staggering-new-death-toll-for-syrias-war-470000/ (accessed May 2, 2016).

Booth, Ken, ed. 2011. *Realism in World Politics*. New York: Routledge.

Borger, Julian, and Bastien Inzaurralde. 2015. "West Ignored Russia's Offer in 2012 to Have Syria's Assad Step Aside." *Guardian*, September 15. http://www.theguardian.com/world/2015/sep/15/west-ignored-russian-offer-in-2012-to-have-syrias-assad-step-aside (accessed April 28, 2016).

Bosco, David. 2009. *Five to Rule Them All: The UN Security Council and the Making of the Modern World*. Oxford: Oxford University Press.

———. 2014. *Rough Justice: The International Criminal Court in a World of Power Politics*. Oxford: Oxford University Press.

Bostdorff, Denise M. 2008. *Proclaiming the Truman Doctrine: The Cold War Call to Arms*. College Station: Texas A&M Press.

Bourne, Angela, and Michelle Cini. 2000. "Exporting the Third Way in Foreign Policy: New Labour, the European Union, and Human Rights Policy." In Little and Wickham-Jones, *New Labour's Foreign Policy*, 168–85.

Box-Steffensmeier, Janet M., and Bradford S. Jones. 2004. *Event History Modeling*. Cambridge: Cambridge University Press.

Brautigam, Deborah. 2009. *The Dragon's Gift: The Real Story of China in Africa*. Oxford: Oxford University Press.

Broomhall, Bruce. 2003. *International Justice and the International Criminal Court: Between Sovereignty and the Rule of Law*. Oxford: Oxford University Press.

Bueno de Mesquita, Bruce. 1996. "The Benefits of a Social-Scientific Approach to Studying International Affairs." In *Explaining International Relations since 1945*, edited by Ngaire Woods, 49–76. Oxford: Oxford University Press.

Buergenthal, Thomas. 1997. "The Normative and Institutional Evolution of International Human Rights." *Human Rights Quarterly* 19 (4): 703–23.

Bugajski, Janusz. 2008. *Expanding Eurasia: Russia's European Ambitions*. Washington, DC: Center for Strategic and International Studies.

Bukovansky, Mlada, Ian Clark, Robyn Eckersley, Richard Price, Christian Reus-Smit, and Nicholas J. Wheeler, eds. 2012. *Special Responsibilities: Global Problems and American Power*. Cambridge: Cambridge University Press.

Bull, Hedley. 1977. *The Anarchical Society*. New York: Columbia University Press.

Buller, Jim, and Vicky Harrison. 2000. "New Labour as a 'Good International Citizen': Normative Theory and UK Foreign Policy." In Little and Wickham-Jones, *New Labour's Foreign Policy*, 168–85.

Busby, Joshua W. 2010. *Moral Movements and Foreign Policy*. Cambridge: Cambridge University Press.

Buzan, Barry. (2010) 2001. "China in International Society: Is Peaceful Rise Possible?" *Chinese Journal of International Politics* 3: 5–36.

Carr, E. H. 1939. *The Twenty Years' Crisis, 1919–1939*. New York: St. Martin's Press.

Carrubba, Clifford J., Matthew Gabel, and Charles Hankla. 2008. "Judicial Behavior under Political Constraints: Evidence from the European Court of Justice." *American Political Science Review* 102 (4): 435–52.

Carter, Phillip. 2015. "Why Foreign Troops Can't Fight Our Fights." *Washington Post*, October 4.

Cassese, Antonio. 2003. *International Criminal Law*. Oxford: Oxford University Press.

——. 2004. "The Role of International Courts and Tribunals in the Fight against International Criminality." In *Internationalized Criminal Courts*, edited by C. Romano, A. Nollkaemper, and J. Kleffner, 3–13. Oxford: Oxford University Press.

——. 2009. "The International Criminal Court Five Years On: Andante or Moderato?" In *The Emerging Practice of the International Criminal Court*, edited by C. Stahl and Göran Sluiter, 21–30. Leiden: Martinus Nijhoff.

Castle, Stephen. 2011. "Mladic Arrest Opens Door to Serbia's Long-Sought European Union Membership." *New York Times*, May 26. http://www.nytimes.com/2011/05/27/world/europe/27union.html?_r=0 (accessed January 28, 2015).

CEH (Comisión para la Esclarecimiento Histórico). 1998. *Memoria del Silencio: Tz'inil Na'tab'al*. Guatemala: Comisión para la Esclarecimiento Histórico.

Cha, Victor D. 2002. "Hawk Engagement and Preventive Defense on the Korean Peninsula." *International Security* 27 (1): 40–78.

Chayes, Abram, and Anne-Marie Slaughter. 2000. "The Future of the Global Legal System." In *The United States and the International Criminal Court*, edited by Sarah B. Sewall and Carl Kaysen, 237–47. Lanham, MD: Rowman and Littlefield.

Christopher, Paul. 1994. *The Ethics of War and Peace: An Introduction to Legal and Moral Issues*. Englewood Cliffs, NJ: Prentice Hall.

CIA (Central Intelligence Agency). 1988. "USSR: Domestic Fallout from the Afghan War." Sov-88-10009CX, February. http://www.foia.cia.gov/sites/default/files/document_conversions/89801/DOC_0000500659.pdf (accessed April 21, 2016).

CICC (Coalition for the International Criminal Court). 1998a. "'Rebellious' Rome Conference Demands Curbs on Security Council Veto Power." *On the Record*, June 23.

——. 1998b. "French Position on War Crimes Sours French Support for Prosecutor, Reparations Provisions." *On the Record*, July 11.

Clark, Ian, and Christian Reus-Smit. 2013. "Liberal Internationalism, the Practice of Special Responsibilities and Evolving Politics of the Security Council." *International Politics* 50 (1): 38–56.

Clark, Phil. 2008. "Law, Politics, and Pragmatism: The ICC and Case Selection in the Democratic Republic of Congo and Uganda." In *Courting Conflict? Justice, Peace, and the ICC in Africa*, edited by Nicholas Waddell and Phil Clark. London: Royal African Society, School of Oriental and African Studies, University of London.

Clark, Roger S. 2010. “Negotiating Provisions Defining the Crime of Aggression, Its Elements and the Conditions for ICC Exercise of Jurisdiction over It.” *European Journal of International Law* 20 (4): 1103–15.

Clarke, Walter. 1997. “Failed Visions and Uncertain Mandates in Somalia.” In *Learning from Somalia*, edited by Walter Clarke and Jeffrey Herbst, 3–19. Boulder, CO: Westview Press.

Clausewitz, Carl von. 2008. *On War*. Edited and translated by Michael Howard and Peter Paret. Princeton, NJ: Princeton University Press.

CNN (Cable News Network). 2012. “Obama Warns Syria Not to Cross ‘Red Line,’” August 21. http://www.cnn.com/2012/08/20/world/meast/syria-unrest (accessed April 27, 2016).

Cohen, Nick. 1999. “The Great Balkan Lie.” *New Statesman*, April 26. http://www.newstatesman.com/node/134611 (accessed June 6, 2014).

Cole, Wade. 2005. “Sovereignty Relinquished? Explaining Commitment to International Human Rights Covenants, 1976–1999.” *American Sociological Review* 70 (3): 472–95.

Conot, Robert E. 1983. *Justice at Nuremberg*. New York: Carroll and Graf.

Conway-Lanz, Sahr. 2006. *Collateral Damage*. New York: Routledge.

Crawford, Timothy W., and Alan J. Kuperman, eds. 2006. *Gambling on Humanitarian Intervention: Moral Hazard, Rebellion and Civil War*. New York: Routledge.

Creta, Vincent M. 1998. “The Search for Justice in the Former Yugoslavia and Beyond.” *Houston Journal of International Law* 30: 381–418.

Cronin, Bruce, and Ian Hurd, eds. 2008. *The UN Security Council and the Politics of International Authority*. New York: Routledge.

Cronin-Furman, Kate. 2013. “Managing Expectations: International Criminal Trials and the Prospects for Deterrence of Mass Atrocity.” *International Journal of Transitional Justice* 7: 434–54.

Cryer, Robert. 2005. *Prosecuting International Crimes: Selectivity and the International Criminal Law Regime*. Cambridge: Cambridge University Press.

Daniels, Philip. 1998. “From Hostility to ‘Constructive Engagement’: The Europeanization of the Labour Party.” *West European Politics* 21 (1): 72–96.

Danner, Allison Marston. 2001. “Constructing a Hierarchy of Crimes in International Criminal Law Sentencing.” *Virginia Law Review* 87 (3): 416–501.

Danner, Allison, and Erik Voeten. 2010. “Who is Running the International Criminal Justice System?” In *Who Governs the Globe,* edited by Deborah D. Avant, Martha Finnemore, and Susan K. Sell, 35–71. Cambridge: Cambridge University Press.

Davis, Christina L. 2009. “Overlapping Institutions in Trade Policy.” *Perspectives on Politics* 7 (1): 25–31.

de Guzman, Margaret M. 2012a. “How Serious Are International Crimes? The Gravity Problem in International Criminal Law.” *Columbia Journal of Transnational Law* 51 (1): 18–68.

———. 2012b. “Choosing to Prosecute: Expressive Selection at the International Criminal Court.” *Michigan Journal of International Law* 33 (Winter): 265–320.

Deitelhoff, Nicole. 2009. “The Discursive Process of Legalization: Charting Islands of Persuasion in the ICC Case.” *International Organization* 63 (1): 33–65.

Des Forges, Alison. 1999. *Leave None to Tell the Story: Genocide in Rwanda*. New York: Human Rights Watch.

Djilas, Aleksa. 1991. *The Contested Country*. Cambridge, MA: Harvard University Press.

Dodd, Vikram, and Ewen MacAskill. 2000. "Labour Drops 'Ethical' Tag." *Guardian*, September 4. http://www.theguardian.com/politics/2000/sep/04/ethicalforeignpolicy.economy (accessed June 10, 2014).

Dong, Jingbo. 2009. "Prosecutorial Discretion at the International Criminal Court: A Comparative Study." *Journal of Politics and Law* 2 (2): 109–14.

Downes, Alexander B. 2008. *Targeting Civilians in War*. Ithaca, NY: Cornell University Press.

Doyle, Michael W. 1997. *Ways of War and Peace: Realism, Liberalism, and Socialism*. New York: W. W. Norton.

Doyle, Michael W., and Anne-Marie Gardner. 2003. "Introduction: Human Rights and International Order." In *The Globalization of Human Rights*, edited by Jean-Marc Coicaud, Michael W. Doyle, and Anne-Marie Gardner, 1–19. New York: United Nations University Press.

Dunne, Tim, and Nicholas J. Wheeler. 2000. "The Blair Doctrine: Advancing the Third Way in the World." In Little and Wickham-Jones, *New Labour's Foreign Policy*, 61–76.

Dutton, Yvonne. 2013. *Rules, Politics, and the International Criminal Court*. New York: Routledge.

Ehrenfreund, Norbert. 2007. *The Nuremberg Legacy*. New York: Palgrave Macmillan.

Erlanger, Steven. 2001. "U.S. Makes Arrest of Milosevic a Condition of Aid to Belgrade." *The New York Times* (10 March). http://www.nytimes.com/2001/03/10/world/us-makes-arrest-of-milosevic-a-condition-of-aid-to-belgrade.html (accessed Jan. 27, 2015).

Eurostat. 2007. *Panorama of European Union Trade*. Luxembourg: Eurostat.

Evans, Peter, Harold Jacobson, and Robert Putnam, eds. 1993. *Double-Edged Diplomacy*. Berkeley: University of California Press.

Falk, Richard. 2009. *Achieving Human Rights*. New York: Routledge.

Fehl, Caroline. 2004. "Explaining the International Criminal Court: A 'Practice Test' for Rationalist and Constructivist Approaches." *European Journal of International Relations* 10 (3): 357–94.

Ferencz, Benjamin. 1980. *An International Criminal Court, A Step toward World Peace: A Documentary History and Analysis*. Vol. 1. Dobbs Ferry, NJ: Oceana Publications.

Ferencz, Donald M. 2010. "The Crime of Aggression: Some Personal Reflections on Kampala." *Leiden Journal of International Law* 23 (4): 905–8.

Finnemore, Martha, and Kathryn Sikkink. 1998. "International Norm Dynamics and Political Change." *International Organization* 52 (4): 887–917.

Fish, Eric. 2010. "Peace through Complementarity: Solving the Ex Post Problem in International Criminal Court Prosecutions." *Yale Law Journal* 119.

Ford, Stuart. 2011. "How Leadership in International Criminal Law Is Shifting from the U.S. to Europe and Asia: An Analysis on Spending on and Contributions to International Criminal Courts." *Saint Louis University Law Journal* 55: 953–99.

Franceschet, Antonio. 2009. "Four Cosmopolitan Projects: The International Criminal Court in Context." In *Governance, Order, and the International Criminal Court: Between Realpolitik and a Cosmopolitan Court*, edited by Steven Roach, 179–204. Oxford: Oxford University Press.

Franck, Thomas M. 1990. *The Power of Legitimacy among Nations*. Oxford: Oxford University Press.

Gardam, Judith Gail. 2004. *Necessity, Proportionality and the Use of Force by States*. Cambridge: Cambridge University Press.

Garrard-Burnett, Virginia. 2010. *Terror in the Land of the Holy Spirit: Guatemala under General Efraín Ríos Montt, 1982–1983*. Oxford: Oxford University Press.

Garrett, Geoffrey, and Barry R. Weingast. 1993. "Ideas, Interests, and Institutions: Constructing the EC's Internal Market." In *Ideas and Foreign Policy*, edited by Judith Goldstein and Robert O. Keohane, 173–206. Ithaca, NY: Cornell University Press.

Garrett, Geoffrey, R. Daniel Kelemen, and Heiner Schulz. 1998. "The European Court of Justice, National Governments, and Legal Integration in the European Union." *International Organization* 51 (1): 149–76.

Gearan, Anne. 2014. "Inspectors Find Signs Syria Used Chlorine." *Washington Post*, June 19.

Geddes, Barbara. 2003. *Paradigms and Sandcastles*. Ann Arbor: University of Michigan Press.

Ginsburgs, George. 1998. *Moscow's Road to Nuremberg: The Soviet Background to the Trial*. The Hague: Kluwer Law International.

Glasius, Marlies. 2006. *The International Criminal Court: A Global Civil Society Achievement*. New York: Routledge.

Goldberg, Jeffrey. 2016. "The Obama Doctrine." *Atlantic*, April. http://www.theatlantic.com/magazine/archive/2016/04/the-obama-doctrine/471525 (accessed April 21, 2016).

Goldsmith, Jack. 2003. "The Self-Defeating International Criminal Court." *University of Chicago Law Review* 70 (1): 89–104.

Goldsmith, Jack, and Stephen D. Krasner. 2003. "The Limits of Idealism." *Daedalus* 132 (1): 47–63.

Goldstein, Judith, Miles Kahler, Robert O. Keohane, and Anne-Marie Slaughter, eds. 2001. *Legalization and World Politics*. Cambridge, MA: MIT Press.

Goldstone, Richard. 2004. "A View from the Prosecution." *Journal of International Criminal Justice* 2 (2): 3380–84.

Goldstone, Richard J., and Gary Jonathan Bass. 2000. "Lessons from the International Criminal Tribunals." In *The United States and the International Criminal Court*, edited by Sarah B. Sewall and Carl Kaysen, 51–59. Lanham, MD: Rowman and Littlefield.

Goodliffe, Jay, and Darren Hawkins. 2009. "A Funny Thing Happened on the Way to Rome: Explaining International Criminal Court Negotiations." *Journal of Politics* 71 (3): 977–97.

Goodliffe, Jay, Darren Hawkins, Christine Horne, and Daniel L. Nielsen. 2012. "Dependence Networks and the International Criminal Court." *International Studies Quarterly* 56 (1): 131–47.

Gorokhov, Valery N., and Dmitri Y. Gorovstov. 1998. "NATO Expansion: A View from the State Duma." *Demokratizatsiia* 6 (1).
Gourevitch, Philip. 1998. *We Wish to Inform You That Tomorrow We Will Be Killed with Our Families.* New York: Macmillan.
Grandison, Claire. 2012. "Maximizing the Impact of ICC Preliminary Investigations." *Human Rights Brief,* February 10. http://hrbrief.org/2012/02/maximizing-the-impact-of-icc-preliminary-examinations (accessed March 14, 2014).
Greenhill, Kelly M. 2010. "Counting the Cost: The Politics of Numbers in Armed Conflicts." In *Sex, Drugs, and Body Counts: The Politics of Numbers in Global Crime and Conflict,* edited by Peter Andreas and Kelly Greenhill, 127–58. Ithaca, NY: Cornell University Press.
Grotius, Hugo. (1625) 1962. *The Law of War and Peace* (De jure belli ac pacis). Translated by Francis W. Kelsey. Reprint, Indianapolis: Bobbs-Merrill.
Grover, Sonja C. 2010. *Prosecuting International Crimes and Human Rights Abuses Committed against Children.* New York: Springer.
Gutman, Roy. 1993. *Witness to Genocide.* New York: Macmillan.
Gvostev, Nikolas K., and Christopher Marsh. 2014. *Russian Foreign Policy: Interests, Vectors, and Sectors.* Thousand Oaks, CA: CQ Press.
Hafner-Burton, Emilie. 2008. "Sticks and Stones: Naming and Shaming the Human Rights Enforcement Problem." *International Organization* 62 (4): 689–716.
——. 2009. *Forced to Be Good: Why Trade Agreements Boost Human Rights.* Ithaca, NY: Cornell University Press.
Hafner-Burton, Emilie, and Kiyoteru Tsutsui. 2005. "Human Rights Practices in a Globalizing World: The Paradox of Empty Promises." *American Journal of Sociology* 110 (5): 1373–1411.
Hall, Christopher Keith. 1997. "The First Two Sessions of the UN Preparatory Committee on the Establishment of an International Criminal Court." *American Journal of International Law* 91 (1): 177–87.
——. 1998. "The Third and Fourth Sessions of the UN Preparatory Committee on the Establishment of an International Criminal Court." *American Journal of International Law* 92 (1): 124–33.
Harmon, Mark B., and Fergal Gaynor. 2004. "Prosecuting Massive Crimes with Primitive Tools: Three Difficulties Encountered by Prosecutors in International Criminal Proceedings." *Journal of International Criminal Justice* 2 (2): 403–26.
Hartley, Thomas and Bruce Russett. 1992. "Public Opinion and the Common Defense: Who Governs Military Spending in the United States?" *American Political Science Review* 86 (December): 905–15.
Hasenclever, Andreas, Volker Rittberger, and Peter Mayer. 1997. *Theories of International Regimes.* Cambridge: Cambridge University Press.
Hathaway, Oona A. 2005. "Between Power and Principle: An Integrated Theory of International Law." *University of Chicago Law Review* 72 (2): 469–536.
Hauslohner, Abigail. 2014. "Shiite Turkmens Recount Slaughter in Northern Villages." *Washington Post,* June 24.
Hawkins, Darren G., David A. Lake, Daniel L. Nielson, and Michael J. Tierney. 2006. "Delegation under Anarchy: States, International Organizations, and Principal-

Agent Theory." In *Delegation and Agency in International Organizations*, edited by D. Hawkins, D. Lake, D. Nielson, and M. Tierney, 3–38. Cambridge: Cambridge University Press.

Hayden, Robert M. 1999. "Biased 'Justice': Humanrightsism and the International Criminal Tribunal for the Former Yugoslavia." *Cleveland State Law Review* 47: 549–73.

Hee-Kyung, Suh. 2013. "Mass Civilian Killings by South Korean and U.S. Forces." In *Truth and Reconciliation in South Korea*, edited by Jae-Jung Suh, 39–67. New York: Routledge.

Heller, Kevin John. 2011. *The Nuremberg Military Tribunals and the Origins of International Criminal Law.* Oxford: Oxford University Press.

Henkin, Louis. 1979. *How Nations Behave: Law and Foreign Policy.* New York: Columbia University Press.

——. 1996. *The Age of Rights.* New York: Columbia University Press.

Hirsch, Francine. 2008. "The Soviets at Nuremberg: International Law, Propaganda, and the Making of the Postwar Order." *American Historical Review* 113 (3): 701–30.

Hirsch, John L., and Robert B. Oakley. 1995. *Somalia and Operation Restore Hope: Reflections on Peacemaking and Peacekeeping.* Washington, DC: United States Institute of Peace.

Hoile, David. 2014. *Justice Denied: The Reality of the International Criminal Court.* London: Africa Research Centre.

Holsti, Oli. 1996. *Public Opinion and American Foreign Policy.* Ann Arbor, MI: University of Michigan Press.

Hoopes, Townsend, and Douglas Brinkley. 1997. *FDR and the Creation of the UN.* New Haven, CT: Yale University Press.

Horowitz, Solis. 1950. "The Tokyo Trial." *International Conciliation* 45 (November): 473–584.

Howland, Todd, and William Calathes. 1998. "The UN's International Criminal Tribunal: Is It Justice or Jingoism for Rwanda? A Call for Transformation." *Virginia Journal of International Law* 39 (1): 135–67.

Hughes, Chris, and Sarah Newey. 2013. "Slaughter of the Innocents: Syria Genocide Outrage." *Daily Mirror*, August 22.

Human Rights Watch. 2009. *Up in Flames: Humanitarian Law Violations and Civilian Victims in the Conflict over South Ossetia.* New York: Human Rights Watch, January.

Hurd, Ian. 2008. *After Anarchy: Legitimacy and Power in the United Nations Security Council.* Princeton, NJ: Princeton University Press.

IDMC (Internal Displacement Monitoring Centre). 2016. "Syria IDP Figures Analysis." http://www.internal-displacement.org/middle-east-and-north-africa/syria/figures-analysis (accessed May 2, 2016).

Ignatieff, Michael. 2001. *Human Rights as Politics and Idolatry.* Princeton, NJ: Princeton University Press.

Ikenberry, G. John. 2001. *After Victory: Institutions, Strategic Restraint, and the Rebuilding of Order after Major Wars.* Princeton, NJ: Princeton University Press.

ILC (International Law Commission). 1950. *Yearbook of the International Law Commission, 1950*. Vol. 2. New York: International Law Commission, United Nations.

International Commission of Inquiry on Darfur. 2005. *Report of the International Commission of Inquiry on Darfur to the United Nations Secretary-General*. Geneva: International Commission of Inquiry, January 25. http://www.un.org/news/dh/sudan/com_inq_darfur.pdf (accessed July 12, 2012).

Ishay, Micheline. 2008. *The History of Human Rights*. Berkeley: University of California Press.

Jackson, James O. 1995. "No Rush to Judgment." http://www.writing.upenn.edu/~afilreis/Holocaust/balkans-atrocities.html (accessed February 10, 2012).

Jackson, Robert. 2000. *The Global Covenant: Human Conduct in a World of States*. Oxford: Oxford University Press.

Jacobson, Harold K., and Michel Oksenberg. 1990. *China's Participation in the IMF, the World Bank, and GATT*. Ann Arbor: University of Michigan Press.

Jo, Hyeran, and Beth Simmons. 2014. "Can the International Criminal Court Deter Atrocity: An Analysis of Violence against Civilians in Civil Wars." Paper presented at the International Studies Association Meeting, Toronto, Canada.

Johnson, Scott T. 1998. "On the Road to Disaster: The Rights of the Accused and the International Criminal Tribunal for the Former Yugoslavia." *International Legal Perspectives* 10: 111–92.

Jokic, Alexsander. 2001. *War Crimes and Collective Wrongdoing*. Malden, MA: Blackwell.

Kalyvas, Stathis. 2006. *The Logic of Violence in Civil War*. Cambridge: Cambridge University Press.

Kang, David C. 2007. *China Rising: Peace, Power and Order in East Asia*. New York: Columbia University Press.

Katzenstein, Peter, ed. 1996. *The Culture of National Security*. New York: Columbia University Press.

Kaufmann, Chaim. 1996. "Possible and Impossible Solutions to Ethnic Civil Wars." *International Security* 20 (4): 136–75.

Keck, Margaret E., and Kathryn Sikkink. 1998. *Activists beyond Borders*. Ithaca, NY: Cornell University Press.

Kelley, Judith. 2007. "Who Keeps International Commitments and Why? The International Criminal Court and Bilateral Non-Surrender Agreements." *American Political Science Review* 101 (3): 573–89.

Kennedy, Paul. 1987. *The Rise and Fall of the Great Powers*. New York: Random House.

Keohane, Robert O. 1982. "The Demand for International Regimes." *International Organization* 36 (2): 325–55.

———. 1984. *After Hegemony*. Princeton, NJ: Princeton University Press.

———. 1986. "Reciprocity in International Relations." *International Organization* 40 (1): 1–27.

———. 2006. "Institutional Design and Power." Typescript. Princeton University.

———. 2008. "Institutional Design and Power." *Yale Journal of International Affairs* (Winter): 4–15.

Kim, Pauline T. 2011. "Beyond Principal-Agent Theories: Law and the Judicial Hierarchy." *Northwestern University Law Review* 105 (2): 535–75.

Koremenos, Barbara, Charles Lipson, and Duncan Snidal. 2001. "The Rational Design of International Institutions." *International Organization* 55 (4): 761–99.

Korman, Sharon. 1996. *The Right of Conquest: The Acquisition of Territory by Force in International Law and Practice.* Oxford: Oxford University Press.

Krasner, Stephen D. 1985. *Structural Conflict: The Third World Against Global Liberalism.* Berkeley, CA: University of California Press.

——. 1991. "Global Communications and National Power: Life on the Pareto Frontier." *World Politics* 43 (3): 336–66.

——. 1999. *Sovereignty: Organized Hypocrisy.* Princeton, NJ: Princeton University Press.

Kress, Claus, and Leonie von Holtzendorff. 2010. "The Kampala Compromise on the Crime of Aggression." *Journal of International Criminal Justice* 8: 1179–1217.

Ku, Julian, and Jide Nzelibe. 2006. "Do International Criminal Tribunals Deter or Exacerbate Humanitarian Atrocities?" *Washington University Law Quarterly* 84: 777–833.

Kull, Steven, and Clay Ramsay. 2003. "U.S. Public Opinion on Intervention in Bosnia." In *International Public Opinion and the Bosnian Crisis*, edited by Richard Sobel and Eric Shiraev, 69–106. Lanham, MD: Lexington Books.

Kuperman, Alan J. 2000. "Rwanda in Retrospect." *Foreign Affairs* 79 (1): 94–118.

——. 2001. *The Limits of Humanitarian Intervention.* Washington, DC: Brookings.

——. 2008. "The Moral Hazard of Humanitarian Intervention: Lessons from the Balkans." *International Studies Quarterly* 52 (1): 49–80.

——. 2009. "Rethinking the Responsibility to Protect." *Whitehead Journal of Diplomacy and International Relations* (Winter–Spring): 19–29.

Labour Party. 1997. *New Labour: Because Britain Deserves Better.* London: Labour Party.

——. 2001. *Ambitions for Britian.* London: Labour Party.

Lake, David. 2009. *Hierarchy in International Relations.* Ithaca, NY: Cornell University Press.

——. 2011. "Why 'Isms' Are Evil: Theory, Epistemology, and Academic Sects as Impediments to Understanding and Progress." *International Studies Quarterly* 55 (2): 465–80.

——. 2013. "Theory Is Dead, Long Live Theory: The End of the Great Debates and the Rise of Eclecticism in International Relations." *European Journal of International Relations* 19 (3): 567–87.

Lake, David A., and Robert Powell, eds. 1999. *Strategic Choice and International Relations.* Princeton, NJ: Princeton University Press.

Lake, David A., and Donald Rothchild. 1998. "Ethnic Fears and Global Engagement." In *The International Spread of Ethnic Conflict*, edited by David A. Lake and Donald Rothchild, 339–50. Princeton, NJ: Princeton University Press.

Lampton, David. 1994. "America's China Policy in the Age of the Finance Minister: Clinton Ends Linkage." *China Quarterly* 139 (September): 597–621.

Lanteigne, Marc. 2009. *Chinese Foreign Policy: An Introduction*. London: Routledge.

Larson, Deborah Welch. 1985. *The Origins of Containment*. Princeton, NJ: Princeton University Press.

LCHR (Lawyers' Committee for Human Rights). 1997. "Prosecuting Genocide in Rwanda: A Lawyers' Committee Report on the ICTR and National Trials." http://www.unwatch.com/rwanda.html (accessed March 9, 2014).

Lee, Roy S., ed. 1999. *The International Criminal Court: The Making of the Rome Statute*. The Hague: Kluwer Law International.

Legro, Jeffrey W. 2007. "What Will China Want: The Future Intentions of a Rising Power." *Perspectives on Politics* 5 (3): 515–34.

Lepard, Brian D. 2010. "How Should the ICC Prosecutor Exercise His or Her Discretion? The Role of Fundamental Ethical Principles." *John Marshall Law Review* 43 (3): 553–67.

Logan, Carolyn J. 1996. "U.S. Public Opinion and the Intervention in Somalia." *Fletcher Forum for World Affairs* 20 (2): 155–80.

Little, Douglas. 1993. "The Making of a Special Relationship: The United States and Israel, 1957–68." *International Journal of Middle East Studies* 25 (4): 563–85.

Little, Richard, and Mark Wickham-Jones, eds. 2000. *New Labour's Foreign Policy: A new moral crusade?* Manchester, UK: Manchester University Press.

Luckscheiter, Jochen, and Kirsten Maas-Albert, eds. 2012. *A Fractious Relationship: Africa and the International Criminal Court*. Cape Town: Heinrich Böll Stiftung.

Lynch, Colum. 2011. "U.N. Blasts Syrian Leaders on Human Rights." *Washington Post*, August 18. https://www.washingtonpost.com/blogs/checkpoint-washington/post/un-blasts-syrian-leaders-on-human-rights/2011/08/18/gIQAvduBOJ_blog.html?tid=a_inl (accessed April 27, 2016).

MacArthur, Douglas. 1964. *Reminiscences*. New York: McGraw-Hill.

Machiavelli, Nicolo. (1512) 1998. *The Prince*. 2nd ed. Translated by Harvey C. Mansfield. Chicago: University of Chicago Press.

March, James G., and Johan Olsen. 1989. *Rediscovering Institutions: The Organization Basis of Politics*. New York: Free Press.

Marrus, Michael. 1997. *The Nuremberg War Crimes Trial, 1945–46: A Documentary History*. Boston: St. Martin's Press.

Martin, Lisa. 1992. Interests, Power, and Multilateralism. *International Organization* 46 (4): 765–92.

Maswood, Javed. 2007. "Developing Countries and the G20 in the Doha Round." In *Developing Countries and Global Trade Negotiations*, edited by Larry Crump and Syed Javed Maswood. London: Routledge.

Matas, David. 1994. *No More: The Battle against Human Rights Violations*. Toronto: Dundurn Press.

McCormack, Timothy L. H., and Sue Robertson. 1999. "Jurisdictional Aspects of the Rome Statute for the New International Criminal Court." *Melbourne University Law Review* 25.

Mearsheimer, John J. 2001. *The Tragedy of Great Power Politics*. New York: W. W. Norton.

——. 2006. "China's Unpeaceful Rise." *Current History* 105 (April): 160–62.

Mearsheimer, John, and Stephen M. Walt. 2013. "Leaving Theory Behind: Why Simplistic Hypothesis Testing Is Bad for International Relations." *European Journal of International Relations* 19 (3): 427–57.

Meernik, James. 2003. "Victor's Justice or the Law? Judging and Punishing at the International Criminal Tribunal for the Former Yugoslavia." *Journal of Conflict Resolution* 47 (2): 140–62.

Melander, Erik. 2016. *Organized Violence in the World 2015*. UCDP Paper No. 9. Uppsala, Sweden: Uppsala Conflict Data Program.

Melvern, L. R. 2000. *A People Betrayed: The Role of the West in Rwanda's Genocide*. New York: Zed Books.

Meron, Theodor. 1997. "Answering for War Crimes: Lessons from the Balkans." *Foreign Affairs* 76 (1): 2–8.

Meyer, Henry. 2015. "Putin Sees a Chance for Assad to Stay in Power in Syria." *Bloomberg News*, December 29. http://www.bloomberg.com/news/articles/2015-12-29/putin-sees-assad-chance-to-stay-as-u-s-pursues-syria-settlement (accessed April 28, 2016).

Milner, Helen V. 1997. *Interests, Institutions, and Information*. Princeton, NJ: Princeton University Press.

Minear, Richard H. 1971. *Victors' Justice: The Tokyo War Crimes Trial*. Princeton, NJ: Princeton University Press.

Minow, Martha. 1998. *Between Vengeance and Forgiveness: Facing History after Genocide and Mass Violence*. Boston: Beacon.

——. 2002. *Breaking the Cycles of Hatred: Memory, Law, and Repair*. Princeton, NJ: Princeton University Press.

Miscamble, Wilson D. 2011. *The Most Controversial Decision*. Cambridge: Cambridge University Press.

Moghalu, Kingsley Chiedu. 2006. *Global Justice: The Politics of War Crimes Trials*. Westport, CT: Praeger Security International.

Monroe, Kristen Renwick. 1996. *The Heart of Altruism: Perceptions of a Common Humanity*. Princeton, NJ: Princeton University Press.

Moravcsik, Andrew. 1997. "Taking Preferences Seriously: A Liberal Theory of International Politics." *International Organization* 51 (4): 513–53.

Moreno Ocampo, Luis. 2009. "The International Criminal Court in Motion." In *The Emerging Practice of the International Criminal Court*, edited by C. Stahl and Göran Sluiter, 13–19. Leiden: Martinus Nijhoff.

Morgenthau, Hans. 1985 [1948]. *Politics among Nations*. 6th ed. New York: McGraw-Hill.

Morphet, Sally. 1995. "The Influence of States and Groups of States on and in the Security Council and General Assembly, 1980–94." *Review of International Studies* 21 (4): 435–62.

Morris, Virginia, and Michael P. Scharf. 1995. *An Insider's Guide to the International Criminal Tribunal for the Former Yugoslavia: A Documentary History and Analysis*. Irvington-on-Hudson, NY: Transnational.

Morrison, J. Stephen, and Alex de Waal. 2005. "Can Sudan Escape Its Intractability?" In *Grasping the Nettle: Analyzing Cases of Intractable Conflict,* edited by Chester A.

Crocker, Fen Osler Hampson, and Pamela Aall. Washington, DC: United States Institute of Peace.

Mueller, John. 2009. "War Has Almost Ceased to Exist: An Assessment." *Political Science Quarterly* 124 (2): 297–321.

Mufson, Steven. 2015. "'Assad Must Go': These Three Little Words Are Huge Obstacle for Obama on Syria." *Washington Post*, October 19. https://www.washingtonpost.com/business/economy/assad-must-go-these-three-little-words-present-a-huge-obstacle-for-obama-on-syria/2015/10/19/6a76baba-71ec-11e5-9cbb-790369643cf9_story.html (accessed April 27, 2016).

Nairn, Alan. 1993. "The Roots of Torture: U.S. Complicity and the Need for Change." In *Confronting the Heart of Darkness*, edited by Shari Turitz, 4–10. Washington, DC: Guatemala Human Rights Commission/USA.

Neier, A. 1998. *War Crimes: Brutality, Genocide, Terror, and the Struggle for Justice*. New York: Times Books.

Nichols, Michelle. 2014. "U.N. Inquiry Chief Wants North Korea Hauled before International Court." Reuters, February 17. http://www.reuters.com/article/2014/04/17/us-northkorea-un-idUSBREA3G2DC20140417 (accessed June 24, 2014).

Nye, Joseph S. 2004. *Soft Power*. New York: Public Affairs.

Office of the Prosecutor. 2013. "Draft Policy Paper on Preliminary Investigations." (November). https://www.icc-cpi.int/iccdocs/otp/OTP-Policy_Paper_Preliminary_Examinations_2013-ENG.pdf.

ODHAG (Oficina de Derechos Humanos del Arzobispado de Guatemala). 1999. *Never Again: Recovery of the Historical Memory Project, the Official Report of the Human Rights Office, Archdiocese of Guatemala*. Maryknoll, NY: Orbis Books.

Olson, James S., and Randy Roberts. 1998. *My Lai: A Brief History with Documents*. New York: Palgrave Macmillan.

Oneal, John R., and Bruce Russett. 1997. "The Classical Liberals Were Right: Democracy, Interdependence, and Conflict." *International Studies Quarterly* 41 (March): 267–94.

Onuf, Nicholas. 2012. *A World of Our Making: Rules and Rule in Social Theory and International Relations*. Reprint, New York: Routledge.

Organski, A. F. K., and Jacek Kugler. 1980. *The War Ledger*. Chicago: University of Chicago Press.

OTP (Office of the Prosecutor). 2010. "Draft Policy Paper on Preliminary Investigations." The Hague: International Criminal Court. http://www.icc-cpi.int/NR/rdonlyres/9FF1EAA1-41C4-4A30-A202-174B18DA923C/282515/OTP_Draftpolicypaperonpreliminaryexaminations04101.pdf (accessed March 13, 2014).

Pace, William R., and Mark Thieroff. 1999. "Participation of Non-Governmental Organizations." In *The International Criminal Court: The Making of the Rome Statute*, edited by Roy S. Lee, 391–98. The Hague: Kluwer Law International.

Page, Benjamin I. and Robert Y. Shapiro. 1983. "Effects of Public Opinion on Policy." *American Political Science Review* 77 (March): 175–90.

Park, Madison. 2014. "China, North Korea Slam U.N. Human Rights Report as 'Divorced from Reality.'" CNN World, March 18. http://www.cnn.com/2014/03/18/world/asia/north-korea-human-rights-response (accessed June 24, 2014).

Payton, Autumn Lockwood. 2009. "Tying Down Gulliver: How Weak States Control the Design of International Institutions." PhD dissertation, Department of Political Science, Ohio State University.

Pejic, Jelena. 1998. "Creating a Permanent International Criminal Court: Obstacles to Independence and Effectiveness." *Columbia Human Rights Law Review* 29 (Spring): 291–354.

Peskin, Victor. 2005. "Beyond Victor's Justice? The Challenge of Prosecuting the Winners at the International Criminal Tribunals for Yugoslavia and Rwanda." *Journal of Human Rights* 4 (2): 213–31.

——. 2008. *International Justice in Rwanda and the Balkans.* Cambridge: Cambridge University Press.

——. 2009. "Review: The Politics of Constructing the International Criminal Court: NGOs, Discourse, and Agency." *Law and Politics Book Review* 19 (1): 14–20.

Piccigallo, Philip R. 1979. *The Japanese on Trial.* Austin: University of Texas Press.

Polachek, Solomon William. 1980. "Conflict and Trade." *Journal of Conflict Resolution* 24 (1): 55–78.

Politi, Mauro. 2001. "The Rome Statute of the ICC: Rays of Light and Some Shadows." In *The Rome Statute of the International Criminal Court: A Challenge to Impugnity*, edited by M. Politi and G. Nesi, 7–16. Farnham, UK: Ashgate.

Pollack, Mark. 2003. *The Engines of Integration: Delegation, Agency, and Agency Setting in the European Union.* Oxford: Oxford University Press.

Posner, Eric A., and Miguel F. P. de Figueiredo. 2005. "Is the International Court of Justice Biased?" *Journal of Legal Studies* 34 (2): 599–630.

Price, Richard. 1997. *The Chemical Weapons Taboo.* Ithaca, NY: Cornell University Press.

——. 2004. "Emerging Customary Norms and Anti-Personnel Landmines." In *The Politics of International Law*, edited by Christian Reus-Smit, 106–30. Cambridge: Cambridge University Press.

Putnam, Robert. 1988. "Diplomacy and Domestic Politics: The Logic of Two-Level Games." *International Organization* 42 (3): 427–60.

Raghavan, Sudarsan. 2013. "At the Scene of 1996 Horror, a New Arc of Despair." *Washington Post*, November 8.

Raustiala Kal and David Victor. 2004. "The Regime Complex for Plant Genetic Resources." *International Organization* 58 (2): 277–309.

Reynolds, David. 1986. "A 'Special Relationship'? America, Britain and the International Order since the Second World War." *International Affairs* 62 (1): 1–20.

Rhodes, Richard. 1995. "The General and WWII." *New Yorker*, June 19.

Risse, Thomas, Stephen C. Ropp, and Kathryn Sikkink, eds. 1999. *The Power of Human Rights.* Cambridge: Cambridge University Press.

Roberts, Hannah. 2002. "Mental Health, Truth, and Justice in Guatemala." *Lancet*, March 16.

Robertson, Geoffrey. 2012. *Crimes against Humanity: The Struggle for Global Justice.* New York: New Press.

Robinson, Simon. 2006. "The Deadliest War in the World." *Time*, May 28. http://www.time.com/time/magazine/article/0,9171,1198921,00.html (accessed June 6, 2012).

Röling, B. V. A., and Antonio Cassese. 1993. *The Toyko Trial and Beyond: Reflections of a Peacemonger*. Cambridge: Polity Press.

Ross, Robert S., Allen S. Whiting, and Harry Harding. 1990. "China's Foreign Relations after Tiananmen: Challenges for the U.S." *NBR Analysis* 1 (3): 5–32.

Rotberg, Robert I., and Dennis Thompson, eds. 2000. *Truth v. Justice*. Princeton, NJ: Princeton University Press.

Rovera, Donatella. 2012. "Who Will Document Syria's Atrocities?" *Washington Post*, May 31.

Roy, Denny. 1998. *China's Foreign Relations*. Lanham, MD: Rowman and Littlefield.

Rudolph, Christopher. 2001. "Constructing an Atrocities Regime: The Politics of War Crimes Tribunals." *International Organization* 55 (3): 655–91.

Ruggie, John Gerard, ed. 1993. *Multilateralism Matters*. New York: Columbia University Press.

Rummel, Rudi J. 1994. *Death by Government*. New Brunswick, NJ: Transaction.

———. 1997. *Power Kills*. New Brunswick, NJ: Transaction.

SáCouto, Susana, and Katherine A. Cleary. 2008. "The Gravity Threshold of the International Criminal Court." *American Journal of International Law* 23 (5): 807–54.

Sandholtz, Wayne. 2008. "Creating Authority by the Council." In *The UN Security Council and the Politics of International Authority,* edited by Bruce Cronin and Ian Hurd, 131–53. New York: Routledge.

Schabas, William A. 2004. "United States Hostility to the International Criminal Court: It's All about the Security Council." *European Journal of International Law* 15 (4): 701–20.

———. 2006. *The UN International Criminal Tribunals: The Former Yugoslavia, Rwanda, and Sierra Leone*. Cambridge: Cambridge University Press.

———. 2008. "Prosecutorial Discretion vs. Judicial Activism." *Journal of International Criminal Justice* 6 (4): 731–61.

———. 2010. "Victor's Justice: Selecting 'Situations' at the International Criminal Court." *John Marshall Law Review* 43 (3): 535–52.

———. 2011. *Introduction to the International Criminal Court*. 4th ed. Cambridge: Cambridge University Press.

Scheffer, David M. 2012. *All the Missing Souls: A Personal History of the War Crimes Tribunals*. Princeton, NJ: Princeton University Press.

Schiff, Benjamin. 2008. *Building the International Criminal Court*. New York: Cambridge University Press.

Schirmer, Jennifer. 1998. *The Guatemalan Military Project: A Violence Called Democracy*. Philadelphia: University of Pennsylvania Press.

Schmitz, David F. 2006. *The United States and Right-Wing Dictatorships, 1965–1989*. Cambridge: Cambridge University Press.

Schnall, Marianne. 2009. "The Atrocities Committed against Women and Girls in the Congo Defy Imagination." http://www.alternet.org/reproductivejustice/125612/the_atrocities_committed_against_women_and_girls_in_the_congo_defy_imagination/ (accessed February 9, 2012).

Schonfeld, Zach. 2014. "Are Syrian Barrel Bombs Really Worse than Normal Weaponry?" *Newsweek*, February 12. http://www.newsweek.com/are-syrian-barrel-bombs-really-worse-normal-weaponry-228913 (accessed June 25, 2014).

Schrag, Minna. 1995. "The Yugoslav War Crimes Tribunal: A Prosecutor's View." *Duke Journal of Comparative and International Law* 6 (1): 187–95.

Seybolt, Taylor B., Jay D. Aaronson, and Baruch Fischhoff, eds. 2013. *Counting Civilian Casualties*. Oxford: Oxford University Press.

Sharp, Jeremy M. 2013. *U.S. Foreign Aid to Israel*. CRS Report 7-5700. Washington, DC: Congressional Research Service.

Sieff, Kevin. 2016. "Child Suicide Bombings Surge in West Africa." *Washington Post*, April 13.

Sikkink, Kathryn. 2011. *The Justice Cascade*. New York: W. W. Norton.

Sil, Rudra, and Peter J. Katzenstein, eds. 2010. *Beyond Paradigms: Analytic Eclecticism in the Study of World Politics*. New York: Palgrave Macmillan.

Silber, Laura, and Alan Little. 1997. *Yugoslavia: Death of a Nation*. New York: Penguin Books.

Silverman, Jon. 2012. "Ten Years, $900m, One Verdict: Does the ICC Cost Too Much?" *BBC News Magazine*, March 14. http://www.bbc.co.uk/news/magazine–17351946 (accessed August 20, 2012).

Simmons, Beth. 2009. *Mobilizing for Human Rights*. Cambridge: Cambridge University Press.

Simmons, Beth, and Allison Danner. 2010. "Credible Commitments and the International Criminal Court." *International Organization* 64 (2): 225–56.

Simonovic, Ivan. 1999. "The Role of the ICTY in the Development of International Criminal Adjudication." *Fordham International Law Journal* 23 (2): 440–59.

Simons, Marlise. 2009. "Long Sentences for Atrocities in Sierra Leone." *New York Times*, April 8. http://www.nytimes.com/2009/04/09/world/africa/09leone.html (accessed February 9, 2012).

Slaughter, Anne-Marie. 2004. *A New World Order*. Princeton, NJ: Princeton University Press.

Sly, Liz, and Joby Warrick. 2012. "Houla Massacre Raises the Stakes on Syria." *Washington Post*, June 4.

Smith, Bradley. 1982. *The American Road to Nuremberg: The Documentary Record 1944–1945*. Stanford, CA: Hoover Institution Press.

Smith, Charles Anthony. 2012. *The Rise and Fall of War Crimes Trials*. Cambridge: Cambridge University Press.

Smith, David. 2012. "New Chief Prosecutor Defends the International Criminal Court." *Guardian*, May 23. http://www.theguardian.com/law/2012/may/23/chief-prosecutor-international-criminal-court (accessed January 21, 2015).

Smith, Julianne. 2008. *The NATO-Russia Relationship: Defining Moment or Déjà Vu?* Washington, DC: Center for Strategic and International Studies, November.

Smith-Cannoy, Heather. 2012. *Insincere Commitments*. Washington, DC: Georgetown University Press.

Snyder, Jack, and Leslie Vinjamuri. 2003–4. "Trials and Errors: Principles and Pragmatism in Strategies of International Justice." *International Security* 28 (3): 5–44.

Stahn, Carsten. 2009. "Judicial Review of Prosecutorial Discretion: Five Years On." In *The Emerging Practice of the International Criminal Court*, edited by C. Stahl and Göran Sluiter, 247–80. Leiden: Martinus Nijhoff.

Steinke, Ronen. 2012. *The Politics of International Criminal Justice*. Oxford: Hart.

Stigen, Jo. 2008. *The Relationship between the International Criminal Court and National Jurisdictions*. Leiden: Martinus Nijhoff.

Stone, Randall. 2011. *Controlling Institutions: International Organizations and the Global Economy*. Cambridge: Cambridge University Press.

Stone Sweet, Alec, and Thomas Brunell. 2012. "The European Court of Justice, Noncompliance, and the Politics of Override." *American Political Science Review* 106 (1): 204–13.

Struett, Michael. 2008. *The Politics of Constructing the International Criminal Court*. New York: Palgrave Macmillan.

——. 2012. "Why the International Criminal Court Must *Pretend* to Ignore Politics." *Ethics and International Affairs* 26 (1): 83–92.

Tabak, Shana. 2009. "Article 124, War Crimes, and the Development of the Rome Statute." *Georgetown Journal of International Law* 40 (3): 1069–1100.

Tallberg, Jonas. 2002. "Delegation to Supranational Institutions: Why, How, and with What Consequence?" *West European Politics* 25 (1): 23–46.

Taylor, Ian. 2006. "China's Oil Diplomacy in Africa." *International Affairs* 82 (5): 937–59.

Taylor, Telford. 2008. "The Nuremberg Trials." In Perspectives on the Nuremberg Trial, edited by Guénaël Mettraux, 372–407. Oxford: Oxford University Press.

——. 2012 [1992]. *The Anatomy of the Nuremberg Trials: A Personal Memoir*, e-Book edition. New York: Knopf.

Thomas, Dylan. 1953. "Do Not Go Gentle into That Good Night." *The Poems of Dylan Thomas*. New York: New Directions.

Thucydides. [431 BC] 2009. *The Peloponnesian War*. Translated by Martin Hammond. Oxford: Oxford University Press.

Trainin, Aron N. 1944. *Ugolovnaia Otvetstvennost Gitlerovtsev* [The criminal responsibility of the Hitlerites]. Edited by A. Y. Vyshinskii. Moscow.

Tsygankov, Andrei P. 2013. *Russia's Foreign Policy*. 3rd ed. Lanham, MD: Rowman and Littlefield.

UN (United Nations). 1994. Report of the International Law Commission on its Forty-Sixth Session, Draft Statute for an International Criminal Court. UN Doc. A/49/10, May 2–July 22.

——. 2010. *Democratic Republic of the Congo, 1993–2003: Report of the Mapping Exercise Documenting the Most Serious Violations of Human Rights and International Humanitarian Law Committed within the Territory of the Democratic Republic of the Congo between March 1993 and June 2003*. New York: United Nations, August. http://www.ohchr.org/Documents/Countries/CD/DRC_MAPPING_REPORT_FINAL_EN.pdf (accessed August 22, 2016).

——. 2011. *Report of the United Nations Commissioner for Human Rights on the Situation of Human Rights in the Syrian Arab Republic*. UN Doc. A/HRC/18/53, September 15. http://www.ohchr.org/Documents/countries/SY/Syria_Report_2011-08-17.pdf (accessed April 27, 2016).

——. 2014. *Report of the Commission of Inquiry on Human Rights in the Democratic People's Republic of North Korea*. UN Doc. A/HRC/25/63, February 7. http://www.ohchr.org/EN/HRBodies/HRC/CoIDPRK/Pages/ReportoftheCommissionofInquiryDPRK.aspx (accessed June 24 2014).

UNHCR (United Nations High Commissioner for Refugees). 2016. Syria Regional Refugee Response. http://data.unhcr.org/syrianrefugees/regional.php (accessed May 2, 2016).

U.S. Department of State. 2006. *Human Rights Report 2006*. http://www.state.gov/j/drl/rls/hrrpt/2006/78759.htm (accessed July 11, 2012).

Valentino, Benjamin A. 2005. *Final Solutions: Mass Killing and Genocide in the Twentieth Century*. Ithaca, NY: Cornell University Press.

——. 2006. "The Perils of Limited Humanitarian Intervention: Lesson from the 1990s." *Wisconsin International Law Journal* 24 (3): 723–40.

——. 2011. "The True Costs of Humanitarian Intervention." *Foreign Affairs* (November–December).

Van de Looy, Judith. 2006. "Africa and China: A Strategic Partnership." ASC Working Paper No. 67. Leiden: African Studies Centre.

Van Schaack, Beth. 2010–11. "Negotiating at the Interface of Power and Law: The Crime of Aggression." *Columbia Journal of Transnational Law* 49: 505–601.

Vaubel, Roland. 2006. "Principal-Agent Problems in International Organizations." *Review of International Organizations* 1 (2): 125–38.

Vickers, Rhiannon. 2000. "Labour's Search for a Third Way in Foreign Policy." In Little and Wickham-Jones, *New Labour's Foreign Policy*, 33–45.

Voeten, Erik. 2008. "The Impartiality of International Judges: Evidence from the European Court of Human Rights." *American Political Science Review* 102 (4): 417–32.

Walsh, Bryan. 2006. "Unearthing Atrocities." *Time*, January 30. http://www.time.com/time/magazine/article/0,9171,1154251,00.html (accessed February 9, 2012).

Walsh, Declan. 2004. "Atrocities in Sudan." ZNet, April 27. http://www.zcommunications.org/atrocities-in-sudan-by-declan-walsh (accessed July 9, 2012).

Walt, Stephen M. 1997. "The Progressive Power of Realism." *American Political Scienc Review* 91 (4): 931–35.

——. 2002. "The Enduring Relevance of the Realist Tradition." In *Political Science: The State of the Discipline*, edited by Ira Katznelson and Helen Milner, 197–234. New York: W. W. Norton.

Walter, Barbara F., and Jack Snyder, eds. 1999. *Civil Wars*. New York: Columbia University Press.

Waltz, Kenneth N. 1979. *Theory of International Politics*. Reading, MA: Addison-Wesley.

Walzer, Michael. 1977. *Just and Unjust Wars*. New York: Basic Books.

Wedgwood, Ruth. 1999. "The International Criminal Court: An American View." *European Journal of International Law* 10 (1): 93–107.

Weiss, Thomas G. 1995. "Overcoming the Somalia Syndrome: 'Operation Rekindle Hope?'" *Global Governance* 1 (2): 171–87.

Weller, Marc. 2002. "Undoing the Global Constitution: UN Security Council Action on the International Criminal Court." *International Affairs* 78 (October): 693–712.

Wendt. Alexander. 1999. *A Social Theory of International Politics*. Cambridge: Cambridge University Press.

——. 2001. "Driving with the Rear-View Mirror: On the Rational Science of Institutional Design." *International Organization* 55 (4): 1019–49.

Weschler, Lawrence. 2000. "Exceptional Cases in Rome: The United States and the Struggle for an ICC." In *The United States and the International Criminal Court*, edited by Sarah B. Sewall and Carl Kaysen, 85–114. Lanham, MD: Rowman and Littlefield.

Wheeler, Nicholas J., and Tim Dunne. 1998. "Good International Citizenship: A Third Way for British Foreign Policy." *International Affairs* 74 (4): 847–70.

White, Colin, Lene Hansen, and Tim Dunne, eds. 2013. "The End of International Relations Theory?" Special issue. *European Journal of International Relations* 19 (3).

Wickham-Jones, Mark. 2000. "Labour Party Politics and Foreign Policy." In Little and Wickham-Jones, 93–111, *New Labour's Foreign Policy*.

Williams, Carol J. 2001. "World Leaders Hail Milosevic Arrest as End of Turbulent Era." *Los Angeles Times*, April 2.

Williams, Paul. 2002. "The Rise and Fall of the Ethical Dimension: Presentation and Practice in New Labour's Foreign Policy." *Cambridge Review of International Affairs* 15 (1): 53–63.

——. 2004. "Who's Making UK Foreign Policy?" *International Affairs* 80 (5): 909–29.

——. 2005. *British Foreign Policy under New Labour, 1997–2005*. New York: Palgrave.

Wilson, Scott, and Joby Warrick. 2011. "Assad Must Go, Obama Says." *Washington Post*, August 18. https://www.washingtonpost.com/politics/assad-must-go-obama-says/2011/08/18/gIQAelheOJ_story.html (accessed April 27, 2016).

Wimmer, Andreas, ed. 2004. *Facing Ethnic Conflicts: Toward a New Realism*. Lanham, MD: Rowman and Littlefield.

Wippman, David. 2004. "The International Criminal Court." In *The Politics of International Law*, edited by Christian Reus-Smit, 151–88. Cambridge: Cambridge University Press.

——. 2006. "The Costs of International Justice." *American Journal of International Law* 100 (4): 861–81.

Wu, Chengqui. 2009. "Sovereignty, Human Rights, and Responsibility: Changes in China's Response to International Humanitarian Crises." *Journal of Chinese Political Science* 15 (1): 71–79.

Wu, Xinbo. 2001. "Four Contradictions Constraining China's Foreign Policy Behavior." *Journal of Contemporary China* 10 (27): 293–301.

Wybrow, Robert. 2003. "British Attitudes toward the Bosnian Situation." In *International Public Opinion and the Bosnian Crisis*, edited by Richard Sobel and Eric Shiraev, 33–68. Lanham, MD: Lexington Books.

Yeh, Kungchia. 1993. "Foreign Trade, Capital Inflow, and Technology Transfer under the Open Door Policy." In *China in an Era of Deng Xiaoping: A Decade of Reform*, edited by Michael Y. M. Kau and Susan M. Marsh, 124–54. Armonk, NY: M. E. Sharpe.

Young, Oran R. 1999. *Governance in World Affairs*. Ithaca, NY: Cornell University Press.

Zhao, Quansheng. 1996. *Interpreting Chinese Foreign Policy*. Oxford: Oxford University Press.

Zimmermann, Andreas. 2008. "Article 124: Transitional Provision." In *Commentary on the Rome Statute of the International Criminal Court: Observers' Notes, Article by Article*, edited by Otto Triffterer, 1767–68. Baden-Baden, DE: Nomos Verlagsgesellschaft.

Zorya, Yuri, and Natalia Lebedeva. 1989. "The Year 1939 in the Nuremberg Files." *International Affairs* 10 (October): 117–29.

Index

Milton Keynes UK
Ingram Content Group UK Ltd.
UKHW012315250823
427508UK00002B/26/J

9 781501 705526